SET
THE
BOY
FREE

SET
THE
BOY
FREE

JOHNNY MARR

The Autobiography

CENTURY

1 3 5 7 9 10 8 6 4 2

Century
20 Vauxhall Bridge Road
London SW1V 2SA

Century is part of the Penguin Random House group of companies
whose addresses can be found at global.penguinrandomhouse.com.

Jacket design by Mat Bancroft and Laura Turner.

First published by Century in 2016

www.penguin.co.uk

A CIP catalogue record for this book is available from the British Library.

ISBN 9781780894324 (hardback)
ISBN 9781780894331 (trade paperback)

Set in 13.25/16.75 pt Fournier MT Std
Typeset by Jouve (UK), Milton Keynes
Printed and bound by Clays Ltd, St Ives plc

Penguin Random House is committed to a sustainable future for our business, our readers and
our planet. This book is made from Forest Stewardship Council® certified paper.

For Angie

Contents

CONTENTS

Emily's

I stood outside, gazing up, on one of those mornings when the sun scorched the pavement and Mancunians used to say it 'cracked the flags'.

It was summer 1968, I was nearly five years old, and every day we would walk past Emily's corner shop and my mother would have to stop and wait while I stared up intently through the window at the little wooden guitar leaning on the shelf between the mops, buckets and brooms. My mother had got used to having to stop at Emily's, and she and my father had wondered about their son being so taken with the toy guitar. It was always the same – we'd stand outside the shop while I gazed up – until that morning, when my mother took me inside and gave the money for it to Emily, who took the guitar down from the shelf and handed it to me.

From the moment I got my first guitar, I had it with me

wherever I went, carrying it around the way other kids carried their toy fire engines and dolls. I don't know why I had to have it, but I was besotted with it, and from then on I can't remember a time when I didn't have a guitar.

Ardwick Green

I was born on Halloween, 31 October 1963, in Longsight, Manchester, and then moved with my parents, John and Frances Maher, to a house in the inner-city area of Ardwick Green.

We lived there at 19 Brierley Avenue, in a row of seven houses, with a car mechanic's garage at one end and eight houses facing us on the other side of the street. Our front door opened into the main room, which had a little fireplace and a black-and-white television, but we spent most of our time in the back room, where the radio was. Next to the back room was a small kitchen. The toilet was in an outhouse in the yard outside, and hung up on the wall of the back room was a tin tub that we used to take a bath in, in front of the fire. Upstairs was my parents' bedroom, and behind that was the room where me and my sister slept.

In the winter, my parents would put overcoats on top of us to keep us warm.

The street was a mixture of working-class families of different nationalities: English, Indian, Irish, and a stern old Polish man called Bruno who had fled the Nazis in the war. At the opposite end of the street there was a tyre factory, with a fire escape hanging down from one of the walls.

My parents were from a small town in Ireland called Athy, in County Kildare. My mother was born Frances Patricia Doyle and was the third youngest of fourteen children. She had grown up there in a three-room house, and at fifteen she moved to England to be with her four sisters and two brothers who had gone there to work. One time, she went back to Kildare to visit her family and went to a dance, where she met my father; he was two years older than her. She returned to Manchester, and my dad followed her, and they were married eight months later.

My father was born John Joseph Maher. He never knew his own father, and he left school at thirteen to work on a farm, driving a tractor and sowing corn, to support his younger brother and three younger sisters. After arriving in Manchester he eventually found work in a warehouse and sent for his siblings and my grandmother to come over to England so that the family could all be together.

Many of my mother and father's brothers and sisters began to start families in Manchester. They were all in their late teens and early twenties. Lots of babies were being born, and there was a feeling of discovery as they all learned how to get by and make new lives in this new city.

My mother was eighteen when I was born. I was named John Martin Maher, after my dad and my mother's favourite saint. Our household was extremely Catholic, and my mum was especially religious. Mass was never missed, and at our front door there was a font with holy water. I spent a lot of my early years among statues and crosses and prayers, and there was a constant backdrop of religion in our house that felt very mysterious and deeply otherworldly.

Eleven months after I was born my sister Claire came along, which meant we were known as 'Irish twins' on account of there being less than a year between us. It was good being one of a pair, and I liked having a sister for company. There were a lot of kids on the street, so there was always something going on. I was more introverted than my sister and was happy to spend time sitting on the pavement, poking an old ice-lolly stick into the tar on the road while I watched the other kids playing. Claire's favourite trick was to switch all the milk and deliveries around in the morning on the neighbours' doorsteps, so she could watch them all knocking on each other's doors to exchange their groceries as a bit of farcical comic slapstick. She was upbeat and outgoing and would chase after anyone with a broom if they crossed us. These things pretty much summed my sister up; she was funny and sweet, but you didn't mess with her, and I was always impressed with the things about her that were different from me.

Both my parents were extremely hard-working. My dad never said too much around the house, although he was sociable in the community and well liked. He had needed to be tough as a boy, as he'd grown up without a father in a little household in the country, and to me he was a strong, brooding presence, doing whatever it took to bring up his own family. After working in the warehouse he took a job laying gas pipes in the road. He would leave the house at six in the morning to be picked up by a gang of his mates in a lorry, and then he'd be out digging all day. I was aware that my dad's job was very physical, but he seemed to like to be out working. When he got home he'd be covered in black dirt from head to foot, and when he was getting cleaned up my mother would leave to get the bus to go to her job as a cleaner at the Royal Infirmary. She was always really busy.

Living in Ardwick meant inner-city housing and the remnants of the post-Industrial Revolution; it was a mixture of streets and factories. The railway tracks ran over the arches across the road from us, and we'd see the trains going in and out of town. In between the railway tracks and our street was an area of derelict land called 'the croft'. It had been a bomb site, and it was where Gypsy families sometimes settled in their caravans. I'd see the Gypsy kids on the croft and think it must be great to be living like that. They were wild and didn't have to go to school; they were let loose to do what they wanted. It looked lawless and dangerous living on the croft, and one day I worked up the courage to sneak over to talk to them. There was a small bonfire going, and a few adults hanging around, and when I asked where they'd come from it was strange to discover that there were people who didn't really belong anywhere. At night they'd be having parties and playing music really loudly on the radios in their caravans, with the trains going by.

Around the corner from us was a little park called Ardwick Green, which gave the area its name. My mother would take Claire and me to play on the swings and roundabouts there on our way back from town. I loved it as it was the only green place around, and we went there a lot, but it was also a skinhead hang-out and they were usually on the lookout for people they could beat up. Sometimes there would be drunks and down-and-outs lying around, and at other times teenagers would be wandering about, usually scruffy and with very long hair, and seemingly very confused. Later I would discover they were hippies, but at the time I just thought they were down on their luck.

Two streets away was the Manchester Apollo, which was a big 1930s art deco theatre that had become an ABC cinema. On some Saturday mornings I'd go with Claire to watch grainy old black-and-white sci-fi and cowboy films, and every time I'd get a new badge with 'ABC Minors' on it. Once in a while there would be a flash car parked outside the front, and a crowd of people would be gathered around to catch a glimpse of whichever British actor or TV personality was there, making a glamorous appearance on the pavement. The biggest attraction in Manchester in the 1960s, though, was Belle Vue fun park, a couple of miles up the road. It was billed as the 'showground of the world' and boasted a circus, which I thought was amazing, and a zoo, which was really grim, and the famous Kings Hall, where all the big 1960s pop acts like Manfred Mann, The Kinks and The Animals played.

Nearly all of my time as a child was spent with my extended family from Kildare. My dad's family of five and my mum's family of fourteen meant that there were a lot of aunts and uncles and an ever growing number of cousins. I was often at my gran's, or at one of my relatives' houses, and as more babies arrived everyone relied on each other for support and help with looking after the kids. Sometimes I would be enlisted to keep an eye on the younger ones, even though I was only a little kid myself.

My Aunt Josie and Uncle Patsy Murphy lived in the next street from us with my cousin Pat, who was a few years older than me. Pat had come over from Ireland and liked messing around with bikes. I would bring my toy guitar to their house and he would show me whatever new tunes he had worked out on his harmonica. Two doors up from them were my Uncle Christie and Aunt Kathleen with their three young boys, Chris, John and Brian. One mile over the other side of the railway was where my Aunt May lived with her husband Denny and my cousins Dennis, Ann, Mark, Geraldine and Jane, and a few doors down from her was my dad's youngest sister, Ann, with her husband, Martin, and my youngest cousin, Siobhan. Two of my mother's sisters lived a few miles away in Chorlton, and we'd get on the bus to visit them: Aunt Cathleen, Uncle Timmy and cousins Michael, Paul, Joseph and Tim; and Aunt Tess and Uncle Christie Brennan and cousins Gerry, Tony, Martin, Mary and Shane. Having so many relatives gave us all our own community and a shared sense of background and history that made us seem like a tribe.

One morning I was in our back room, sitting on the floor and messing around with some toys, when my mum dashed in with my Aunt May. There was a Dansette record player on a cupboard and I watched them hovering over it excitedly as my mum put on a 45rpm record with a red label. The record dropped on to the turntable and I heard a simple guitar figure as 'Walk Right Back' by The Everly Brothers started to play. I watched the two women closely while they shared the song, and I saw my mother as a music fan. I loved the sheer joy they took in playing the record. When it was finished they pressed the switch again and the song started over. They continued playing it, pointing out bits and singing along, until I knew all of the song myself. I'd never seen anyone playing the same record over and over again, and I'd never seen anyone identifying bits of the music as it played. It was an infectious pop song with a cheerful sound and great voices, but the best thing to me about the Everly Brothers record was the loud guitar hook. After that, I listened for the same thing on every record I heard.

Our house always had music going. My parents were both obsessed about singers and bands, and my mother bought records all the time. She would compile her own pop charts and compare her predictions with the real Top 20. One Saturday she decided she had to get a new record that was out, and me and Claire walked around all the shops with her to find it. Everywhere we went the record was sold out, but she was determined to get it and we ended up walking the three miles into Gorton to the last shop she could think of. When we got there the shop was closing, but they had the record and she made them stay open so she could buy it.

If it wasn't the records being played at home, then it was the music on the radio. My mother would stand me on a chair in front of it and I'd be there for hours while the UK Top 30 blared at me. Anything that had a distinctive guitar part would have me transfixed, and from the age of four I knew all the words to the songs in the charts, whether they were by Love Affair, The Four Tops or anyone else. Standing in front of the radio became a habit, and my mother could leave me and get on with the housework without having to worry about where I was.

Television was another source of music. Many of the TV programmes that were around were light entertainment shows designed for the whole family, like *Sunday Night at the London Palladium* or the *Happening for Lulu* show, and I would wait expectantly through the comedians, magicians and dance routines in the hope that whatever pop act was on might include someone holding an electric or acoustic guitar. Sometimes a band would appear with the full complement of instruments, and I'd study their guitars regardless of who they were or what song they were playing. If you were really lucky it would be a real pop band like Amen Corner or The Move, but there was also plenty of disappointment when some solo act appeared on their own in soft focus, singing some soppy ballad with the sound of the BBC orchestra behind them.

I've no idea if music is something that you're born with or is bred into you, but the fascination I had with music was something completely personal and natural, and I knew that if I wanted to be the real thing then my wooden guitar would have to be electric, or at least look like one. I carefully took the strings off it and laid it down on the concrete back-room floor. I got a tin of my dad's household paint and painted my guitar white with a huge old paintbrush, and then I stuck two beer-bottle tops on it to look like volume and tone knobs. I got white paint all over me and most of the floor, but I felt like I had stepped up a level and I thought it looked fantastic.

As we lived within walking distance of the city centre, we were always going into town to Lewis's, the big department store, on the corner of Market Street. The roads in the city were noisy with the lorries and buses, but I loved seeing all the buildings and the busy streets, and there were always a lot of interesting-looking people in Piccadilly Gardens. When we got to Lewis's we'd take the escalators to the fourth floor where all the electrical items were, and my mother would leave me on my own to look at the amplifiers. She was used to my obsession with guitars, but she was starting to think there was something a bit strange about a child wanting to stand and look at big black boxes with speakers in while his mother went to do the shopping.

Claire and I went to school at St Aloysius, a 1960s single-floor prefab building on Stockport Road, just past the bus depot. I wasn't crazy about school, but I was smart enough to get by. People at school would often get the pronunciation of my name wrong. I would be called *Ma-her* and *May-er* and even *Mather*. It was annoying, and I never really understood why it was so difficult to get my name right. It happened at the dentist and at the doctor's too – it happened everywhere.

My teacher was called Mr Quinlan. He was an eccentric man who brought a big green parrot called Major to school with him every day. Major was a big talker and had a cage in the classroom, and every hour Mr Quinlan would let him fly around the room, causing mayhem and landing on pupils' heads. Most of us were amused by it, but my sister hated it and it gave her a phobia of birds for the rest of her life.

It could be a bit edgy around Ardwick, and even as a little kid I had to watch myself. I was in the street one day when a much older kid grabbed me for no reason and started pounding my face into the pointed tail lights of a parked Ford Anglia car. I couldn't get away, and Claire ran to the house to get someone. When he eventually stopped, blood was gushing all down my face. My mother came out and because we didn't have a car or a phone she ran down to the main road and straight into the traffic, and stood holding her hand out in front of an oncoming car. The car stopped and she shouted for the driver to take us to the hospital. When we got there, a doctor stitched up the gash over my nose, which left a permanent scar.

I was always over at my gran's. She liked a drink and was good fun and she let the kids run a bit wild. Gran lived near the Apollo with my dad's young brother Mike and my Aunt Betty, and her house would often end up in a party. My Uncle Mike was just in his teens, and because he was so young he was more like an older brother than an uncle. Mike seemed to have it all: he was doted on by his older siblings and he had the latest clothes and gadgets. He had moved from Kildare, and with no father around and my gran being so free he could do whatever he wanted, and he made the best of it. It was great having someone older to hang around with, especially someone who could do what they wanted. He took me with him to the Belle Vue Aces' speedway races on Saturday nights, and he was a major George Best fan. I thought Mike was the coolest thing going.

Other things close to home were much more disturbing, however. Being a child around Ardwick and Longsight in the 1960s, it was impossible to not be aware of the Moors Murders. The horror of what had happened had rocked the whole country, but the shock of it was felt even more acutely in the North West, where the events took place. The pictures of Myra Hindley and Ian Brady seemed to be an ongoing fixture in the newspapers and on the television, and I picked up half-heard details from the adults' conversations about tortured children and tape recordings. Depravity was a diffi- cult thing to fathom, but I realised that something monstrous was going on, and it was even worse that one of the victims, Keith Bennett, had lived nearby and had been on his way to a house near my gran's when he was taken.

Around at my gran's I would see some musical instruments that belonged to my Aunt Betty and her friends. Betty was the main musician in the family, and she knew a lot of the Irish musicians who were playing in bands around Manchester. She was great to hang out with and she could pretty much get a tune out of anything. All my relatives were well aware of my obsession with music, and regardless of me being a child they talked to me like I was a grown-up. There were a lot of get-togethers, and a lot of smoking and drinking. No subjects were off-limits, and no type of language either.

A lot of nights there were parties, with everybody playing instruments and singing. I would hang around the adults in anticipation, taking in the wildness and hearing the banter and conversations about who turned round to who and 'told them to feckin' feck off'. They were lively nights, and I sat on the floor, watching and listening to handsome men and pretty young women rocking as the night got more raucous and the bottle caps flew off. One of the benefits of being around young Irish people at the time was that my parents weren't into the traditional music and rebel songs – they thought that belonged to another generation. My family liked pop music, rock 'n' roll and country music. Hearing the guitar riffs on the rock 'n' roll songs made a big impression on me, and I was always trying to work out what it was I was hearing. The more I noticed the guitars, the more alluring it all was, and the combination of the sound and the wild exuberance it brought out in everyone made me want to make music myself that would evoke the same kinds of feelings.

My gran was usually up for dancing, and by dancing I mean jiving, and jiving fast. All the chairs and tables were moved back, and she was up and off like a demon, elbows swinging and shoulders bouncing as she whirled around the floor. I was seven at the time and it was an amazing sight. Not all of the men would get up, but if my dad was in the mood and the right Elvis Presley song came on he and my mum would jive, and I thought they were fantastic.

As the night wore on it would be time for the instruments to come out, and everyone would sing songs. My dad's sister May would sing a couple, and then my Auntie Ann would sing. I liked the songs Ann sang, like 'Black Velvet Band', and I'd be waiting for it to be her turn. She had a poignant way of putting a song across, a way of singing that was tinged with sadness. Then my dad would take out a harmonica and give it to me and show me how to play the tune. In those late nights, sitting around with everyone playing and singing, the slower tunes took me to somewhere else, to a place of yearning and a beautiful melancholy that I understood but that was only expressed in music. In those melodies I discovered a different side to life, and the outside world faded out. It was something I thought was real and unspoken, and I learned that you could chase that feeling down. The music was my way into somewhere, as well as a way out.

I saw my first electric guitar in the Midway pub on Stockport Road in Longsight. The pub had a big room at the top where we used to go for parties, and Betty would hire her friend's band, The Sweeneys, to play. The parties at the Midway were great. The adults treated it as a big night, and everyone was dressed up in the new fashions. At the start of the night the room would be practically empty, as most people would be in the pub downstairs. Me and Claire would hang around upstairs waiting for the band to arrive, drinking fizz with our cousins Dennis and Ann while 'The Israelites' by Desmond Dekker and 'Baby Come Back' by The Equals played to the coloured lights.

When the band arrived, I'd watch them carrying their instruments up the stairs and then set up their equipment on the stage, waiting for the big moment when the guitar player went over to his case and took out his Fiesta Red Stratocaster. It was the most valuable-looking thing I'd ever seen, beautiful and shiny and contoured — it was better than a car, better than a jukebox, better than anything. Watching the band getting ready to play was amazing to me. It seemed like quite a serious business getting everything working right, and because they were grown-ups it appeared to be a job, a profession – and if that was a profession, why would anyone ever want to do anything else?

The band started their set when everyone was good and ready to start partying. It would all be uptempo for the first part of the night, a mixture of chart songs and some songs by the Irish club singers. I'd watch all of the band, but the guitar player was the one I really scrutinised as he flicked the switches and turned the knobs on his Strat.

One time, when they finished the first set and the band took a break, I remember, as usual, I had one thing on my mind: I had to see that guitar up close. I loitered around, just watching the case, so I could be there when the guitarist came back to open it. When he approached the stage and saw me waiting, he asked me if I wanted to take a look. He snapped open the lock and lifted the lid and there it was, right in front of me: shiny, red and chrome, with its strings and switches in its lined case, a totally otherworldly treasure. I examined it for as long as I could. It was beautiful.

My parents often went out to clubs in Manchester to see bands. The two main places were the Airdri and the Carousel, which were predominantly for the Irish community. In the 1960s, the club culture for the Irish in Manchester was still centred around showbands, which played a mixture of American rock 'n' roll, country and western, and ballads. The main frontman would be someone like Joe Dolan or Johnny McEvoy, and the backing bands would be The Big 8 or The Mainliners. Me and Claire were used to our parents going out, it was part of their routine, and I loved seeing them getting ready and the smell of my mother's perfume when she gave me a kiss on the way out of the door.

I would stay up with my Aunt Josie until they got back, and then I'd hear all about the bands and the songs and my mother would say, 'John, you would've loved the guitarist.' Sometimes, if it was one of the more well-known acts, my mum would have taken her autograph book. She'd tell me about meeting the artists to get a signed photo, and the excitement of it all made it seem like going out to see a band was the best and most glamorous thing that could ever happen.

As time went on, I was more aware that I came from the inner city. I had relatives who lived much further out of town, and when we took the long bus ride out to visit them it was a different world. Their lives were more about the hills and trees, and mine was streets and roads and walking around the city centre.

All my family went back to Ireland quite a lot. We'd get the night train from Victoria station in Manchester to Holyhead in Wales, and then get on the boat to Dublin. I'd stand on deck in the middle of the night with my dad in the blustering wind and look out at the moon on the sea. My dad would have me and my sister inside his overcoat, and it felt like an amazing adventure.

Kildare couldn't have been more different from Ardwick. My relatives lived in little cottages spread out along country lanes, surrounded by green fields. You boiled the water from a well in a big pot over a fire, and there was a barrel in the back garden with rainwater that you washed your hair in. I cycled around the lanes with my Aunt Josie, and I saw a lot of nature for the first time and played by a river. I didn't quite know what I was supposed to do in a field, but I came to like the calm of the country and the smell of the wood fires wafting across the fields in the evenings. It was nice to know my roots and see what life was like for the generation before me.

Back home, I was playing on my own one day when two scooters stopped at the end of the street with three older boys on them, and they called me over. As I approached them, I noticed that they were all dressed alike, with short hair, and one of them was wearing a shiny suit. I had my football with me, and one of them asked me if I wanted to sit on his scooter. He lifted me on to the back, revved it up and showed me where the side panels had been taken off so you could see the engine. I liked the scooter, but the thing I really noticed was the boys' clothes. One of them had a red rose sewn on to the pocket of his coat. I asked him what it was, and he said, 'That's the Lancashire Rose. See this?' he went on, pulling his coat open to show me the red lining. 'It's a Crombie.' Then he lifted up his shoe and said, 'These are called Royals, and you have to have these laces.' I looked at his red-and-black woven laces and saw that one of his friends was wearing the exact same type. When I noticed his black shirt with its button-down collars, the boy took off his suit jacket to show me the pleat that ran down the back and said, 'This is a Black Brutus.' I don't know why, but it seemed important to them that I had the right information about all of this, and I felt like I'd been given some secret knowledge. I watched them ride off and I thought they looked fantastic.

I ran to my house and shouted, 'Dad . . . Dad . . . I want a Crombie . . . can I get a Crombie?' My dad had no idea why his eight-year-old son was going mad about an overcoat. 'A Crombie?' he said. 'A Crombie coat, you mean?' 'Yeah,' I said, 'you have to sew a rose on it.' My dad was laughing and said, 'You're not getting a Crombie, that's a man's coat.' He thought I was mad, and then I turned to my mum and said, 'Mum . . . I have to get some Royals.'

Having a lot of industrial buildings around gave me plenty of opportunity for exploration, and one night me and some boys were climbing on the roof of a car mechanics workshop. There was a block of three old brick garages, and the roofs were made of corrugated iron that sloped up and down beside each other like mountain peaks. It was late at night and I thought nobody was in the buildings, but when I heard someone start yelling at me from below I jumped from one roof on to another and went straight through it. I spun around in blackness and saw the skylight above me, and then I woke up on the floor with my mother and some workmen standing over me as I was being lifted into an ambulance. The ambulance raced through the traffic with the siren blaring, and I was in and out of consciousness. I'd fallen thirty feet and was saved by a mechanic who'd broken his hand when he'd tried to catch me. I'd landed in a five-feet gap between huge sheets of glass and a forklift truck, and if I'd fallen a couple of feet either side it would've all been over. When we got to the hospital we learned that the man who'd saved me had come off worse in terms of broken bones. He was standing in the hospital corridor in shock and kept saying, 'He just came through the roof . . . he just came through the roof,' while my mother was thanking him for saving me.

Petrol Blues

I 've always said that when my family moved from Ardwick to Wythenshawe, eight miles away, it was like we'd moved to Beverly Hills. I was eight years old when my parents announced that we would be leaving our house as part of the inner-city clearance scheme, and to me it felt like we were finding the new frontier. My mother also announced that I'd be getting a new baby brother or sister soon. It was all exciting and very mysterious. Wythenshawe was a working-class area in the suburbs of south Manchester, and was the biggest housing estate in Europe.

It was Easter when we moved, which meant that the days were getting longer and the weather was good. My dad's boss gave my mum and my sister and me a lift in his car while my dad hauled our furniture in an uncle's van. Our new council house had three bedrooms upstairs and one main room downstairs, with a big window leading on to a garden at the back, and a small garden at the front. There was central heating, and best of all there was an inside toilet and a bath-room with a real bath, so we didn't need to fill up the tin tub any more, like we'd done in the old place.

All my relatives decided to move to new places that were closer to Ardwick, and although my gran and some of my other relatives would come to visit, the rest of the family started to go their own way. There were a number of other families from our street that had been relocated with us, and the new houses on our square made an instant community. Whereas in the old place I'd spent a lot of time on my own on our little street or in the house with the radio, there were now kids everywhere. I started playing all around the estate, which included lots of empty houses that the more intrepid of us were able to explore before the rest of the neighbourhood moved in. It felt like another beginning for us – new oppor-tunities in a brand-new environment.

Although the new community was just as diverse as the one we'd left behind, with British, Asian, Jamaican and Irish fami-lies all thrown in together, the early 1970s was a time of serious violence and racism in the UK, and was made all the worse for some Irish people with the media reports of bombings and terrorism on the mainland. I was in a friend's house one after-noon when his mother started complaining very loudly about one of the families on the estate. Her tone became nastier, and when she finished her tirade with a scathing 'Irish pigs', I realised it was meant for me. I was shocked: it felt like a vicious attack on my family. My parents had no political affiliation with anyone and were well respected. Claire and I had been called 'Irish pig' before by kids, and I had brushed it off as ignorance, especially as I was born in England, but being called one by an adult was hard to take.

My new primary school, the Sacred Heart, was a twenty-minute walk from our house. One of the benefits of my sister and me being so close in age was that it was slightly less of an ordeal being the new kids. As usual my sister fitted in quickly and got into the swing of things without too much fuss, whereas I felt like I'd migrated to the North Pole – my new environment seemed so bewildering. In the 1970s Wythenshawe had a reputation for being violent, but compared to Ardwick everyone seemed sophisticated and well mannered. It was nice, but also a bit strange. I was used to other kids being volatile and unpredictable; I wasn't used to them being polite and taking a positive interest in me.

Some of the Sacred Heart kids were a bit wary of us and acted like Claire and I were exotic curiosities because of the way we looked. Since we were little the two of us had been obsessed by clothes. We took note of what was in the shops and what everybody was wearing on the street, and our parents both had to work just to keep their kids from total meltdown should her platforms shoes not be high enough or his jacket need wider lapels. When we turned up for the first day of school we didn't realise we were supposed to be wearing a regular uniform. I was wearing a wool sweater with stars on that, believe it or not, was called a 'star jumper', and Claire had on a check jacket that looked like a shirt and was called . . . yes, a 'shirt jacket'. We were more suited to a disco than the school playground, but we were up-to-date and it got me attention from girls, which I liked, and also from some of the teachers, which I didn't.

Going to school in the suburbs changed things for me. In Ardwick I'd been quiet and was sensitive to what was going on around me. It wasn't always a good thing, and I often felt strangely uneasy without knowing why. Pop culture became all-consuming and more meaningful to me than anything else, and I related to it as if it were a portal to another dimension, one that made more sense to me than the world I actually lived in. My dream was that I would be able to escape there if I got good enough on the guitar. The move to Wythenshawe made me more confident, and I started to notice that I was around people who considered it a good thing that I took playing music so seriously.

My new teacher was called Miss Cocane. She was a very modern woman in her late twenties who smoked cigarettes after school in the classroom and who, ironically, was as intense as her name suggested. She could be stern, but she took an interest in me and would often ask about how I was progressing on the guitar. She spotted a creative side in me that no one else had really noticed. One afternoon I was leaving class when she called me back to talk to her. I stood beside her desk, hoping I wasn't in trouble, and listened attentively as she lit a cigarette and said, 'You have something that you should be aware of. What do you think about being an artist?' I listened to what she was saying and it sounded good. 'You can go two ways,' she continued, 'you can get bored and get into trouble, or you can find something you like and be good at it, and be an artist.' She sounded kind and concerned, and I knew she was serious. 'But it's not easy,' she said. 'You have to really work hard.' What she was saying was a revelation, but it seemed logical. 'You want to play the guitar, but we don't teach that in this school,' she said – which wasn't a problem for me as I didn't even know there was such a thing as guitar lessons – 'but you can do something else, and if you show me that you've worked hard at it you can bring your guitar to school. What else do you like?'

I had to think about that. No one had ever asked me that question before. I wanted to give her a genuine answer, so after pausing to think for a minute I said, 'Colours.'

'Colours?' she said. 'What colours? Trees? Nature? What do you mean?' She was intrigued.

I thought again, a bit unsure of how to reply. 'Bikes,' I said, 'and . . . clothes.'

She laughed, but I was sincere and she said, 'Right, of course.'

I walked home, thinking hard about our conversation. An artist . . . it sounded good, and it felt good, as if a door had been shown to me, a door that was wide open.

My answer about colours and bikes and clothes wasn't actually as abstract as it sounded. I'd become fascinated by colours, and I would obsess about a specific shade of green or blue in the way that I did about songs. It started in Ardwick when my dad got me a bike he'd bought off a mate. My Uncle Mike had showed me how to take it apart and respray it, and what had been an old purple junker had been transformed into a stunning machine of metallic bronze, which was a colour I didn't even know existed. A few weeks later I sprayed my bike metallic gold, then silver with dark red touches, and then another colour, and on and on it went. I loved painting bikes. I would examine the colours up close and would be mesmerised by them, and I wondered why I'd get a different feeling from one colour to another one.

When it came to clothes my environment couldn't have been more perfect. Working-class people are mad about fashion: they use their clothes to express who they are and who they want to be. If it's not exactly 100 per cent true that 'clothes maketh the man', then it's definitely a fact that clothes can maketh the man look a bit more interesting to girls and to other boys too.

The trends in my neighbourhood changed rapidly – you had to be fairly vigilant to keep up. Sometimes it was just about a colour, and this was the case with Oxford bags: extremely wide trousers that covered your shoes and came in an array of colours that became more desirable with every passing week. Dark red Oxfords were referred to by everyone as 'wines', and I coveted and obsessed over the vibrant 'electric blues' and beautiful 'bottle greens' until my parents bought me a pair just to shut me up. Best of all though were the 'petrol blues', a shade so perfect it would always be my favourite colour, and I would go to a shop in Moss Side called Justin's just to look at them. When it came to colours, however, nothing was ever as beautiful as the jackets and trousers called 'tonics', which were made from pieces of cloth that changed from gold to green, or maroon to blue, and which were so sublime that I sometimes thought of them as supernatural.

My favourite place for clothes was the Wythenshawe Park Fair, which came to the neighbourhood for three days every Easter. It was a ten-minute walk from my front door and was the highlight of the year for kids from all over south Manchester, who came to find adventure and engage in all sorts of teenage activity while trying to avoid the inevitable threat of violence that could break out at any time. Every minute was action-packed, and I'd be there from when the first ride started in the morning until the last ride stopped at night. I'd hang around the Speedway and the waltzers and take in everything. Girls would be screaming as they whizzed by, and 'Blockbuster!' and 'School's Out' would blare out from loud-speakers above the racket and commotion. There was a brand-new movement in pop music that was reclaiming the brash energy of rock 'n' roll and was built on trashy guitars, tribal drums and stomping beats, and I loved it. The bands all dressed garishly, with lots of make-up. They had names like Sweet, Bowie and Roxy, and played songs with titles like 'Teenage Rampage' and 'All the Young Dudes'. It was for rowdy young kids looking for excitement, and it went under the name of glam rock.

The best new band of all for me was T.Rex. Their song 'Jeepster' was the first record that I bought with my own money. I found it in Rumbelows, a furniture shop that sold electrical items and record players that were known as 'stereo-grams'. I'd gone in there because I knew they sold records cheap, and in a box of ex-chart singles I came across this amazing record. The label had a picture of a guy with a guitar on it; he was standing in the grass with his bandmate and was obviously wearing make-up. I was nine and I'd never seen anyone look like that before. I handed over my ten pence, and as I walked home I kept taking it out of the paper bag to look at it. When I got to the house I raced to the front room, switched on the family record player and put it on. The song kicked off with a drumbeat and then a guitar and handclaps. It sounded like people were playing in some room somewhere, not at all like the other pop songs that were around with their orchestras and pianos and boy-band harmonies. This song sounded odd, more alluring, a bit weird. Then I heard the singer's voice: '*You're so sweet, you're so fine . . .*' I pictured the enigmatic man in the make-up on the label, and he sounded like he looked. Within seconds the record got to the hook '*Girl, I'm just a Jeepster for your love*' and hit an unexpected chord change that was strange and moody. Forty-five seconds into it I was already planning on playing it again. I was on a journey. Hearing 'Jeepster' for the first time wasn't about hearing a song, it was about discovering a sound. I didn't care what he was singing about, it just sounded right with the music. The phrase that jumped out was '*You've got the universe reclining in your hair*', which to a nine-year-old was odd but striking. Somehow it all made sense.

Marc Bolan became my idol. I collected every poster and photo of him I could find, usually from girls' magazines like *Jackie*, and I went to the cinema to see his film *Born to Boogie*. Like George Best and Bruce Lee, Marc Bolan was small, audacious and good-looking, but best of all he was a pop star who played the guitar. He was also about to go on a creative streak, releasing a string of brilliant hit singles that would make him one of the most important figures of the decade. In 1972, not long after I bought 'Jeepster', T.Rex released the single 'Metal Guru', a record I thought was so beautiful, it sounded like it came from another world, yet was strangely familiar to me. I watched him perform it on *Top of the Pops*, and was so ecstatic after seeing it that I got on my bike and rode off down the roads until I got lost, then had to find my way home when I came back to my senses. Shortly after this I started to think about how Bolan had changed the spelling of his name from *Mark* to *Marc*, and it gave me an idea. If I ever changed my name from the seemingly unpronounceable *Maher*, a good way to spell it would be *Marr*.

Buying 'Jeepster' as my first record was a total fluke. It could have worked out differently had it not been for the picture of Bolan and Mickey Finn on the label. There's no doubt that I would have been a Marc Bolan fan eventually, but the significance of owning that first record at that point in my life went deeper, as 'Jeepster' and the B-side 'Life's a Gas' became the first songs I taught myself to play on the guitar, and that started me on the road to writing songs of my own.

A year earlier, my dad had taken me to Reno's guitar shop on Oxford Road and bought me a new acoustic. It was decent enough to play properly, and the practice I was putting in was starting to pay off. I didn't have my own record player, so I'd drag my parents' one off the sideboard in the front room and into the middle of the floor, and when everyone was out or in the kitchen I'd sit and learn from the records I'd bought or borrowed from my friends from the estate – usually Mark Johnson and Mike Gallway, who had the same tastes as me. In studying the records closely I picked up incidental things about arrangements and production, and I noticed that different instruments would come in and out for effect or that a vocal line would be doubled with a guitar or organ to make it stronger. The records in the early 1970s were unconventional and quirky, and instead of focusing solely on what the guitars were doing I would try to play what I was hearing on the whole record, giving me an accidental 'one-man band' approach. When the constant playing on the floor in the front room finally got too much for the rest of the family, they'd send me into the hallway so they could watch television, until eventually I got my own record player.

For me, having my own record player in my room was like a scientist getting his own laboratory, and I made the most of it. Now I could experiment all I wanted, and although I was sharing my room with my new baby brother, he would have to grow to love it.

My brother Ian's arrival was a new chapter for the family, and it brought us all even closer together. My parents were delighted, and it was especially nice for me and Claire to have a new sibling to fuss over. Having Ian around made me more grown up. Not only were Claire and I given the responsibility of chipping in and looking after him whenever it was required, but I was now a little boy's much older brother and it was a role I liked. I doted on Ian and he would follow me everywhere.

My family usually went away to North Wales for two weeks in the summer to stay in a caravan. We still didn't have a car, so we'd get a lift from a neighbour or my dad's boss; the journey always seemed to take for ever. I liked those times in the caravans. It was a nice break from work for my dad, and my mother could relax on the beach as Claire and I played with Ian in the dunes. We'd stay out by the sea all day until it was getting dark, and then we'd go up a long, steep road to a pub at the top, pushing Ian in the pram. We'd spend the evening in the family room round the back, and I'd stand on a chair in front of the jukebox all night, taking money off people to make their selections. Every so often Ian would toddle over with ten pence from my mum and dad for me to play something myself. At closing time we'd head back down the hill to the caravan, my dad carrying me on his shoulders, and we'd play cards and have something to eat. It was at times like these that I was aware that my parents were a little bit different from other kids' parents. They were still young, and would stay up late, having a drink. They were pretty laid-back.

My dad got involved with the local social club and he would take me and Claire with him when he went to see bands to book them. We'd go on a Sunday afternoon to a club some-where out of town, and my dad would buy us Cokes and crisps and we'd sit with a bunch of agents and club owners while the bands and singers would audition. The acts would come out in their stage gear and do their routines and sing the hits of the day. I'd watch them plugging in their equipment and messing around with echo machines and I thought it was like being in the music business.

My best friend on the estate was Chris Milne. He had moved from Ardwick at the same time as us, and he lived just six houses away from me on the square. Chris was a blast. He was funny and outgoing and he liked pop music too, and we were put in the same class at Sacred Heart. His family were original Mancunians, warm-hearted with a lot of banter and an open-door policy, which meant I went round to his house a lot. We'd often play things from his sister Catherine's record collection, which included an album by The Supremes. Chris had three main interests: Rod Stewart, Manchester City football club and girls – all of which meant that he was a great best mate.

Chris and I would hang out together, and when we'd finished kicking a football around I'd bring my T.Rex collection over to his house, which now included 'Ride a White Swan', 'Metal Guru' and 'Children of the Revolution', plus some Sweet and David Bowie. Chris would play me his Faces records, I'd find tracks off The Supremes' *Greatest Hits*, and he would sing along to everything. I don't know who suggested we should form a group – maybe Chris wanted to sing with his mate who was a guitarist, or more likely it was the other way around – but either way it seemed like the obvious next step to me, so I dedicated myself to learning how to write a song that Chris could sing. My first efforts at songwriting were basically steals from Bolan, which was impressive seeing as I had no idea what he was singing about. I doubt that he knew himself. I was able to do it without too much difficulty though, and with some songs of my very own and my mate singing, all I had to do now was find some other eleven-year-olds to make up the rest of the band. But before I could do that, Chris and I had to put world domination on hold. We had somewhere else to go: Maine Road, home of Manchester City FC.

Terraces

I was ten when I first went to see Manchester City. I was already well into football, but hadn't yet committed to either City or Manchester United. All my family and relatives were United fans, and they had assumed I would be falling into line. My Uncle Mike had even supplied me with one of his United shirts, which for some reason I never got round to wearing. Don't get me wrong, I thought George Best was a totally cool dude, but everyone knew that. I'd even been to a United match, with my cousin Martin and my Uncle Christie, when United played Chelsea at Old Trafford and lost one-nil. But instead of it enticing me into the Red Devils' fraternity, the experience had the total opposite effect: when I got into the ground, I just didn't like . . . the vibe. I don't know why, but I just didn't go for it. The next week Chris Milne and I took off on our own to watch Man City, and within a mile of their ground at Maine Road I knew I was in the right place and that the world would be forever sky-blue. There was another reason I became a Manchester City fan, and that was because at the time City were the better team. It was fortuitous for me that I was at the right age at a rare time when the blue side of Manchester was the more successful. I started going to the games when City were in their heyday and had legendary players like Mike Summerbee, Francis Lee and Colin Bell. I loved the fact that my team were formidable and had style. Things would get even better with the arrival of Dennis Tueart from Sunderland. He was tricky and tenacious, and had the right amount of flash and attitude to go with it. Dennis Tueart became my footballing hero, and would take his place in Manchester City folklore by scoring the winning goal in a Wembley cup final with an overhead kick. The only way he could have been any cooler was if he had been playing a Gibson Les Paul while he was doing it.

Going to a football match in Britain in the early 1970s was scary for a kid, and like nothing else at all. It was a parade of tribalism, boorishness and aggression. Boys and men with feather cuts and skinheads pounded the streets in boots and braces, and with scarves tied to their wrists and belts, in a procession of loud menace. No one gave a damn about your size. If you were in, you were all in, and if it kicked off, which it always did, then no one cared that you were ten or eleven or whatever, you'd better run and be prepared to give someone a kicking or get a kicking like everyone else – either that or make sure you stayed well on the fringes. Getting jostled around on the terraces amidst all the older blokes pushing and shouting abuse was an education. On the terraces you'd see men with earrings, dyed hair and shaved eyebrows; customised trousers called 'skinners', turned up to the shins, with twenty-four-hole Doctor Martens, and home-made tattoos done with a pin and Indian ink. It was all completely eye-opening to me.

I went to every home game, and sometimes I'd get to an away game. Going to away games was downright perilous, as you were venturing into enemy territory and asking to get beaten up. I went to watch City at Middlesbrough, and from the moment I got off the coach at Ayresome Park I knew it was a mistake. After the game the City fans were fenced in the car park, while a couple of hundred Middlesbrough fans were baying for us and attempting to pull down the gates that were keeping them out and us in. After five minutes one of the fences got destroyed, and as the gates crashed down a horde of monsters rushed at us. It was total panic. I got caught in the swarm of City fans and was swept out on to the street with everyone screaming and shouting and policemen on horseback charging about the place. I darted across the road and ran at top speed until, completely lost and alone, I came to a side street. I carried on to the end, and as I got there a young Middlesbrough fan ran into the street from the opposite direction and stopped right in front of me. We looked at each other for a few seconds and neither of us knew what to do. I didn't want to get beaten up, and I didn't want to try to beat anyone else up either. I sized up the enemy: we were about the same age and he was scared; we were both in the same predicament. I instinctively put my hands up and made it obvious I didn't want any trouble, then he stuck his hand out to shake mine. He took the red-and-white silk scarf from around his wrist and said, 'Do you wanna swap scarves, mate?' Getting a scarf from an opposing fan at an away game usually meant taking a scalp from a battle. I took his scarf and gave him mine off my wrist, and he patted me on the shoulder as we both took off in opposite directions. I ran frantically around more streets until I eventually hitched a ride home from some City fans in a van.

I went to other away games and I got chased a few times, but I never got another scarf and I never had to give one away either. I kept the scarf from the Middlesbrough kid and wore it at some City games. People assumed it was a trophy, but I knew otherwise and I liked the way I'd got it.

Wythenshawe

The six-week summer holiday break was the schoolkid's ultimate reward. After school broke up, a whole six weeks of freedom from the rigours of school would stretch gloriously before me, and I'd anticipate adventures – some planned, some a mystery, but either way I knew something was bound to happen.

The 1975 summer holidays were significant for me as I'd finished at Sacred Heart Primary School and it would be the last big break before starting at St Augustine's Grammar School, which I'd got into after passing the eleven-plus entrance exam. On the first day of the holidays it had become a custom for a bunch of us boys and girls to head out on our bikes to the River Bollin, which was about a ten-mile ride away. That year, after a day of swimming in the river and hanging out in the sun, we started to cycle home as fast as we could. I was on a second-hand racing bike that was too big for me, which I'd painted purple. We flew up a steep hill, and as we shot down the other side at top speed I leaned forward to pull the brakes and my foot slipped into the front wheel. The bike jammed instantly, and I somersaulted over the handlebars and into the air, followed by the bike, and then crashed on to the brand-new road, skidding along at full speed and ripping a lot of the skin off my arms and my back. When I came to a stop and my friends helped me up, I noticed my friend Mike turning green when he saw my mangled wrist and my hand flopping around in the wrong direction. All I could do was to ride the seven miles to the nearest hospital while trying to use my arm in order to stay on the bike.

When we got to the hospital and the shock wore off I was in agony, and I was rushed into the operating theatre to fix my right arm, which was broken in two places. When the doctors were done I had a huge plaster cast on it, and was told it would come off after six weeks, which meant I'd have it for the rest of the holidays, right up until I started my new school. A nurse said to me, 'That's so unlucky, breaking your arm on the first day of the holidays,' but all I could think of was, *How am I going to play the guitar?*

The holidays were torture, as not only could I not play the guitar, but I couldn't ride my bike either. I'd sit by my record player and listen to a pile of 7-inch singles, but not being able to play along with them was really frustrating. There was one record that came out that summer that I listened to incessantly: 'Disco Stomp' by the intriguingly named Hamilton Bohannon.

The guitar in it was hypnotic and infectious, and I couldn't wait to work it out as soon as my arm was healed. Not being able to play meant that I had to focus on something else, so I taught myself vocal harmonies by singing along to The Hollies' *Greatest Hits*, which had the added bonus of some good guitar parts by Tony Hicks.

The day finally came when I could have the cast taken off and start my new secondary school. I left the hospital and walked into class late, wearing the new regulation navy-blue blazer, which the school had just changed from the traditional blue with pink stripes, and which had been the bane of previous pupils' lives – as well as being known to rival schools as 'pyjama boys', the owners of said striped blazer stood out a mile and would often get beaten up for wearing it. I adapted my new uniform so that it looked suitably modern: my tie was as wide as possible and my trousers were 14-inch flares. I also appeared to be much taller than I actually was, as under my flares were shoes called wedges, with giant platform soles, in regulation black.

I was ambivalent about going to St Augustine's. On the one hand I was supposed to feel privileged to be there on account of its former academic achievements, which was something the school were never slow to remind you of; but on the other hand all of my friends who hadn't passed the entrance exam were at the less prestigious and far more appealing St Paul's Secondary School down the road. The other thing I had a problem with was that St Augustine's was an all-boys school, and having been around girls all my life it was a bit of a shock and something that took me a while to adapt to.

The headmaster of St Augustine's was the infamous Monsignor McGuiness, aka Spike, who had been given his nickname on account of his enormous hooked nose, and was known for liberally dispensing six of the best to boys with a leather strap. He was an imposing barrel of a man who loomed over us in the corridors in his clergyman robes, giving off an air of holy menace and completing the sinister look with his shiny black hair, scraped back in the style of a fat vampire. It was also common knowledge that he was usually very drunk, and you would notice this if you had the misfortune to encounter him. The Monsignor's title meant that in the Catholic Church he ranked higher than a priest but lower than a bishop, which the school regarded as practically the same as having their own man in the Vatican. That the neighbourhood and therefore the school was becoming more working class was a source of consternation to Spike, and he tried to maintain the appearance of upper-class entitlement and old-style English elitism, despite the fact that the school so obviously didn't warrant it. The teachers, who were referred to as 'masters', were required to wear gowns at all times, with some of the more enthusiastic electing to parade around with mortarboard hats on their heads, like it was Oxford in the 1940s and not actually Manchester in the 1970s. There was also the depressing matter of the school's reputation for physical violence by teachers on pupils, which I saw plenty of, and the rumours of sexual abuse, which I'd heard whispers about and which was eventually found to be all too true, with at least one teacher convicted and serving a prison sentence some years later.

I took to the business of grammar school well enough and tried to learn to adapt. For the first time I was around some kids from middle-class and upper-class backgrounds, and I discovered that a nice house and exotic holidays might sound great but privilege can sometimes make you timid. It was also the first time I'd met kids whose parents had divorced, which was something that you never heard of in working-class circles. Some boys were intimidated and I felt sorry for them; I was relieved that I didn't feel like that myself. After a while I found I was only interested in a few subjects, English literature being one of them. It was inspiring to discover W. H. Auden and T. S. Eliot and to learn about the classics, and I liked something in all of the poetry that we studied.

The very first art lesson was memorable. The teacher, Mr Addis, started off with an explanation of the Union Jack and why it was such a poor design. I warmed to the theme immediately, having always disliked the national flag for its association with racist skinheads, and viewing it as aesthetically lazy and charmless. Mr Addis then instructed us to design our own national flag, and I took to the task enthusiastically by painting a ship on to a white, blue and maroon background; someone then pointed out to me this was a flag designed entirely for people from Manchester, as the ship signified the Manchester ship canal. The teacher thought it was a good design though, and from then on I would visit the art room as much as possible at break times to paint and to make collages.

Aside from English and art – and maths, which for some reason I found I was good at – the only other things that engaged me in school were football and music. I got on the football team and was put on the right wing on account of being small and fast. I liked being a winger, it suited my mentality. I enjoyed being speedy and swerving around, getting chased down and chasing something down. I had little interest in being up front in the centre, and was more than happy to leave that to someone else to make a big deal about. I liked the tricky stuff and making something happen, being flash on the side and then setting up your mate up front, and if the centre forward wanted to run around taking all the glory, then fine. To me the winger was cooler, and I felt the same way about guitarists and singers.

Getting on the football team was a blessing and a curse. It gave you a bit of status and was fun while you were doing it, but it also meant that you had to give up your Saturday mornings to play, something I was not at all eager to do. The games teacher who ran the team was particularly sadistic and took my attitude as insolence. He would go out of his way to single me out and punish me by sending me on long runs, which wasn't actually a problem for me as I didn't mind running at all.

Every so often the bus ride to school would be notable if not downright spectacular because of the presence of one passenger. Wayne Barrett would get on at Sharston Baths and make his way to the back of the bus, wearing a polka-dot blouse and black velvet pants, with a bright green Ziggy Stardust haircut and shaved eyebrows. Aside from his image, he was notorious for being tough and had the distinction of being the only person expelled from St Augustine's purely for being a badass. I'd seen so-called boot boys and effeminate glam

42

rockers before, but never as the same person. Wayne Barrett was the lead singer of the local band Slaughter and the Dogs, and he walked on to the 371 like he was walking onstage at Madison Square Garden.

One downside of coming from Wythenshawe was that its reputation for violence was well deserved. You had to watch yourself walking through subways or cutting across parks in case you bumped into the wrong people, and you had to be especially streetwise if you were carrying a guitar. One evening, coming back from a mate's, I took a detour across some derelict land near my house and saw two hooligans in the distance. They were people I knew but were also the type of guys who would be friendly one day and jump you for no reason the next. As I walked past them, hoping it was one of their friendlier days, I felt a chunk of brick hit me on the back of the head and heard a dull buzz in my ears as another rock hit me on the side of the face. I couldn't let myself run, something in me wouldn't allow it, and I knew that if I did they'd come after me and give me a kicking. Blood was coming down from the gash in my head and was all over my hands when I got to my house, and my mother took me to the hospital once again to get my head stitched up. I'd see the guys who did it knocking around, and they both acted like nothing had happened. It was just the way it was.

My friend Tony was a beautiful creature, another Bowie fan, with a blonde Ziggy haircut, high cheekbones, and green eyes like a Siamese cat. He wore red Oxford bags with white platforms and a black Harrington jacket. Tony was three years older than me and was the first guy I knew who was openly gay. The trends and times meant that boys who looked like girls, and girls who looked like boys, were fairly commonplace, especially if you were into David Bowie, and plenty of straight men were fashionably camp and effeminate. Tony came from a family of three brothers who were all hard and rarely needed to show it. Most people assumed that you shouldn't mess with Tony, because of his brothers, but they would find out that he didn't need protecting by anyone anyway. Tony wasn't camp but he was cutting and had a serene self-possession that gave him a feline poise and inscrutability. A lot of boys found him intimidating, and most of the girls I knew were either in love with him or wanted to be him.

We were together a lot, and it got some people talking, which didn't bother me at all – we had a lot of things in common and plenty to talk about. The two of us were in Piccadilly Gardens one Saturday afternoon just after I'd had my hair cut. We were waiting at the bus stop when two big uglies with north Manchester accents came over and started making cooing noises and blowing kisses. I looked at Tony's face as he continued talking to me, and I could see he was aware of the situation. 'Eh,' said one of the lads, 'are you queers?' They were obviously up for a fight. I readied myself for the inevitable as Tony continued to talk to me with his back to the goons and appeared to be ignoring their remarks until one pushed him in the back and said, 'Eh, y'fuckin' queer.' With that, Tony grabbed my head and kissed me on the lips for what seemed like a very long time, then spun around and attacked the biggest of the two with really hard punches to the face until the lad went on to his knees. He then grabbed the other guy, who was backing off, punched him very hard in the face and threw him down into the road full of traffic. I thought the guy was going to be killed, and as we ran off towards the train station Tony turned to me and said, 'That was nice' and then, laughing, he added, 'Don't worry, I won't do it again.'

On the train home in my platforms and Budgie jacket, I looked at Tony and thought about 'All the Young Dudes': '*Now Lucy looks sweet 'cause he dresses like a queen. But he can kick like a mule, it's a real mean team.*' I loved the song, and there was no doubting it, pop music was for me and my friends.

The first show I ever went to see was Slaughter and the Dogs at the Wythenshawe Forum. Fronted by Wayne Barrett and Mick Rossi, this band were local heroes and had built up a following of kids from all over south Manchester. I got into the show because my friend's brother was in the support band, Wild Ram, who would soon change their name to The Nose-bleeds. Although I was only twelve years old, my parents were relaxed about where I went and assumed I knew what I was doing even if I didn't. The atmosphere in the Wythen-shawe Forum was a riot. Slaughter and the Dogs were introduced by Tony Wilson, who I recognised from being on the TV, and during their set 300 kids threw themselves and each other around in a way that was both dancing and fighting at the same time. I stayed on the outskirts of the fray, just watching it all. Slaughter were exactly what their audience needed, a young band from the same streets who looked like stars, and with a guitar player in Mick Rossi who knew what he was doing and was blazing a trail. Very soon afterwards they changed their style and image, but to me they were best and most true to themselves as street glam kids. I saw them at their teenage peak, and it was a great first show for me to see.

I don't know what would have happened had I stayed in Ardwick, because in Wythenshawe there were kids everywhere playing music. Different parts of the estate were represented by fledgling bands with names like Moonchild, The Freshies, Four Way Street and Sad Cafe, and there were at least two bands called Feedback. It may have been the times or because of the sudden migration of kids into the area, but wherever I went I'd hear about someone with a guitar or drum kit. Maybe it was because I was looking out for it, or maybe it was looking for me.

West Wythy

'I hear you're forming a band – you should get me in on drums.' That was how Bobby Durkin introduced himself to me. I was happy to have encountered a drummer so easily, and I knew he was good because he told me so: 'I'm good. Come around to mine on Saturday and we'll have a jam.' Bobby was a likeable fella with black Bolan hair and, like me, he came from an Irish family. He was a typical drummer, outgoing and full of energy. This meant that I now needed to get an electric guitar so that I could be heard, and acquiring one became my main preoccupation.

I had been going into a guitar shop in the nearby town of Altrincham religiously every Saturday so I could be around the guitars and hear the owner's stories of life on the road as the soundman for The Sweet. I never had the money to buy strings or plectrums, but my devotion to the place was such that eventually the boss, Duncan, let me make cups of tea for him and run out for sandwiches and cigarettes. After several weeks of free labour my persistence paid off and Duncan agreed to give me a discount on a second-hand Red Vox Ace that I'd set my heart on and which happened to be the cheapest guitar in the shop. My mother said that if I got a paper round and saved the money then she and my dad would help out. I delivered papers twice a day and saved up all the money I got, and with my parents chipping in I bought my first electric guitar for £32.

Dave Clough was the first real guitarist that I knew. He was sixteen and he dressed like his hero Nils Lofgren in scarves and patterned shirts. I'd met him at the youth club, which was the haunt of Claire and her friends and all the switched-on kids. It was known as 'West Wythy' – or 'West Wivvy' as we all pronounced it – on account of it being held in West Wythenshawe College. Like the fair, West Wythy was a place to dress up and hear music. Open three nights a week, it was a hotbed of hormones and fashion.

It was important that I got there early, because before the DJ started his set at seven thirty I would hang out with a gang of older boys who stood around the jukebox, playing old records that I wouldn't hear anywhere else. It had been a while since I'd seen people playing old records, and it was fascinating to watch these older boys make selections in the manner of connoisseurs. I'd look into the jukebox as an old Decca or Track label spun around. 'Wishing Well' by Free, 'Crosstown Traffic' by Jimi Hendrix, 'Substitute' by The Who and, best of all, 'The Last Time' by The Rolling Stones introduced me to a musical philosophy and the sorts of records where the guitar was the star. The older guys in West Wythy regarded themselves as real guitar players, and regardless of the fact that I was a little kid they treated me as a junior one of them, and that was something that meant everything.

There was one kid at West Wythy who didn't play or sing but was very cool. Andrew Berry had a dark red soulboy haircut and wore peg trousers and a black cap-sleeved T-shirt with the word 'Roxy' on it. Growing up with three sisters, he had worked out that the best way to meet girls was to cut their hair, and he was already a great hairdresser by the time he was fifteen. Andrew and I really got along. He was sharp and funny, and he carried himself as if he was a cut above the scruffy musicians. We started to look out for each other, and we would make time to talk whenever we could.

I needed an amp so I could play with Bobby Durkin, and Dave Clough let me borrow his. It was a nice gesture, and unusual for someone to part with their precious amp for an afternoon. Bobby's was a lively Irish household, with his little twin brothers running around and his older brother Billy making dry quips about us being 'on *Top of the Pops* tomorrow'. I squeezed myself and the amp up the staircase and into the bedroom, and as I stood in front of the drums I plugged the guitar into the amp. I held the guitar and heard a buzz and a crackle and then *Kraanng!* I hit the chord and the drums kicked in, and I was playing an electric guitar along with someone else, just like a band. It was happening, I was a real musician. I played with Bobby for the rest of the afternoon. We were rough, but it felt good and I could have carried on doing it all night.

The word got around about me and Bobby playing, and I soon got a recommendation about someone with a guitar who was interested in playing with us. Kevin Williams lived over the railway bridge on the estate. Lanky and sporting nerdy spectacles, he didn't quite fit the image of the rock star, but it didn't bother him one bit as he was a natural showman who gallivanted around the neighbourhood, entertaining everyone with songs and jokes he'd memorised from television and things he had come up with himself. Kevin and I went through some songs from a Beatles book at his house and I saw that he was good, so I started looking for a place for us to practise while coming up with some songs that we could all play.

The front of our house was on a busy dual carriageway opposite Brookway High School, which was a big modern place from the 1960s that most of the local kids attended. I wanted to go to Brookway rather than St Augustine's as it was outside my front door, but my mother was having none of it as it wasn't a Catholic school and it had a reputation for devilment, which to me made it sound even better. Almost everyone I knew went to Brookway, so it was only a matter of time before I met the rest of Dave Clough's friends, who were in a band called Four Way Street. The main man of the band was a talented guitarist and singer called Rob Allman. Rob was a middle-class kid with supportive parents who let their son and his friends rehearse in the hallway of their house. I was invited over to see them play. All the band were nice, but a little curious about the visitor sitting on the stairs while they rehearsed, especially as I had adopted the look of a mini Keith Richards and was smoking cigarettes, which I had become an expert at in recent months. The band ran through the rock songs of the day, like 'Jumpin' Jack Flash' and 'All Right Now'. I took it all in, and liked seeing how it all worked.

My attention then turned to their other guitarist, called Billy, who knew he was cool and seemed to be taking it more seriously than the others. While all the young musicians who were around at the time were copying their heroes, Billy Duffy had a unique way of playing, whether by accident or design. I'd never seen anyone look that serious when they played. When the band finished, Billy and I got talking and he was the one out of all of them with whom I had an affinity.

I started spending more time at Rob's. His parents were kind, and the house became a creative haven for me and Billy and a few others who played guitar. I don't know why I was accepted by the older guys, other than the fact that I could play quite well and had mastered 'Rebel Rebel' better than anyone else. Being around them was an education. They were clued up, acerbic and sarcastic, and soon I was able to play everything they could. It was unusual for a bunch of older kids to nurture someone so much younger. Maybe it was because I could take care of myself, or maybe they just liked having a little urchin hanging around.

Rob Allman was brilliant and musically gifted, with an ego that made him an obvious frontman and a prodigious enthusiasm for alcohol. I would go over on a Saturday night and he'd have a bag containing six cans of toxic syrup called Carlsberg Special Brew, which made you so deranged you'd have been better off sniffing glue on a merry-go-round. I would hang in there after drinking two cans and try to get through a Neil Young song or 'While My Guitar Gently Weeps' before dropping my guitar on the floor and running to throw up outside. Sometimes I didn't make it.

The atmosphere around Rob's was more like a salon for musicians, and everyone had their own influences and specialist subjects: Billy's favourite guitarists were Mick Ronson, and Paul Kossoff from Free; Rob was into Neil Young and Richard Thompson; and there were a lot of guitar players that we all liked, such as Nils Lofgren, Pete Townshend and Bill Nelson. I was very into Keith Richards and was a Rolling Stones fanatic, having discovered their 1960s Decca singles on the West Wythy jukebox. My first impression of Keith Richards was from seeing his image on the cover of the *Through the Past, Darkly* album at someone's house. When I learned that the guitar on the records came from the same person in the photograph, and I then became aware of his reputation as an outlaw outsider, I was fascinated. He seemed totally heroic, and his role in coming up with riffs and driving his band was like a beacon to me. People forget just how freaky Keith Richards was in the late 1960s and early 1970s. He was a freaky dangerous guitar player, and he could write a riff better than anyone.

The other big influence on me at this time was Rory Gallagher. I found his albums in record shops and I knew I would like him. Lots of bands at that time were remote and shrouded in Tolkienesque imagery or had a sound that was swamped with organs and all kinds of nonsense. Rory Gallagher was Irish and someone I could relate to. He had a beat-up guitar, played stripped-down lo-fi rock and was the walking definition of musical integrity. He seemed to live for playing the guitar, and to me he represented the idea that if you wanted you could live all of your life in a room with your guitar and an amp and that could be your world forever.

We all read the music press and discussed everything that was going on, and then one day something was different. There had been a gig in town the night before by a new band from London called Sex Pistols, and some of the older guys had gone. I heard there had been a big fight with people throwing pint glasses and chairs, and it sounded a nightmare, but then I saw Billy and got another side to the story. He was raving about this band, who played loud short songs and were really young. He was saying, 'They were really good, John . . . really good' as an indisputable fact, and it was obvious that the Pistols had affected him. Then I heard about the opening band, called Buzzcocks, who were from Manchester and had a broken guitar, and within a single day I realised that something had changed. The first punk song I heard was 'Boredom' by Buzzcocks on a 7-inch EP called *Spiral Scratch*, which my friend's older brother had bought. I picked up the record and looked at the cover, and turning it over the first name I saw was John Maher, who played the drums. I had to change the spelling of my surname. It had already been decided.

In the meantime I was making progress with my own guitar playing and starting to develop a style that I liked and that I was even able to identify as being my own. I always switched between playing acoustic and electric – to me it meant that you were more complete; I thought I should be equally good on both. One time, I was sitting round at Rob's, playing a riff, when Billy came in and said to me, 'James Williamson?' I hadn't heard that name before and asked him what he meant. 'That riff . . . it sounds like James Williamson,' he said. I was a bit bothered by that, as what I was playing was something I was turning into a song, but I could see he genuinely thought it sounded like someone else and I wanted to know who this James Williamson was. 'It sounds like something off *Raw Power* by Iggy and the Stooges,' Billy said, 'you'll love it.' I made a mental note to check this record out. If there was someone out there who played this way, then I wanted to hear it.

The next time I was in Virgin Records, I leafed through the *S* section for Stooges, looking for *Raw Power*. Wow! What the hell was that cover?! The picture was unbelievable, strong, a weird creature, totally unlike anything else I'd ever seen. I held it and something told me I needed it. I bought it for £3.30, and on the bus ride home I kept looking at the sleeve, trying to imagine what it would sound like. I got home, put the record on in my bedroom and heard 'Search and Destroy' for the first time. It blew my mind, and I wondered why the whole world hadn't already told me about the track, then the next song started, 'Gimme Danger', and there it was . . . the acoustic guitar sounding like what I'd been playing. How could that be? This sounded to me like the greatest ever group, heavy, sexy, dirty, like the best older brothers someone like me could ever find, and James Williamson's playing was perfection. I played the whole album over and over, and hearing it I knew I was on the right path and that everything I already felt was real. Iggy and the Stooges were going to a place I really wanted to be; *Raw Power* shone a light.

Having my own band with the full line-up of me, Chris, Kevin and Bobby was exciting, and I couldn't wait to get going. I plucked the name 'Paris Valentinos' from the air and it stuck.

Now that punk had come along all the fashions had changed, and Claire pierced my ear for me by taking a sewing needle and stabbing it straight through my left earlobe without even bothering to put ice on it beforehand. The other requirement for being in a band was to dye your hair various colours, and we would steal bottles of hair dye from the supermarket and change our hair colour almost every week. After I got into Johnny Thunders and New York Dolls, I started cutting my hair myself and took to always wearing eye liner, which didn't go down well with the teachers at St Augustine's. I also insisted that they change the spelling of my name on the register to *Marr* instead of *Maher*, but they refused, so I just put *Marr* on the front of my schoolbooks and refused to answer if a teacher called me *Ma-her* or *Ma-yer* when they took the register.

Bobby had persuaded the Sacred Heart school to let Paris Valentinos use their hall to practise once a week, and we had the whole place to ourselves. What he didn't tell us was that in return he had agreed to us playing hymns in the church next door for the congregation at the Sunday evening service. We duly complied and tried to look solemn as we strummed through the hymns, until a few weeks later the priest decided he was better off without us because we were often giggling uncontrollably and Kev was chatting up the girls in the choir.

I still didn't have an amp, so I would share Kevin's Vox with him and we'd plug the microphone into the PA system that the school used for assembly. After all the wishing and fanta-sising, it was good to finally get down to the business of actually being in a band and learning how to do it, although it wasn't all excitement: sometimes Bobby couldn't get his dad to bring his drums, and I'd have to motivate the others to come and practise when there was a disco on somewhere nearby.

The first gig we played was in the summer of 1977, at a street party for the Queen's Silver Jubilee. I'd been seeing a girl called Denise for a few weeks, and she told me that her dad wanted someone to play and asked me if the band could do it. When we got to her house there were a couple of tables set up on the street for a stage, with a few gangs of kids lingering around, eyeing up the drum kit. Chris spotted a crate of lager and promptly set about it, and Kevin produced a bottle of cider.

When the appointed time came for us to make our debut, we staggered into the sunshine and on to the tables and kicked off with a wobbly rendition of Thin Lizzy's 'Don't Believe a Word', which luckily featured Kevin on lead vocals, as Chris, our singer, was stumbling around, out of it, on the pavement behind. We followed this with 'Jumpin' Jack Flash' and Tom Petty's 'American Girl' before we had to stop and get off the stage to push the tables back together. All in all it wasn't going so badly, and we introduced Chris as he made a few comedy attempts to get up on to the tables. Once he was up, he hung on to the mic stand and addressed the twenty people scattered around the road with a flamboyant 'Good evening, people' before launching into a confusing version of 'Maggie May'. He then had to be carried off by the rest of us before reaching the end of the second verse. It was a good day. We went home feeling triumphant and drunk. I knew we were scrappy and I felt like a kid, but at least I was a kid in a band.

The only thing I needed now was an amp of my own, and I heard that Billy Duffy had just got a new Fender amp after joining The Nosebleeds. I nagged him to sell me his old Falcon practice amp, and eventually he agreed to part with it for £15. When I got it home after carrying it the two miles from his house, I found that he'd put his pink shirt in the back which I'd been pestering him to give me for weeks.

At home, my parents watched me coming and going, buzzing around, trying to get my band going and becoming even more independent. My dad and I left each other to do our own thing, and that's how we got along. He'd get in from laying pipes, and I'd either go out, or stay in my room, listening to records and practising. I was starting to get fairly rebellious, but we managed to co-exist; it suited him and it suited me. My mum was a bit more involved in what I was doing, but she left me to get on with my life in my own way. I was fourteen and the oldest child, and she was taking care of Ian, who was just starting school, and she'd also gone back to work in a post office.

One day my dad asked me if I fancied going out to do a

week's work with him in Liverpool. He was working on the road near Quarry Bank school, where John Lennon had gone, and aside from thinking that the pop culture connection might tempt me, he also thought it would be good for me to get out and do some proper work in the school holidays. I thought he was mad to even suggest it, but he was persistent and after a while I realised that the money would be useful, so I agreed. At five thirty on Monday morning he woke me up. It was still dark. I immediately wondered why the hell I was awake and getting into my dad's van. After an hour's drive I fell out of the van and on to the pavement, where my dad said to me, 'See down there?'

I looked down the road to where he was pointing. 'Yeah?' I said.

'We're going to dig all the way down there – all the way – and by Friday no one will know we've even been here.'

I looked down the street to where he was pointing. It was a really long way. I dragged all the heavy equipment out of the van and I was already really muddy before I'd even started. I got my head down and got on with digging the road. A couple of my dad's mates showed up each day and watched a lad with dyed hair and bracelets wrestling with a jackhammer while looking like a mini New York Doll. Every day I'd get in the trench and lay the gas pipes, and every day, driving back in the van, I'd fall asleep with my head up against the window. It was knackering. At the end of the week the road was back to normal and my dad handed me £125. That was pretty good – it was certainly more money than I'd ever owned. It was hard-earned, and my dad did it every day – that really impressed me.

After a few years of St Augustine's I was starting to learn how the school worked and how to work it. Like every guitar player through the ages, I was good at art and good at English, and could do well enough in most things if only I found them worthy of interest. I wanted very much to like history classes, but in those days everything you were taught in a Catholic school had a Catholic agenda, and so history was mainly indoctrination in martyrs and saints. My parents would get the same comments about me from the teachers: 'He's intelligent and is letting himself down' and 'He won't apply himself to the work.' A couple of the more right-on teachers tried a more positive approach, telling me that I could be a leader, which was well-meaning but I didn't really know why they said it.

My head was so full of songs and bands that nothing my teachers or parents said could make me think my future was going to be anything other than music. I would put a record on in my room before I left the house for school in the morning while Ian was downstairs getting ready. 'Cracked Actor' off *Aladdin Sane* was a favourite. I'd turn it up really loud and Claire would be in the bathroom, shouting, 'John! John! Turn it down! Turn it down, will yer! I'm trying to do my hair.' Why 'Cracked Actor' hindered her styling process so much I don't know, but she took her hair very seriously.

I would turn records up as loud as they would go and play them over and over while staring at the label going around. It could have appeared crazy to my family, but they were used to it and understood it. I'd continue to stand and listen in my blazer, holding my school bag, and then I'd have to run out of the front door and across the road to jump on to the bus. I'd find somewhere upstairs near the back, lean my head against the window and keep the song in my head until the bus got to school. It was a useful technique that helped me get through the day – it was like I was wearing invisible headphones.

Most of the boys at my school were all right. One of the most enduring things from school was learning to recognise the different personalities that crop up. Some were loudmouths and some were quiet types. There were one or two kids who were genuinely funny and a few who were irritating. Those who were most irritating were the ones who made a craft of it. I always wondered what mentality you had to have to be like that, and I suspected those who craved constant attention were not entirely OK with themselves.

I didn't have a problem making friends, but there wasn't anyone that I felt I had very much in common with. Then, one day, I was standing around at break time when a boy walked up to me, looked at the Neil Young badge I was wearing and said, '"Tonight's the Night"', or more accurately he sang it in the same voice that Neil Young did, which was impressive and also hilarious. He was called Andy Rourke, and was in different classes from me and was the only other kid in my year who didn't have a regulation haircut. We struck up a conversation about records and discovered that we both played guitar. That information was enough for us to take the conversation further, and Andy invited me round to his house the following day. He said that his mum would pick me up.

I was waiting outside our house with my guitar when a large white car pulled up. Andy's mother got out – she looked a bit like a Mancunian Elizabeth Taylor – and the electric car boot magically opened. I put my guitar in the boot, climbed in the back seat and said hello to Andy. I'd never been in an executive company car before, and I immediately saw that Andy's background was somewhat different from mine. We drove to his house, a nice semi-detached in the suburb of Ashton-on-Mersey, and went straight up to his bedroom to play guitar.

One of the first things I noticed was a huge mural of a Crosby, Stills, Nash & Young album cover that his mother had painted on the wall. I was impressed that he knew the album, and even more impressed that he had a mother who had painted an album cover on his wall. Andy shared his room with one of his three brothers, Phil, who also played guitar, and he offered to let me try out the Eko acoustic that was leaning against the wall. I took the guitar and played 'Ballrooms of Mars' by T.Rex. I knocked a couple of riffs around and then Andy played Neil Young's 'The Needle and the Damage Done'. His playing was assured and accomplished, and it was obvious that he was a natural musician. We passed the guitar backwards and forwards and in those moments Andy and I made a connection that would take us through times and places we couldn't even imagine. We started hanging around in school a bit, smoking cigarettes at break times and talking about bands and songs, then he'd go to his classes and I'd go to mine.

Town

I would go to the record shops and bookshops in Manchester
city centre every Saturday without fail. Most of the bookshops were shabby affairs, with a shifty-looking proprietor
who would eye you suspiciously like you were after a sleazy
paperback or he wanted you out if you didn't. I'd inspect the
second-hand paperbacks by J. G. Ballard and William
Burroughs with titles like *The Drowned World*, *The Wind from
Nowhere*, *The Naked Lunch* and *Junky*, and wonder what it was
all about, and then I'd look around and see older guys in their
late teens hanging around by themselves with serious
expressions.

Rare Records on John Dalton Street was a compulsory
stop: there you'd find row upon row of meticulously arranged
gems from the 1950s to the present day – although I usually
went in on my own as my mates couldn't comprehend why

I would even listen to a Dusty Springfield record, let alone buy one.

Some of my mates were prodigious thieves. I'd come out of a shop oblivious to anything that had happened, and then around the corner be presented with an album cover pulled from under a sweater, or be shown a pair of jeans underneath the jeans they were already wearing. My friend Marv was so supremely gifted, he once laid out five pairs of sunglasses on the bus: one from each coat sleeve, one from each sock, and one from the hood of his jacket. It was like a magic trick. Everyone stole album covers from the record shops. Phoenix Records in the student precinct was the easiest, as it was out of the way and the pungent smell in the air meant the staff were sufficiently . . . preoccupied. We'd be in there, seemingly browsing the latest offerings by Jethro Tull or Ted Nugent, while Marv would be deftly slipping any number of half-decent record sleeves up the front of his jumper and inside his jacket. I went in there once to buy a Mott the Hoople album, but couldn't because Marv had already nicked the cover.

A few of my friends were into heavy rock and prog music, but even though there were guitars in it I just couldn't get into it. I didn't like old-looking guys playing flutes or anything to do with dragons and robes. I would go around to someone's house to check out their records and hear a lot of classical keyboard players noodling about, and what guitar playing there was sounded like it was going around in circles and didn't appear to have a point – or if there was a point it was to show that the musician had been practising a lot. I also noticed that in the heavy rock scene there were never any girls – it was a girl-free zone – and that's never a good sign.

My parents went out every Friday night and sometimes on a Saturday too. Claire and I were meant to be babysitting Ian and would sit in front of the TV and innocently say goodbye, then as soon as the tail lights of my parents' car disappeared at the end of the road, a gang of kids would pile in the back door with bottles of cider and we'd have a party. Claire's friends would be in her room, and me and my mates would be in mine. Ian would love it as we'd let him stay up watching whatever TV he wanted.

One night, when me and my friends were listening to Neil Young and sitting around devoutly with my red light bulb on, I heard the usual pounding of disco music coming from my sister's room next door. Claire liked other sorts of music, but she really liked disco and she really liked to dance. As I tried to persevere with the introspective meditations of *After the Gold Rush*, my sister opened my door and, after surveying the scene, declared, 'You look like you're having a good time' and danced off. I followed her into the disco next door. The music was amazing, uplifting and melodic, and the guitar playing immediately caught my attention. It was by a band called Chic, and the guitar player was called Nile Rodgers. I was totally hooked and listened to Chic for weeks until I knew every note. I loved the harmonic chord changes as much as the infectious rhythm in the guitar playing, and I worked out that when Nile Rodgers plays, you hear his heart in one hand and his soul in the other.

The first punks I saw in Manchester were in Market Street

in 1976. It was a startling thing – not for the usual reasons like scruffy leather jackets and spiked-up hair, but because the first punks in Manchester looked like small, effeminate thugs. Their hair was short, which was strange at the time, and they usually wore blazers. Leather jackets would come later, after everyone saw The Ramones. The punks I met had stud earrings and drainpipe jeans, V-neck sweaters with no shirt underneath and plastic sandals or baseball boots, and they knew they looked weird.

My parents usually let me go wherever I wanted. I was always out, at youth clubs, or at someone's house, listening to records. I rarely stayed in the house, and if I did I was in my room, practising, until Ian had to go to bed, then I'd find somewhere to go. All the bands came to Manchester and it was an important city on the live scene. The word would go around that someone was playing, and I would head down to the Free Trade Hall or the Apollo and make my way around the back where about seven or eight lads would be waiting to sneak in. There was a big set of double doors at the Free Trade Hall, and we'd stand around until the opening act started, then a few boys would push one door as hard as possible while someone else would try to get their hand inside to pull the bolt off the inside. Once the doors flew open, the doorman, an old boy who'd been at the place for years, would try in vain to grab the tearaways charging at him, but he never caught anyone. Sometimes we just kicked and kicked at the doors until the poor old fella came to see what was going on and we'd rush him before he could do anything about it. Once inside, we'd dash into seats or hover about as inconspicuously as possible until the security men gave up the search. I saw everyone who came to town whether I liked them or not, and I always got in.

Someone told me that the old blues band Fleetwood Mac were playing at the Apollo. I knew of Fleetwood Mac from 'Albatross', a slow instrumental track from the sixties, and I also knew the riff from their song 'Oh Well'. I assumed they were a bunch of old long-haired blokes, but I didn't have anything else going on so I walked over to the Apollo and waited around on my own. As I was standing by the side doors, a huge Bentley pulled up beside me and a very tall man stepped out with two beautiful blonde women, one on each arm, and a big glass of red wine in his hand. They walked up to me and the man raised his glass of wine, then smiled and made a gesture as if to say, *Yeah, son, this really is as good as it looks*, before the three of them walked through the doors. I stood in awe, stunned by the beauty of the young women, and I thought to myself, 'I am definitely going to do that for a living.' I had to see what the show was like, and we kicked open the doors just as they started. The guitarist was flailing away on a white Les Paul while one of the girls, who was the lead singer, was spinning around. It was very good and quite commercial, and nothing at all like an old blues band. They finished the set with the single 'Go Your Own Way', which I'd heard on the radio, and a few weeks later their album *Rumours* took over the world.

Almost everyone hanging around the gigs and estates took drugs. There was plenty of teenage drinking around too, but smoking hash, or 'draw', was really the thing and it became an intrinsic part of life. The other local pastime was taking magic mushrooms. They grew in abundance on Brookway Fields and we would boil them up into a psychedelic brew, and then wander around Wythenshawe, hallucinating. Gangs of girls and boys would hang around outside the shops at night when there was nowhere else to go. I'd be stood in a shop doorway with a few of Claire's friends and some kids would come around the corner tripping and be climbing on the dustbins and rolling around on the floor and have no idea where they were. Some people became psychotic and were to be avoided for fear of a random confrontation or a never-ending conversation, and some would be walking around the estate in sunglasses and sandals like it was California at the height of summer.

Aside from it being something to do, I liked psychedelics and altered states, and when Patti Smith came into my life, with her transcendental poetry, quoting Rimbaud and William Blake, I was really good to go. When I was fourteen I went to see Patti Smith at the Apollo, and I was so looking forward to it I bought a ticket in advance. Her album *Horses* had been a huge influence on everyone, and she'd even had a chart hit with 'Because the Night'. I was a big fan of the album *Radio Ethiopia*, especially the singing, which had pure rock 'n' roll abandon, and I played the album every day. Through being a fan of Patti Smith I found out about CBGB's and the New York scene with The Voidoids, Talking Heads and Television, whose guitarist, Richard Lloyd, was brilliant.

I went on my own to the Patti Smith show, but when I got there I saw Billy Duffy with a couple of guys in the bar. I went over and he introduced me to Howard Bates from Slaughter and the Dogs; Phil Fetcher, who I recognised from Wythenshawe; and a guy with glasses called Steven Morrissey, whose name I'd heard because he was in a new version of The Nosebleeds with Billy. I said hello and then went to see what was happening inside the hall.

I was stood right at the front when Patti Smith came on with her band, and it was like witnessing an incantation. I thought she was on another plane. The show was electricity, rock 'n' roll and ritual, and the stage seemed like a different dimension, one I knew I had to live in myself. The next day the world felt different. It was another sign along the road.

One of the great things about punk was that it was easy to customise your school uniform. I got a torn white shirt from the jumble-sale box in the Sacred Heart one night when we were rehearsing, and for the first time ever all the boys in school were trying to find the original old St Augustine's blue blazers with pink stripes that were now de rigueur and the height of street fashion.

Going to school started to become more and more like an inconvenience for me. My older friends had left Brookway and would be making plans to do interesting things during the day while I had to sit in a room with boys I had nothing in common with, being patronised by teachers who to me were unimpressive and not even doing a decent job of it. I started to skip out of school a couple of hours early in the afternoon and go into Central Library in town, or stay at home some mornings and go into lessons later in the day. The school would ask for a letter from my parents and I'd tell them I'd bring one and then not bother.

I'd have to stick around all day, though, if I wanted to play football. I liked playing football and liked all the lads on the team, but I didn't much care for it when I had to trek up north somewhere to another school on a Saturday morning. Trials were being held to get on the team for Manchester Boys, and the school put me up for them. I went over to try out, and got picked. After that I went over to try out for Man City's youth team. It was a big deal to go to the training ground and see some of the players coming and going. Witnessing the dedication of the boys who wanted to be footballers made it even more obvious to me that I was a musician, and the fact that I was the only person wearing eye liner on the pitch said it all. I didn't hear any more from them. I played for a couple of seasons with a bunch of great guys in a Sunday league team in my neighbourhood, but I was much more into music and to me football was just a good game.

One afternoon, a teacher told me that I had to attend a meeting with him the next morning. It sounded serious, and when I got there Andy Rourke was waiting too. I assumed we were in trouble, but then the teacher informed us both that Andy would be moving to my class, and that he wanted me and him to stick together. His parents had just split up and he had chosen to deal with the situation by taking lots of drugs and coming into classes smashed. It was a tough time for him, and the school was threatening to expel him unless he could pull out of it. The teacher also informed me that my truancy had become unacceptable. So with some prescience and

69

unconventional logic, he reasoned that the best thing for us both would be if me and Andy hung out full-time.

Andy and I took to the new arrangement with gusto. He would get a bus from his house to mine in the morning, and I showed him how to not get on the second bus to go to school. We would wait around the corner until my mum went out to work and then sneak into my house until lunchtime. We'd go into school later on and sit together in classes, and then go back to his house in the evening. Andy's home life was very unusual, as he and his three brothers, all teenagers, were living on their own. His dad was often away and his mother lived in Spain. His younger brother, John, was twelve, and Andy and I were fourteen. His next older brother, Phil, was fifteen, and the oldest brother, Chris, was seventeen. We had a comfortable house completely to ourselves and carte blanche to do what we wanted, and what we wanted to do was play music and experiment with drugs.

The relationship between me and my parents had by now become quite turbulent. They disapproved of my noncon-formity and were frustrated by what they saw as my rebelliousness. My dad and I didn't talk much. He was a quiet guy to begin with, but now I was running around, doing what I wanted and not bothering to go to school, he thought I was headed for disaster. As far as my dad was concerned, his son was wild, and he was half right. Things would escalate for my folks when I came home one day and told them I'd joined a notorious band from Whalley Range called Sister Ray.

My own band had been trundling on and rehearsing in the school hall. Chris had lost interest in being a singer, so the band had elected me to take over on vocals and the obvious move was to get Andy in on second guitar. With two guitars and Andy and Kev on backing vocals, the band was more power pop and did songs by The Cars, Bowie's 'Suffragette City', 'Do Anything You Wanna Do' by Eddie and the Hot Rods, and 'Another Girl, Another Planet' by The Only Ones, who had become my favourite band. I liked being the frontman – I was OK with being the leader and I liked having the sound of the band around me. Vocally I was going for something between Johnny Thunders and Patti Smith, and the next step was to turn the riffs I had into songs of our own. Kev, our bass player, told me that Sister Ray had heard about me somehow and had contacted him to ask if I'd be interested in playing with them. They had a new record coming out and were planning on doing some gigs. He warned me that their singer was something of a loose cannon, which sounded ominous, but he told me they were a really good band, so I agreed to meet with them.

Sister Ray had been on the Manchester scene for a couple of years. They were fronted by Clive Robertson, who was known for being a maniac onstage and off, and they'd just had a song out on a compilation album called *Identity Parade*. They were adults, and I wondered how it would work with me playing with them, but they were determined to have me in the band and we set up a rehearsal. Their songs sounded like a cross between Hawkwind and The Stooges, and I liked the idea of playing something so full-on and punky, but I didn't imagine I would stay with them for very long as when we met I found the vibe around them to be heavy in a strange way.

We rehearsed in a grim basement in the red-light district of Whalley Range, and it was claustrophobic, dark and intense. Sister Ray were very loud and had a genuine air of threat about them. At fourteen I was thrown in at the deep end, and hung on to my guitar as each song came at me in a storm of woozy feedback and the singer screamed things like, 'Gimme some pills to swallow down with booze, gonna get me a rope, put it round my neck' – he didn't hold back.

Going over to Whalley Range at night with my guitar was perilous. I always ran to and from the bus stop and tried to time it to the minute so I wasn't standing on the street on my own. We rehearsed for a few weeks, and the next thing I knew it was in the local newspaper that I had joined them and we were playing a gig. The first proper show I ever played was with Sister Ray, and was appropriately enough at the Wythenshawe Forum. A gang of kids came from the estate to witness my debut, including the Valentinos, who predictably sneaked in. It was a fierce set, and a baptism of fire as the singer went mental and got into an altercation with one of the other bands after we played. I left the show with Andy and Bobby and made plans to get back to playing with the Valentinos. I wanted to do my own songs, and I knew that was it for me with Sister Ray.

Angie

Stacking shelves at the Co-Op in Wythenshawe's Civic Centre was not my thing at all, but I needed money. I was only there for four or five torturous weeks, but it was long enough for me to bring myself to the attention of the supervisor, who looked exactly like Margaret Thatcher and acted exactly like Margaret Thatcher and whose name, funnily enough, was Maggie.

The woman loathed all life forms, and her hatred of me and my skinny jeans and pointy shoes knew no bounds. From the first night of my employment she found the most demeaning jobs for me in the hope that I would mess up and have to do it all again – whether it was climbing the highest ladders and stacking 200 cans of dog food, or getting under the counters in the dust and dirt so my non-regulation school uniform would get filthy. Suffice to say I wasn't planning on staying very long.

At the end of January after a week of heavy snow, the bus drivers went on strike, which meant I had to walk the eight miles to the Co-Op. I took off in the freezing cold, and as I passed a bus stop near Brookway High School a few girls shouted to me, 'Johnny, are you going to Gill's party?' I didn't know about a party and I didn't know Gill, so I just replied 'Maybe' and left it at that as I continued on my mission to get to work for my shift.

The evening drew in and got darker, and the sodium lights came on, turning the snow pale orange. There was no one on the streets and hardly any cars on the roads, and as time passed and I walked and walked I got lonely. I'd just turned fifteen, and all I wanted was to get ahead and go somewhere. I didn't want to be walking for miles in the snow on my own to some place where I'd be put down and disrespected just because I had the gall to not hide my dreams. All the while I had the whole of The Only Ones' album going through my head. I loved the band, and I knew every note and word. I felt like I was walking on spirit alone.

When I got to work I got word from one of the women on the checkouts that I had to go and see Maggie. I guessed I was in for some shit, and when I went to the office she said I was fired for being ten minutes late. To have the woman get in my face after the heroic expedition I'd just completed was so ridiculous I started laughing, and then really laughing. That Maggie was getting more annoyed made me giggle all the more, and the more annoyed she got the funnier it all was to me. It was hilarious, I loved it, it was perfect she flipped.

That was me out – cool. However, I didn't know that when

someone left the Co-Op the custom was that you went to the loading bay at the rear to face a firing squad made up of the entire staff, who were armed with a seemingly endless supply of eggs. It was a huge supermarket, so there was a hell of a lot of staff and a hell of a lot of eggs. As soon as I appeared, off they all went, no surrender, on and on, mercilessly, until I was completely covered with eggs. They waved their good-byes and went back to work, laughing their heads off, and I had to get home. The buses still weren't running, and I wouldn't have been let on one anyway, so off I walked, a human omelette in the snow.

A couple of miles from home I was so cold and uncomfortable I decided to go to my mate Danny Patton's place, which was on the way. Danny's family were great. Whenever you turned up at his house, his parents would greet you warmly and they were fun and would let you hang out. They were most amused when I turned up on their doorstep. I went straight to the shower and borrowed some clothes. After I got fixed up, Danny asked me, 'Are we going to Gill's party? There'll be some girls there.'

'Yeah,' I said, 'we're going.'

I went to Gill's house with three of my friends: Bobby the drummer, and the other two who were just pretending to be in a band. The party was a younger and straighter crowd than I was used to, and there was a bit of a fuss that we had turned up. The house was a buzz of teenage sexual frisson; alcohol was going down fast. Gill's parents were away and she was concerned that things were about to get destroyed or stolen. There was also the usual threat of violence from some uglies who planned on killing me when they got drunk enough. I'd got used to that, so I always clocked the nearest escape route out of anywhere, just in case. I was once at a party where a guy I'd never seen before broke a bottle on the sink and came at me really slowly while I backed up the whole flight of stairs. I made it into a bedroom and had to climb out of the window. In those days, being known for being in a band occasionally had its drawbacks.

The party was just getting into the swing of things. I wandered around for a few minutes before settling on a couch in the main room, where Blondie's new LP, *Parallel Lines*, was playing. I sank down next to my drummer and in a few seconds something happened that was to be the most important moment of my life: across the room I noticed a girl standing side-on. I was stunned by how pretty she was, and just like a movie the rest of the room appeared to freeze and I saw a glow around her. All I could think was, 'You have found her.' It was a total knowing. I turned to Bobby and said, 'I'm going to marry that girl.'

It's amazing how the course of your life can change within a few seconds. One moment things are as normal, and then a phone call, a meeting, destiny or fate, and everything is different from then on. I locked into that moment. I had to talk to her, and hoped she'd want to talk to me. I can't remember what I said at first because I wasn't hearing myself speak. I was fascinated by her. She was so beautiful and assured and so totally cool. I could tell she was younger than me, and after saying something I asked when her birthday was. She told me it was in October. 'What date?' I asked her.

'Thirty-first, Halloween,' she said.

'What? We're born on the same day.'

I thought it was beyond a boy and a girl, it was soul to soul. I needed her to like me as quickly as possible, but I couldn't let her see it because I would look an idiot. I found out later that she knew who I was and was into me in the same way. Angie just didn't let on.

For the next few weeks I would just happen to be wherever she was going. When she walked to school in the morning I would be at my window as she went by, wondering if she'd look over. She looked every time and we'd wave to each other. I made sure I was standing by her school gate when she came out at lunchtime to go to the shop. I'd have Andy with me so I didn't appear completely desperate, but she knew I'd be there and I knew she was expecting me. A gang of us would all hang around together – some of her mates and me and Andy – and we all knew it was so me and Angie could spend forty minutes together. Then I'd kill time until three forty-five when I could walk home with her.

This ritual went on for weeks. It didn't matter that I was supposed to be in school myself, it wasn't even a considera-tion. I'd taken to having longer and longer sabbaticals from St Augustine's, and it didn't seem to bother my school that their resident guitar hero was missing. If it was a nice day, Andy and I would look at each other and declare, 'It's too nice to go in today,' and then go outside and walk around Wythenshawe Park. If it was raining, we'd turn to each other and say, 'It's a bit grim to go in today, isn't it?' and stay indoors instead.

If one of us had a crisis of conscience, it would be alleviated by the other until he came to his senses. As long as I turned up at the school registrar's office every now and then with a handwritten note saying 'Dear Sir, Johnny had conjunctivitis' and sign it with some unreadable signature, then everything was fine. When Andy needed a note, I would write one for him. After it became obvious what we were both doing, I wrote, 'Dear Sir, Andy was with Johnny Marr because he had conjunctivitis,' and once I wrote a letter that simply said, 'Andy had conjunctivitis too,' just to see if we could get away with it and because it was funny.

Angie and I started to see more of each other, although Andy was never too far away. He was easy-going as always, and it gave him plenty of opportunities to acquaint himself with a number of Angie's friends, who were interested in their own hormonal activity. He was well happy and kept busy.

The early days of finding each other were magic for me and Angie. One day we snuck off and sat on a wall on the estate with the spring sky behind us, and I laid out the plan for our future: 'We'll get away and get out. I'll put together a band and make records. We'll go to London, and then go around the world. I'm a guitar player and you're a guitar player's girlfriend. That's what we're doing.' She didn't doubt me, and that was amazing and validating. There was no other option for me anyway, and now that I had her it was even more necessary because she needed it too. I believed I could do it. She made me brave.

The policy of my folks towards having friends at my house was very much 'persona non fat chance', but it was open house for Angie. All of my family loved her. They treated her like she was one of us, and approved of her more than they did me. I was all right with that as it meant that she could stay over any time she wanted, which meant all the time, which was perfect, obviously.

Angie's family's attitude towards me was a different matter. Her parents didn't know she had a boyfriend and wouldn't have been pleased about her having one who smoked cigarettes and was about to drop out of school to play guitar full-time. Angie was fourteen and they saw her as a conventional school-girl with a sensible future ahead of her, not the girlfriend of a maverick tearaway who was living the life of one of The Rolling Stones – if the Stones lived on a council estate in south Manchester – and was planning on escaping by whatever means he could.

Angie lived with her mum and dad and her older brother, Pete, and not surprisingly they had started to notice that she had taken to dying her hair jet-black, had become very pale, and appeared to have lost all interest in homework and also food. Within about six weeks of us getting together she looked exactly like a teenage Siouxsie Sioux on the arm of a teenage Johnny Thunders, and wherever we went people would look and look again. We listened to New York Dolls, Psychedelic Furs and The Cramps, and her absolute favourite was Iggy Pop. Although I didn't actually introduce her to cigarettes, I did introduce her to other things like guitars and record covers and gigs, and that was all right – Angie wanted an adventure and she supported all my ideas and curiosities. There were a lot of them.

At Andy's house we would find more and more adventurous ways to smoke pot, with ever more ridiculous results. There was a football pitch behind the back garden, and when the two teams lined up, we would dress up the dog, who was called Dan, in a replica of the home team's kit, complete with a hole in the shorts for his tail, and send him out to play with them. We would wait until a particularly tense moment in the match and then watch Dan go straight for the ball and race around in his kit as the players would try in vain to catch him. All of us would be watching from inside the house and be rolling about in fits of laughter. They'd have to wait until Dan got bored of the game and ran off. What made it all the funnier was that we would do it again the next week. Once, when Dan followed me all the way back to my house late at night, I flagged down a black cab and put him in the back of it. I gave the driver six quid and sent him home, and when the taxi pulled up the dog got out. I had no money left for the week, but it was funny.

One thing that Andy's younger brother John devised was pouring buckets of water on the road when it was freezing cold so it would turn to ice. Then he would hide behind the curtains, peep through the window and watch the cars skidding around the corner. It was a weird prank for a little kid to come up with, and we never considered the seriousness of it, but it was wickedly funny, especially when the obnoxious next-door neighbour came off his bicycle.

It was around this time that I realised my band needed to get more serious if we were going to get anywhere. We played a couple of shows in local youth clubs, but I knew we had to be more dedicated to get as good as I thought we needed to be. One idea was to get Andy to play bass. It seemed obvious to me, as he was totally brilliant whenever he picked up Kev's bass and his approach to the instrument was like no one else. He was reluctant at first, but he became a master bass player within a matter of weeks.

Rob Allman had formed a couple of bands after Four Way Street split up, and he knew that I was serious about what I was doing. He came to one of our rehearsals, and after hearing a couple of my songs he proposed that we start a new group with Andy on bass and Bobby on drums and me and him on guitars and vocals. I wanted to work with Rob because he was so good, and Kev didn't mind not joining as he was getting into acting and would eventually join the cast of *Coronation Street*. We started rehearsing in the back room at Andy's house, and Rob named the band White Dice. I didn't like the name, but it was good to be rehearsing regularly and writing our own songs. Rob brought in his friend Paul Whittle to play keyboards, and the band got very good at arranging vocals and harmonies. Rob was a great musician and I learned a lot about songwriting, but he was a few years older than my band and he would sometimes treat us like we were his subordinates and try to tell everybody what to play. This didn't sit well with me, and he and I would often clash.

One day I walked in from school and the phone rang. I picked it up and someone with a London accent said, 'Is that Johnny Marr? This is Jake Riviera, Elvis Costello's manager.'

'Oh yeah?' I said, assuming it was Bobby on a prank call.

'Is that Johnny Marr?' repeated the caller more assertively. 'This is Jake Riviera, Elvis Costello's manager. I was sent this tape of your band and I think it's really good. I want you to come into the studio.'

I was just about to say 'Fuck off, Bobby Riviera' when I had the realisation that the call might actually be genuine. Here I was in my school uniform, fifteen years old, and I was talking to Elvis Costello's manager. I stood up straight and said, 'Oh, OK, cool.'

The band had recorded a song on to a cassette months before and Rob had sent it to a record company. Jake Riviera had heard it and liked it enough to send us train tickets to London and put us in the studio for a day. The prospect of going into a real recording studio was bewildering, especially as it was at Nick Lowe's house. It was hard to believe it was real, and I had no idea what might happen.

We went to London and made our way to the studio. After waiting for an eternity outside an anonymous-looking house, the door opened and we were greeted by a very sleepy Carlene Carter, who was Nick Lowe's wife and the step-daughter of Johnny Cash. Unaccustomed to being greeted by a beautiful rock goddess in a negligee, we made our introductions and walked through to where the studio was set up for the session. The whole day was surreal and almost too much to process. I was in the recording studio, with classic guitars and amplifiers everywhere, in Nick Lowe's house. The session went by in a blur. We played six songs to the producer, and he decided we should try to complete four. I got to play Elvis Costello's Rickenbacker, which had been left in the hallway, and at ten o'clock we dashed to Euston station to catch the last train back to Manchester and wait for a call to say that Mr Riviera wanted to be our manager. The call never came, but I wasn't disappointed. I didn't expect anything and loved the whole experience.

The band continued for a while and we tried rehearsing in a few different places around Manchester. One place was called T. J. Davidson's Rehearsal Rooms, and in the room above us was Joy Division, who I'd occasionally see loading their gear in and out of the building. They looked very weird and completely different from any other bands around at the time: they appeared to be wearing old men's clothes and their haircuts looked like something from the 1930s. They were dedicated though, and always seemed to be busy gigging and rehearsing.

We continued to practise and tried to find some gigs, but not a lot seemed to be happening. One problem was that the older guys in the band seemed to want to just sit in the pub and talk about doing things, whereas I wanted to get out and do it. I got us a gig at a students' union event, but the night was a disaster. Rob got very drunk, to the point of sabotage, and I knew then that I was going to have to find something else. I was disappointed and sad about it, but we'd been working too hard and the music was too important to me to let it be fucked up. It was a chance to find my own music for my own generation. In my next band I would be the leader, I would play the guitar and write the music, and I would look for a singer to front it.

Stagewear for the Street

To my mind, my schooldays were finally over. I was still fifteen and officially had another year left to go, but I took off for the last time one summer's morning and told Angie that I wasn't going back. She and I walked around town feeling like anything was possible, and I reaffirmed my plans for our future: playing music and going places. I was determined to have a decent group and I knew it had to happen. There was a punk hangover in Manchester. The older generation of musicians acted like they'd won the war, and it was impossible to go out to a gig or a record shop without hearing tales of glory days from some of the people who were hanging around on the scene. I thought some of the punks were hypocrites: they seemed to want the same lifestyle and status as the rock stars they were supposedly out to dethrone. I was bored of what had become of guitar culture too. I had respect for the guitar players who had been pioneers in the sixties, but rock music had become very macho and was desperately out of date to me. I wanted something for my own times, and I was very aware of being young and from a different generation with different values.

My parents weren't going to subsidise me, so I needed to find a job of some sort to get by. Claire was going her own way too and hanging out more with her own circle of friends.

As 1979 went on, Britain began to feel the effect of the new Conservative government, led by Margaret Thatcher. Nick-named 'The Iron Lady', she abolished free milk for schoolchildren and was a woman so contemptuous you really had to wonder if the nation hadn't lost its collective minds in electing her leader of the country. In the short time she had been in power there was already a change in the community I grew up in, as families suffered unemployment and a sense of real apprehension took hold. She had a colossal ego, and her philosophy relied on the very worst aspects of human nature. She knew that if you put people under enough hard-ship, they would turn away from each other in order to protect their own interests. Her vision, like that of all Conservative governments, was truly cynical in that it relied on fear, greed and indifference towards others – like someone choosing their new two-car garage over the needs of the unemployed father of three next door – and the terrible consequences of her vision would affect British people for a very long time.

I started working on Saturdays in a clothes shop called Stolen From Ivor, whose clientele were mostly soul boys. We sold straight-leg jeans and button-down shirts and did a nice line in pastel-coloured sweaters that were popular with the Perry boys, who wanted to look like Bryan Ferry. I didn't wear the clothes in the shop, but I did procure a black leather box jacket which I was able to get with a bit of discount and after I'd hidden it so a customer wouldn't buy it first.

I wasn't going to make enough money working one day a week, so I enrolled temporarily at Wythenshawe College in order to be eligible for a grant of £200, which I gave to Angie to save. I needed to study three subjects, so I chose English, Art and Sociology, but then switched Sociology for Drama as the tutor was cool, and from her I learned some interesting things about writing and staging. My career as a student didn't last very long. The most useful thing I did was spend time around the students' union, and I attended a couple of union conferences in different towns. I liked the politics and I was impressed by the idealism in action of some of the people involved. I became friends with a guy called Tony O'Connor, who gave me a copy of Tony Benn's *Arguments for Socialism*. It was an inspiration. Up until then my political views were instinctive and entirely subjective, based on my upbringing and what I'd observed in my environment. It seemed to me that working-class people weren't supposed to question why their lives were the way they were, and I wondered why there was still a ruling class. Tony Benn's book really enlightened me and set me on the right path. I wanted to find out more.

I was in the shop one Saturday when a girl from a few doors away ran in, in a state, saying that there was a gang of rioters coming our way. For days before there had been battles on the streets of nearby Moss Side, and racial tension in the area

19 Brierley Avenue, Ardwick. 'I was aware that I came from the inner city.'

With my mum and dad. Ardwick, 1967.

Some of The Tribe, sometime in the sixties. My mum and dad second left.

My mum and dad out on the town.

Me and Claire just after I got my first guitar. 'My sister was sweet but you didn't mess with her.'

Art room at St Augustine's, 1977. 'Andy Rourke was the only other kid in my year who didn't have a regulation haircut.'

Claire just back from school. She's smiling because it's Friday, which means dancing.

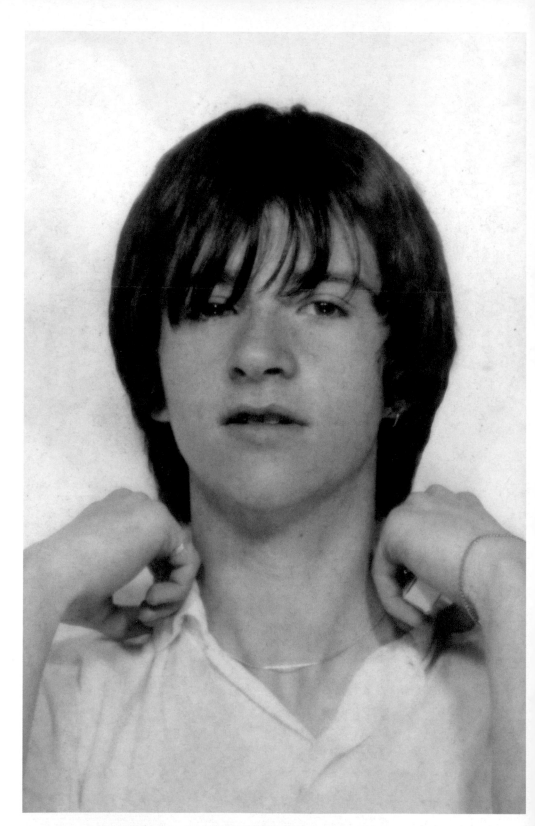

Taken off from school again, aged fourteen. Just after the Patti Smith gig, 1978.

Top: With my brother Ian in 1979, just after I joined Sister Ray.

Below: Billy Duffy in his pink punk shirt that he left in the back of the amp for me.

Top: Back at my parents' working out a new way to write.

Below: Just after Angie and I first met. 'Angie was up for an adventure.'

Working in
X-Clothes. 'What
is everybody
looking at?'

Left: Off to see Iggy.

Opposite: With
Angie one night at
the Ritz, Manchester,
1980. 'She was so
beautiful and so
totally cool.'

A few days after I knocked on Morrissey's door. 'I was wearing baggy 1950s Levis with bike boots.'

Above: Si Wolstencroft. 'Morrissey and I had thought we'd found our drummer. He was good and he looked the part.'

Right: At Drone Studios on day one of The Smiths' official line-up playing together. 'It's a profound irony that the very first thing The Smiths did when they got together was to start laughing uncontrollably.'

was high after reports of excessive force by police. Around a thousand people had attacked the police station and a policeman had been shot with a crossbow. We could hear windows being smashed outside the shop, and as I ran to pull the shutters down alarms were starting to go off. Out front there was chaos everywhere as people ran around, throwing refuse bins at shop windows. My boss grabbed the money from the cash register in a panic, and we locked ourselves in until the police came to get us out.

I didn't like working in Ivor's: the shop was too straight and I felt confined. I'd met a guy who worked in a shop called Aladdin's Cave that sold clothes that were more rock 'n' roll, and he told me there was a full-time job going. I went in to see the boss, and he hired me on the spot. The new job was better: the shop was more underground and the customers were more outsider types. The music was better too, as they played the stuff I liked from the alternative rock clubs. The owner of the shop was a much older guy called Mike who wanted to know everything about my life outside the shop. He'd ask me about where I went and what music I liked, and he was particularly interested in what I wore and why.

I assumed his enquiries were driven by shrewd commercial motives, as he started to sell my type of clothes and then gave Angie a job and borrowed some of her clothes to copy and sell too. It worked for him as each week the shop got busier and it soon became the most popular place for young people in town. Working in a clothes shop was perfect for me. Aside from being around the clothes, it gave me time to play whatever music I wanted all day. Wire, The Cramps, Magazine and

Siouxsie and the Banshees were all on rotation, as were old favourites by Human League and David Bowie. The other thing that was good about working at the Cave was that I got the opportunity to go to Johnson's.

Angie and I had been devotees of Johnson's for a long time. The shop was on the King's Road in London, in the area known as World's End, and I found out about it when Billy Duffy got a job there and I went to visit him. The owner was Lloyd Johnson, a style aficionado and original mod who had started off with a stall in Kensington Market in the late sixties. In 1978 he opened the King's Road shop, not far from Malcolm McLaren and Vivienne Westwood's infamous shop, Sex. The Johnson's style was a reimagining of classic rock 'n' roll retro, something which Lloyd called 'stagewear for the street', and it was worn by bands like Stray Cats, Johnny Thunders and Iggy Pop. The Cave sold some Johnson's clothes. They were expensive, and Angie and I could only afford them by working for weeks in order to pay them off. The Cave also sold clothes that were suspiciously like Johnson's but not the real thing, which neither Angie nor I would have been seen dead in. Eventually I struck up a deal with the boss whereby Angie and I would go to London to pick out things that we liked, and bring them back to sell in the shop, and he would give us free Johnson's clothes in return. Angie would stay at my house and we would get up at five thirty in the morning to catch the train to London. When we arrived at Euston we'd take the Underground train to Sloane Square and walk the length of the King's Road to Johnson's, looking in on a great shoe shop called Robot along the way.

The trips to Johnson's were never anything less than a total event for us. Angie would be in a La Rocka leather bike jacket and leather skirt, Vivienne Westwood shirt and Johnson's bike boots. We would get to Johnson's and Lloyd would welcome us with a friendly 'Aw! Look at these two little lovebirds, aren't they lovely!' and on one occasion he took us to the warehouse to show us some designs he was working on that were inspired by the Japanese kamikaze pilots and that would become his most famous creations. In the shop we'd pick out as much as we could and stuff it into two bin liners each. We'd then stagger back down the King's Road with the bags and make the journey back to Manchester, where Mike would meet us. We'd give him the clothes we'd bought and pick what we wanted for ourselves, which we got on the condition that we wore them in the shop – which we would've done anyway. Pretty soon our friends started to make requests for us to get them clothes from London. We made a couple of trips and were able to sell clothes cheaper than the Cave. It was better than our friends paying inflated prices, and it gave me and Angie a decent income for a while. It also helped to stop counterfeit copies, and suddenly there were a lot of people walking around Manchester looking like Stray Cats.

One day, in 1981, a young man and woman walked into the Cave with clipboards and asked me in a formal tone if I would be interested in appearing on a television show about unemployed youth. I was confused and pointed out that I was employed by the shop, but they went on to say that it didn't matter that I was employed – I was what they needed. The woman ticked off a list of types: 'We've got a punk, a student, a posh girl, a skinhead . . .' They didn't know what I was, but they thought I'd be good on the telly. I'd get £30 for every show for six weeks, and that sounded very good to me. I told them I'd think about it and I'd let them know.

As the couple were leaving, Mike came over and asked me what that was all about. I told him, and Mike, who never missed a commercial opportunity, made a suggestion: 'You should do it. You could wear one of our suits each week. It would be a good advert for the shop.'

Ordinarily I would have joined in the spirit of enterprise and helping out a friend, but I had long since decided that the boss was not someone I wanted to be friends with. 'No, I'm not wearing one of the suits,' I said. 'I'll wear my own stuff.'

'What about a Johnson's suit?' he said. 'You could wear a different one every week.'

That sounded great to me and I pushed it further. 'I'll wear one if you let me keep it,' I said, '. . . and pay me thirty quid.'

He paused to think about it. I couldn't believe he was even considering it. A free Johnson's suit every week – I would've done the TV shows just for one, and now he was considering giving me £30 a week on top of that. 'Twenty quid,' he said.

'OK then,' I replied, and I started planning which Johnson's suits I was going to wear on the telly and what I was going to buy with my £300.

The TV show was called *Devil's Advocate* and was broadcast live every Sunday. I would be sat with ninety-nine other 'youths' while the presenter, Gus Macdonald, introduced topics to do with unemployment and young people in the UK and we'd give our opinions. When I told my parents I was doing it they were impressed that I'd been asked to participate and thought that I must be quite clever. It was a good premise for a show, to give a national platform to unemployed teenagers, but I felt a little weird about being on there when I had a job. My intention was to say very little and leave it to the others who were genuinely more interested in being on the show and genuinely more unemployed too. The producers had a different idea though. They put me on the front row and I sat there in a Johnson's suit that only rock stars could pull off, or indeed afford, until they realised that I wasn't contributing very much. On the two occasions when I did, I mumbled and looked very nervous, like I wanted the camera to go away.

With the money I'd made from the TV show and working at the shop I was able to buy a second-hand black Gibson Les Paul, which was the first proper classic guitar I owned. I'd spend most nights playing it in my bedroom and working on ideas for songs. I'd sit on the floor with my guitar and record ideas on to a cassette while Angie lounged on the bed, flicking through magazines and looking at record covers. Sometimes I would practise on my own and feel like I was getting nowhere and that everything had been done before, but then I'd put a chord in a different place on the neck or change its shape around and would make a discovery. I noticed that certain chords sounded more like how I felt, like I was playing something that was personal to me and that I could relate to. I was looking for things that evoked a sense of yearning but with a kind of optimism, and that started to develop into an identity of my own that I liked. Bit by bit these discoveries became my vocabulary on the guitar, and I was sounding more and more like myself. I had a notion too that if I could I should try to make some kind of statement. Something contrary to everything else I'd already heard before. I just had to find out what I wanted to say.

By now I'd lost touch with Bobby and I'd been told about a really good drummer from south Manchester called Simon Wolstencroft. He heard I was forming a band, and he came round to meet me one evening. Si was very cool. He was the same age as me and very laid-back, he looked great and had a style that was pure bluebeat. I told him that I wanted to form a band that had a rock sound but didn't play actual rock songs – I was interested in something new and groove-based, like Gang of Four or Talking Heads. Si's hero was Topper Headon from The Clash, who at the time were moving along similar lines with songs like 'Radio Clash' and 'The Magnificent Seven'. He was excited about the idea of the band, and he agreed to join on drums.

The first time we got together was in a basement of a carpet shop we'd borrowed from a friend's boss, which was so cold and damp my guitar was crackling and giving me electric shocks. We persevered for a couple of nights until I couldn't take any more and went to find us a room in a new place I'd heard about near town. Decibel Studios was in an old mill building in Ancoats, on the edge of the city centre, and was owned by a French guy called Philippe. The studio was only half built, and Philippe offered to let me use it for free two nights a week if I helped with the building work. I went over every night after working in the shop and within a week of carting bricks and putting up walls we had a place to practise.

The band started off as me, Si and Andy, and my plan was to audition a singer. I didn't want to front the band, and I wanted a four-piece line-up with guitar, bass, drums and vocals. The first night at Decibel we were playing a song called 'Freak Party', which sounded like a kind of new wave Funkadelic, when Si suggested that our song title would be a good name for the band. We were playing a new kind of music that sounded young, and it was a good feeling to be going into the unknown. I felt like I was on the verge of something.

A guy collared me in the shop one day and asked if I knew where he might be able to sell a painting that a friend of his had mysteriously 'found'. I'd made the mistake a few weeks earlier of telling him about a pot dealer who was also a fence, and now he'd come back to me with this business idea. I told him I'd look into it and hoped it would just go away, but he was a forceful and persistent character and I eventually gave in and agreed to introduce him to the fence to shut him up. A few weeks later, I was rehearsing with Freak Party when the door was suddenly kicked off its hinges and three very aggressive, burly men stormed in the room and shouted at us to 'Fucking stop right now!'

We stopped.

'What's your name?' one of them screamed.

'Simon Wolstencroft,' said Si.

'And who are you?' he shouted at Andy.

Andy told them, they all glared at me and one of them barked, 'What's your name?'

'Johnny—' I said, and with that all three of them charged at me and rammed me up against the wall and off my feet.

I had no idea what was going on, but I knew it was serious trouble. One of them went through my pockets and I thought 'It's a bust' – but then I saw that they weren't interested in whatever was in there and knew it had to be something else. Two of them kept me up against the wall. My guitar was still plugged in. *'Klaang!!'* . . . *Klaang!!'* the guitar was blasting through the amp and feeding back massively as they wrestled it off me. Then one of them took off my shoes. 'Uh-oh', I thought, as I realised I was in really big trouble and I would be going to a cell.

Angie was sitting on a desk in the reception outside as two of them dragged me into the corridor. The cops shouted at her 'You stay there!' and I saw the dismay on her face as they hauled me backwards down the iron staircase to the front door. They put me in the back of an unmarked car, and I watched Andy and Si get into another. I still had no idea what was happening and told myself to keep quiet as the cop on the back seat next to me hit me in the ribs every time we sped around a corner.

It was only when we arrived at Longsight police station that I was informed that I was going to be arrested for receiving stolen goods, and the reason it was so serious was because the painting was a famous work by the Mancunian artist L. S. Lowry. I sat on my own in a grubby pale green cell and thought, 'You've really done it now.' I stayed in the cell all night in my leather trousers and my Only Ones T-shirt. A different policeman would come in every couple of hours to kindly let me know that I would be going away for a long while. They seemed to really enjoy telling me, 'You won't be seeing that little bird of yours for a long time,' and were amused that I was in a band and wore make-up. They let me out the next night and I saw a lawyer a couple of days later. He informed me that I would most likely be sent to a juvenile prison for eight months to a year.

Angie and I spent the night before the court date saying goodbye to each other; we were both still in shock. People had been telling me they knew so-and-so who'd look out for me in prison, which was supposed to be comforting, but it wasn't. I had been around some unscrupulous types, but it was just part of growing up in my environment. I couldn't believe that one unthinking step had got me into this situation. It would mean no Angie and no guitar, and a potential prison sentence.

I stood in the magistrates' court and watched everyone else who was involved get sent down. The judge finally came to me and miraculously decided to let me go with a £300 fine. It was incredible: the judge had showed me mercy and I was walking out of there. Standing in that court room that day made me realise more than anything what I was. I was a musician. Not only that but, by my count, getting busted while I was playing my guitar meant at least one million rock 'n' roll points.

Freak Party continued rehearsing at Decibel and we started looking for a singer. We auditioned a couple of people. One guy looked great but insisted on singing 'The Flowers of Romance' over and over until I couldn't take it any more. After what felt like hours we told him, 'Thanks, we'll call you' and he left. Shortly after he became a very successful model; I couldn't listen to 'The Flowers of Romance' for years.

Si told me about a friend he had been in a band with, called Ian Brown. He was the same age as us and was into good music. I asked Si to invite Ian to come and sing with us, but he was in the process of starting a new band of his own. Soon afterwards I got to know Ian. I had a lot of respect for him and we became friends.

I was spending most nights at Andy's, which was becoming a total madhouse. We had continued to live without any boundaries, and though it was fun at first it had got to the point where the place was a lawless free-for-all. I'd been around since Andy's parents first split, and the brothers were like my own. I considered the place a creative refuge as much as an alternative to my own home life, but drug use was becoming more serious with some people there and things were starting to feel dark. I found myself being introduced to some characters that I had a bad feeling about, new kinds of reprobates who had no interest in music and would bring only bad things.

The first alarming sign was when, completely out of the blue, one of my friends said, 'We're getting some heroin tomorrow.' 'What?' I asked, and he continued to talk about scoring smack the next day. I was shocked to see that the others seemed totally OK with it, and then I realised the reason why: they were already smoking it. At that moment I knew that I had to get out and move on, but I didn't know how to do it. I was angry and disappointed with them all, especially Andy, for keeping it from me. There was now a divide between me and Angie and everyone else, and we watched our friends very quickly turn into vampires as the dealer dished out smack all day, lording it over them while they followed him around and laughed at his bad jokes. I hated the dealer not just because of his profession but because he was utterly moronic and knew nothing other than how to sell drugs and steal from people. He wasn't worthy to be around, let alone admired. My friends may have been roguish, but they were young and still quite innocent until the heroin arrived. I carried on the band with Si and Andy, hoping it would all play out and that things would get back to how they were before. I was angry with them for getting into it, but my band was my life and I didn't think I had any other choice.

One night, the three of us drove back to Andy's in Si's car after a rehearsal. I still wanted to find a singer, but it was early days; the music was getting good and I felt something would turn up eventually. When we got there, I walked into the kitchen and saw one of my friends shooting another one of my friends up with heroin. I froze and they looked at me. I just turned around, found Angie and said, 'Let's get our things, we're leaving.' Angie kept asking me what had happened as I stormed upstairs to collect our things, but I was so angry I couldn't speak. I packed our clothes into a bag and we walked out. I didn't say goodbye to any of them. A line had been crossed and there was no more band and no more friends. I didn't know what I was going to do, but whatever it was the next day would be day one.

X

A new shop called X-Clothes was about to open in Manchester. I'd stopped working at the Cave and made a totally clean break with the past; now I needed to find a new job. X-Clothes was an independent company with one shop in Leeds and one in Sheffield. It had built up a loyal following of customers who were into alternative fashion, and was owned and run by a great couple called Sue and Jeremy. They were proud of their independence, and manufactured clothes on their own X-Clothes label as well as representing the best alternative designers like Vivienne Westwood, Susan Clowes and Stephen Linard; their aesthetic was high-end London hip with a bit of punk and rock 'n' roll thrown in. I went for an interview with the owners and their no-nonsense assistant, Gina. It was more of a grilling than an interview, and they asked my opinions on politics, fashion and alternative culture. I was impressed that they were so fastidious and that they wanted all aspects of the shop to be perfect, so when I got home and they called to say I had the job I was fairly elated.

Claire had just left school and was working as a dental nurse, and Angie was working as an assistant at a solicitor's office. I was paying my parents some rent and having to pay off my fine, so I really needed some money. Angie was on a lunch break in town one day when she saw a bundle of cash lying in the street. No one else had noticed it, and when she picked it up and counted it there was £60 there. It was an amazing bit of luck and kept us going until I got my first month's pay.

There would be four of us working in X-Clothes. Lee was the manager; he demanded I show deference to him from my first day, and I decided it would be best not to get on the wrong side of him or he'd make me pay for it. Jules was the assistant manager. She was a real music fan and good at her job, and she and I got along straight away. The other person was Russ, who had moved to Manchester from Sheffield because he was an X-Clothes acolyte and really wanted the job. As the youngest I was assigned all the menial tasks at first, like sorting hangers and moving boxes. It was fine and someone had to do it, but I also recognised that my new boss was putting me in my place just in case I got too above my station.

Starting up the shop from scratch was not just a new beginning for me but for all of us. The day we opened, the place smelled of fresh paint. All of us were style freaks and were excited about what we were selling; we were on board with the aesthetic and we knew a lot of other people in Manchester would be impressed. X-Clothes established itself straight away. Musicians in bands, people from other shops and everyone from the clubs came in to check the place out. The most impressive people in terms of style were the kids from the outskirts of town. I'd thought that anywhere north of the city centre was stuck in the sticks, but there was a bunch of rockabilly kids who'd come in who were so correct in every detail, right down to their socks and choice of hair product, that they could've been in a fifties film. They each had their own favourite star: Gene Vincent, Eddie Cochran, Montgomery Clift. I became friendly with them and even managed to get one of them, who I called Rockabilly Geoff, a Saturday job.

I loved working in town, and I already knew a lot of the customers from Stolen From Ivor and the Cave. It was good for the shop, but it alienated me from the boss. He would clip my wings by sending me out on errands, but I was happy to go along with whatever he threw at me, and I'd smoke a cig and just thought of it as being part of the job.

Adapting to my new situation helped me put the past behind me. Life was still uncertain and I was yet to find new friends, but I was optimistic about starting something different. I missed hanging out with Andy, but he was in a place that I'd had to get away from, and I liked the energy and promise of a fresh situation. I started to think about the music I wanted to make in the same kind of way. I wouldn't write songs with a bass player and drummer in a rehearsal room, I'd do it on my own. I knew I'd be forming a group at some point, but I wasn't inclined to start looking for other musicians yet. I decided to write a whole lot of new songs and get as good as I could at it. I was back in my parents' house and I applied myself to working on melodies and riffs on my own. I got into learning the song structures on girl-group records and Motown singles, and I listened obsessively to records by Phil Spector and worked out how they were put together.

In the shop we took turns playing the music we liked. Russ loved Killing Joke and Fad Gadget and pretty much everything from his home town, so we'd have all the Sheffield bands like Cabaret Voltaire, Human League and Clock DVA, with some Throbbing Gristle thrown in. Jules played The Stooges and The Fall and anything else as long as it was The Velvet Underground. Lee liked The Associates, which impressed me, and also Kraftwerk, but then he'd spoil it by suggesting Frank Sinatra, which for some inexplicable reason was a bit of a thing in the early eighties and was greeted with much derision from the rest of us.

All the bands on Factory Records came into the shop. Tony Wilson asked me one day if I'd be interested in joining Section 25, one of his bands. He gave me a tape and I liked it, but I wanted to have my own band and I told him I couldn't do it. Around this time the graphic designer Peter Saville came in with another guy from Factory called Mike Pickering. They'd just been to a meeting about a new nightclub they were about to build, and mentioned a designer called Ben Kelly and New Order. They pulled out a roll of blueprints and laid them out on the shop counter. It looked impressive, and Mike and Peter were very excited about it. I asked them what the club was going to be called and they said, 'The Haçienda.'

Things were going well, and it was time to find somewhere of my own to live. Money-wise I was making just enough to travel to and from work, and to pay off my fine, so I didn't quite know how I was going to go about it, but I knew it had to be done. It was around this time that Ollie May, who I'd met back in college, started coming into the shop. Ollie wasn't the usual Mancunian X-Clothes customer; he was Swiss and from a comfortable family who had moved to Cheshire in the nicer part of the North West. He was intellectual and quirky in an endearing way, and his grandfather had been a famous Swiss philosopher. We were talking one day and I told him I was looking for somewhere to live. 'You should move into the house I live in,' he said. 'There's a room going on the top floor, ten pounds a week – it's Shelley Rohde's house.' Shelley Rohde was a journalist and TV presenter, and Ollie had been living as a lodger with her and her family for a few months. It sounded perfect, but it seemed a bit odd just to turn up on Ollie's say-so. Ollie assured me that it would be fine though: the family were easy-going and it was a very bohemian kind of household.

I loaded my clothes, records, guitar and an amp into my dad's car, and he drove me to my new home. I'd grown up with the idea that when you were old enough to get a job you left home, or if you didn't get a job you would be kicked out, and I assumed that my dad would be glad to see the back of me. I got my things into Shelley's house and when I said goodbye to my dad I saw in his face that he was sad to see me go.

My room was on the top floor; it was small and had a sloping ceiling, and Ollie's room was across the landing. The rest of the house felt creative with a bohemian air about the place. Along the walls on the stairs were photographs from films and TV shows that Shelley had been involved in, and at the bottom of the stairs was a big framed poster of the biography she had written about the artist L. S. Lowry, which I took as a sign to count my blessings. I didn't see anyone from the family for the first two days, until Shelley's son Gavin came into my room to introduce himself with his younger brother Dan. They were interesting and friendly and into playing music, and I appreciated the welcome. I eventually met Shelley and she was fairly nonchalant about having another lodger living upstairs. We got to know each other, and everyone did their own thing and acted like I'd always been there.

It was inspiring being in an artistic environment and nice to have Ollie across the landing. He was a lively person and busied himself by listening to jazz-funk records at deafening volume. I would hang out with him occasionally, but most of the time I'd be in my room listening to The Shangri-Las and The Crystals and analysing all the Brill Building records I could find. This music seemed to come from a time when pop was more hopeful, and I thought these records were more unusual and better than most of the modern stuff that was around. I bought a cheap sofa bed and I didn't have a television, so my nights were all about music. I'd recently traded my Les Paul for a red Gretsch Super Axe and a Teac cassette machine that had an overdub facility. I'd work on a chord sequence until I was happy with it and then record a second guitar part on top. I would then bounce the two tracks together and experiment with putting more guitars on. I could build up the tracks by bouncing and overdubbing and create my own wall of sound. Eventually I had a lot of tapes of chord patterns and riffs done entirely with guitars, and Ollie and I would listen to them over and over. It was great to have the freedom to work on things, and I really liked having my own domain.

There was only one problem with Shelley's: the cat. It was big and white and was the most malevolent thing I'd ever come across in my life. I'd always had a problem with cats, ever since my parents brought home a scrappy little thing which Claire christened 'Fluffy'. I didn't trust Fluffy, and I didn't understand why I was expected to accommodate a creature who was totally manipulative and wanted to bite me all the time. We would be alone in the house and it would stare at me and play mind games until I gave in or went out of the house altogether. My friend Paul had a cat that controlled everybody in his house. It would preen around with an attitude of 'this is what I want you to do for me' and would then act all innocent and pretend to be nice.

I tried to avoid Shelley's cat whenever I could, but if I had to go into the living room or kitchen it would be lurking, ready to pounce. Its favourite thing was to jump on to the back of the chair you were on and linger behind your head, purring ominously. If you tried to get up or moved suddenly, it would scratch and bite you. I'd be stuck watching a TV show for hours, and Shelley's daughter Michelle would say, 'Oh, look . . . he really likes you!' as beads of sweat trickled down my forehead – until the beast prowled off to terrorise someone else.

Crazy Face

Quite soon after X-Clothes had got going, I started to visit the shop next door, which was called Crazy Face. It was a different kind of place from X-Clothes, slightly more mainstream but with its own distinct identity. It sold more retro, American-influenced clothes, and was by then a successful independent brand, with two other shops in town and a factory too, where they made all the stock and had the main office. I would hang out and chat with the girls who worked there, and I soon noticed that the music that was playing was a very specific mix of original rhythm and blues, rock 'n' roll and soul. One day I asked one of the girls what it was they were playing.

'I don't know, some old thing Joe makes us play,' she said.

'Who's Joe?' I asked.

'The owner, it's all his stuff.'

I'd also noticed that there were a lot of original black-and-white press photos of people like Marlon Brando, Jeanne Moreau, The Shangri-Las and Little Richard. It was pretty unusual in a clothes shop at the time, and I was intrigued about who was behind it all.

One day, when I was on a break, I wandered into Crazy Face and saw an older guy I'd not seen before standing by the counter. He was wearing a beat-up black original leather flying jacket and what seemed to be American railroad baggy work pants, and looked very much like Jack Nicholson in *One Flew Over the Cuckoo's Nest*. As a couple of the girls said hello, he stuck out his hand and said, 'Hi, I'm Joe.' He had a warm way about him, so I put my hand out and said, 'Hi, my name's Johnny . . . I'm a frustrated musician.' It seemed like a normal thing to say, and we struck up a conversation which eventually turned to the subject of the guitar. Joe told me that he owned a Gibson acoustic and that he'd been trying to master the intro to 'My Girl' by The Temptations with not much success. 'I'll show you how to play it,' I said, and he was pleased enough to invite me over to his office across town the next day during lunchtime to show him how it was done.

70 Portland Street was a nice-looking old building on the edge of Chinatown. It had a big, blue, church-style wooden door that led to five floors of machines, with people cutting and assembling patterns everywhere and an empty basement shop downstairs. Joe ran the place with a curious style of both placidity and all-seeing scrutiny. As with his other shop, which was called Tupelo Honey, the name Crazy Face came from a Van Morrison song. The office itself was about a ten-minute

walk from X-Clothes, and about four minutes if I ran, which I usually did in bike boots and with a cigarette in my mouth.

That first day when I went over to hang out with Joe didn't feel like a regular day. He was in his early thirties, and it was unusual to be hanging out with someone that much older than me. Joe was very cool. He was a grown-up, with a family, and ran a business, but he was still a free and easy guy. Here was someone who was talking to me like I was an equal but had already lived a real life. He had been a genuine beatnik in the sixties, and had seen the Stones and The Beatles and The Animals. He'd been to America too, and it seemed like he knew everything. We clicked with each other immediately, and he was as intrigued by me as I was by him.

When I was in his office he handed me his Sunburst Gibson acoustic. I took it, sat down and played Smokey Robinson's 'The Tracks of My Tears'. When I finished he stood up and said, 'Do it again.' I played it again, and when I got to the end he said, 'I've never heard anyone play like that – what are you doing?' I was buzzed that he liked my playing, but I hadn't really considered what I was doing to be anything out of the ordinary. I did it the way I'd taught myself, the way I played everything. Then I played 'My Girl' for him, which was the tune he wanted to learn. He was really impressed and told me that he'd been around a lot of guitar players in the sixties and seventies but had never seen anyone play 'with the tune going and then with another tune going on top'. When Joe told me this, and said it so genuinely, it was the first time I really believed I had something. Until that point it had seemed like everyone I'd been playing with had either assumed that I was totally confident and so were reluctant to give me too much praise, or they felt they were in competition with me for some reason. Either way, I had finally met someone I could believe when they told me I was really good, and that person was Joe Moss.

Morrissey and Marr

L ife in town was fast and exciting every day. It seemed like there were new possibilities in music and fashion for my generation, even if there weren't in employment and industry. Music-wise I was noticing all of the new guitar stuff that was around by Siouxsie and the Banshees, Magazine and Talking Heads, which had developed from the punk scene; as well as the new kind of pop that was turning up by The Associates, Simple Minds and Grace Jones, which drew on the fashions and styles coming out of the nightclubs. This wave of musical diversity was new, and seemed very different from the too-familiar voices of the established post-punk scene, which for people of my age was now starting to feel tired, even if it had been great once upon a time.

Retro culture was starting to develop, with second-hand clothes stores appearing on a few of the back streets. Some of my friends were working in these shops, and if an X-Clothes customer was trying on an item that was the wrong size or too expensive, I would send them around the corner to get it at Reflex, my mate's place, or at the Antique Market. Lee would be annoyed when he found out, but people would then come back to our shop because they trusted me, which would annoy him again.

A club night had started once a week in a place called the Exit, and Angie and I went down there one Saturday night. The place was buzzing with young people, most of whom were shop assistants and hairdressers working in town. The music was loud and the atmosphere was full on, and everyone was all dressed up with somewhere to go. We'd been in there about five minutes when a record came on that immediately hooked me with its scratchy rhythm guitar. I had to know what it was and who it was by, so I weaved my way across the dance floor and over to the DJ, who was elevated in a booth like a preacher in a pulpit. A young man in a pink shirt and with a huge white quiff with a trilby perched on top leaned over and shouted, 'Johnny Marr!', and I realised it was Andrew Berry, the star hairdresser from West Wythy. 'What are you up to?' he shouted.

'Just out on the town,' I bellowed back. 'What's this record?'

'This one playing now? It's Bohannon, "Let's Start the Dance".'

'Ah, Bohannon,' I thought. It was the same kind of guitar I'd heard on 'Disco Stomp', and with that Andrew invited me and Angie into the DJ booth for the rest of the night to choose records, catch up and drink free Harvey Wallbangers. Meeting up with Andrew again was a major moment for both of us. I had never forgotten him – he was charismatic and one of those people that everyone remembers after they meet them. We connected when we were younger and we picked up where we'd left off. After that night we started to meet up every day, and the two of us had a shared sense of adventure and a joint motivation to make something amazing happen.

Angie had left the solicitor's and had got a receptionist's job at Vidal Sassoon, just down the street from me and around the corner from where Andrew was working at Toni & Guy hair salon. She and I would meet up after work and then a bunch of us would go over to a gay club called the Manhattan Sound, in Spring Gardens, where the manager, Dennis, would let us sit around and play whatever we wanted on the record decks before the place got busy. One of the friends who would be out with us was called Pete Hunt, and there was another friend who was Pete Hope. They were usually together and were therefore always referred to as 'the two Petes'.

Pete Hunt ran a record shop in south Manchester called Discount Records, and one night he told me he was going travelling around Europe and asked if I would keep all the records from the shop in my room at Shelley's until he came back. I was amazed: to have all the records from a record shop in my bedroom was like a dream I would've had when I was eleven. The only snag was that my attic room was small. But I'd worry about that when the time came. The other thing that Pete Hunt told me was that when he was in London the week before, trying to find the Wag Club in Soho, he'd met a guy on the street who was also going to the Wag. They ended up hanging out, and Pete thought that me and his new friend would get along, so he'd invited him up to Manchester to meet me. He also told me that the guy had made an amazing record and that his name was Matt Johnson. He sounded interesting, and I was impressed to hear that he'd made a record. A few days later Pete played me Matt's album, which was called *Burning Blue Soul*, and when I heard it I was even more impressed. It was really innovative, experimental and very psychedelic. It knocked me out, and I was looking forward to meeting the person behind it.

Pete had invited Matt to stay at his place, and said that after he'd met me we'd all go to Legends, a club in Manchester which on Thursdays played electro and modern guitar music like Cabaret Voltaire, Gang of Four and Psychedelic Furs. The rest of the week it was full of beer monsters dancing to Abba. The sound system and lights were great, and I would go there most Thursdays and would often see the same people each week. Matt arrived and introduced himself, and it was like he and I had known each other forever. He was friendly and inquisitive, and I soon caught on that he was working class and had a fast intellect. He was wearing an old Levi jacket, matching 501s and beat-up boots. We started talking about music, and it turned out that he liked exactly the same chart stuff as I had when I was a kid, and when you're passionate about things that are quirky and you meet someone who likes the same things in the same way, it's powerful and significant. We hung out in Pete's kitchen for a while and compared notes on how we wrote our songs, and when Pete produced his Höfner guitar we passed it back and forth and discovered that a few of our instrumental riffs sounded alike. Matt and I both knew something was happening, and then Matt said to me, 'I'm forming a band, my next records are going to be under the name The The, why don't you join me?'

'OK,' I said, 'if I can work out a way I can live in London, I'm in.'

That was it: I had met a genuine kindred spirit, someone the same age as me who was excited about making a new kind of music. We went into town and hung out at Legends and carried on getting to know each other all night. I meant it when I told Matt, 'I'm in.' I just didn't know in 1982 when or how it might happen.

Pete Hunt finally had all the records from the shop at his house, ready for me to collect. Angie had just passed her driving test and was given the use of her parents' old white VW Beetle for us to get about in. We went round to Pete's and loaded all the albums and singles into the boot and on to the back seat. It took a few trips, but I eventually hauled the whole lot up to my room and stacked them in rows three and four deep until it looked like the hideout of a meticulous hoarder with amazing taste in music.

Angie getting the car coincided with me reacquainting myself with the harmonica. The Beetle was the only place I could practise without driving everyone mad, and she had to put up with me blowing harp along to a tape of the Stones' second album wherever we went. It was great for us to finally be mobile as we could see each other more, and I started getting good enough on harmonica to decide that it should feature in whatever group I put together next.

Having all the records surrounding me in my little room every day was perfect. I was still rushing out each morning and going out to clubs after work, but then I'd spend a few nights in going through piles of albums by The Crystals and The Shangri-Las, or Wire and Can, and then I'd play my guitar until I fell asleep.

Not having a band and getting back to writing on my own was really good for my playing. I was able to explore chord changes without being tied down to a bass player and a drummer. I ended up filling out my chord changes with melodies and little phrases, and was free to go anywhere I wanted. I was also getting away from some of the things that a lot of other guitar players had done up to that point, as a lot of the old standards were out of date and sounded too obvious. I had my little three-track cassette machine that enabled me to put down an idea and then layer a riff over the top, and I became quite good at coming up with things that sounded full without it needing much else besides the guitar.

Eventually I started to get a collection of instrumental pieces together and I ended up with quite a few ideas for songs, which I would play on my guitar when Angie and I were driving about in the Beetle. One night when I was over at Joe's, I told him I wanted to start a new band. I wasn't sure how I was going to go about it, but I knew that the time was right to find a singer. I didn't want to be the frontman. I had been reading everything I could about the Stones' manager Andrew Loog Oldham, and was fascinated by his reputation as a fast-talking visionary; he became as much of an inspiration to me as any musician. Joe listened. He knew the things I was into, and his view was that as long as the guitar was featured and we found someone who could sing well enough and who looked the part, then it could be good. I started checking out people who came into the shop. There were a couple of guys who fancied themselves as singers, but they were either too old or too goth. I asked Tony Wilson if he knew of anyone I could work with, and he was eager to match me up with a girl he had on Factory, but it was all jazz and bongos and I knew I was looking for a guy anyway.

One Saturday I got chatting to a couple from Liverpool who told me that The Bunnymen were splitting up and that I should track down their singer, Ian McCulloch. That sounded great to me: Ian McCulloch would've been at the top of my list of singers at that point. I liked his voice, and his style was not a million miles away from mine. I figured Liverpool was close enough to make it work, and they said they'd get Ian's number from the band's manager, but then the following week I heard that The Bunnymen were advertising upcoming gigs, and it was back to the drawing board.

All the time I was running around town I was thinking about forming the new band. Andrew said that I could play at a fashion show he was planning later in the year, and I knew that I could probably get a gig at the Manhattan Sound in Manchester. Lunchtimes and evenings I'd often go over to Joe's office or house to hang out with him, and he would listen to my plans. One night I told him that the only guy I'd heard was any good was someone called Steven Morrissey, who Billy Duffy, who was now in London, had been in a band with a few years before. I heard myself talking and realised it might be worth trying, even if it was something of a long shot as I hadn't heard anything about him for a long time. All I knew was that he lived somewhere in Stretford and that he had written stuff in the *NME* about New York Dolls. I thought about it for a week or so, and then I started to wonder how I might go about tracking him down.

One night I went over to Joe's to watch a *South Bank Show* programme about the songwriting duo Jerry Leiber and Mike Stoller, which he'd recorded on his VHS video machine. Video recorders were revolutionary at the time, and something of a godsend for music fans and film buffs as you could now watch your favourite band's TV performances or films whenever you wanted; my friends and I would record any music show that happened to be on. Leiber and Stoller had become something of an obsession of mine, having written and produced records by The Drifters, Ben E. King, Elvis Presley and The Shangri-Las, and it was great to get the chance to see a programme about them. At one point Joe turned to me and said, 'Watch this bit.' On the screen, Jerry Leiber was telling the story of how he met Mike Stoller, and how he didn't actually know his future partner but had heard that he was someone who wrote songs. He found out where he lived, went to his house and knocked on the door. Right then I had a eureka moment: I knew exactly what I needed to do. The only snag was that I didn't know where the door was.

The next day happened to be my day off from the shop. I got on a bus to my parents' house and looked for a phone number I had for a guy who lived in Wythenshawe called Phil Fletcher, who I had met a couple of times with Billy. I called

Phil and asked him if he had a number for Steven Morrissey. He told me he didn't, but that the best person to ask would be Steve Pomfret, who lived around the corner from my parents. I walked over to his house and rang his doorbell. Steve, or 'Pommy' as he was known, answered the door and I told him I was looking for Morrissey's address. He went off down the hallway while I waited in the sunshine. When he came back he was holding a piece of paper with *384 Kings Road* written on it. He gave it to me, and when I looked down at it I knew it was part of my life story.

Some things just happen and go by without any meaning, while other things you just know are meant to be. Right then I knew that the band I was putting together would be special; I knew it would be great.

Pommy asked me when I was going round there and I said, 'Now.' Then he asked me if I knew where it was, and I said, 'No'. He thought that was funny, and as he wasn't doing anything he suggested that he come with me. Everyone liked Pommy, he was friendly and a nice guy. I asked him if he knew any bass players, but he didn't, so I asked him if he could play the bass and he said, 'Not really.' We caught up with all the new music we liked, and I spent most of the bus ride to Stretford talking about The Gun Club, who were a new band that I thought were the best thing around.

It was a really beautiful day. Summer had come early and there were long shadows on the pavement as we walked through the south Manchester suburbs. After ten minutes we came to an anonymous but pleasant-looking semi-detached red-brick house with a little swing gate outside. I opened the gate, walked up to the door and knocked. There was no answer, so I waited a bit longer and tried again. Finally I heard someone walking down the stairs and the door opened. A young woman with fair hair and a nice way about her answered, and I said hi and asked if Steven was in. 'I'll just get him,' she said. After a little while a young man appeared.

'Hi,' I said to him, 'my name's Johnny . . . and you know Pommy.'

'Hi Steven,' said Pommy.

'Oh, hi Pommy,' he replied. The first thing that struck me about him was his voice: he spoke quite softly and evenly. I could see he was somewhat bemused by his two unexpected callers, but he was courteous and said to me, 'Hi, nice to meet you.'

'Sorry to just turn up at your door,' I explained, 'but I'm forming a band and I wondered if you were interested in singing?'

'Come in,' he said, surprisingly unruffled for someone who'd just been asked to join a band by a complete stranger on the doorstep. The moment felt good.

I followed Morrissey up the stairs and noticed his clothes. He was wearing suit trousers and a buttoned-up shirt with a T-shirt underneath and a baggy cardigan. His hair wasn't a quiff but was short and fifties-like, and I thought his look was similar to the older guys around the Factory scene like A Certain Ratio, more bookish and intellectual than street. There was a life-size cardboard cut-out of James Dean from the film *Giant* on the corner of the stairs, and I noticed a typewriter as I walked into his room. I was wearing baggy 1950s Levis with bike boots and a sleeveless Johnson's jacket. I was also wearing a flying cap and had a huge quiff dyed different shades of red. I sat on the bed and Pommy sat on a chair on the other side of the room, and then Morrissey, who was stood by his record player, said, 'Would you like to play a record?' I walked over to a box of 7-inch singles that was on a dresser and inspected all the Decca and Pye labels until I came to a Tamla record by The Marvelettes which I liked, called 'Paper Boy'. I took it out and Morrissey said, 'Good choice,' then I flipped it over and put on the B-side, which was called 'You're the One'.

We got talking and I commented on his collection of rare Tamla 45s. He asked if I'd ever been to America, and I raved about Dusty Springfield's 'Little by Little'. He played me Sandie Shaw's 'Message Understood', which I hadn't heard before, and then 'A Lover's Concerto' by The Toys.

Talk turned to Billy Duffy and his ex-girlfriend, Karen Colcannon, who we both knew, and I asked him about what had happened with The Nosebleeds. 'Nothing happened,' he said, 'it was just a lot of waiting around.' I explained that I didn't have the other musicians for the band yet, though I had a couple of people in mind. I thought I might get back in touch with Si Wolstencroft, as he was a good drummer and he looked the part. Morrissey and I were both very much at ease with each other, it wasn't a difficult situation at all, especially considering that I was explaining my hopes and dreams to someone I'd never met before, in his bedroom. It felt totally natural, and although he was a few years older than me there was an immediate understanding and empathy between us.

He knew I was serious and that I could back up what I was saying. While all this was happening, Pommy sat in the corner just taking it all in. He could tell that something special was happening right in front of his eyes. He was completely silent, with a smile on his face.

When it was time for me to leave, Morrissey — or 'Steven' as I was calling him — gave me a few sheets of paper with some words typed on them. 'Songs,' I thought, 'that's what it's about.' I folded them into my jacket pocket and suggested that he call me on the X-Clothes payphone at noon the next day. We said goodbye, and as I went out of the gate and into the sun I thought to myself, 'If he calls tomorrow this band is on.'

The next day at noon the phone rang. We talked for a long time about records and bands and he asked if I'd looked at the lyrics he'd given me. I had. They were for a song called 'Don't Blow Your Own Horn', and I'd kicked around some chords for it but what I was doing wasn't really knocking me out. I didn't consider it to be a problem though, and after some more talk we arranged to get together at my place to start writing some songs. A couple of days went by and then an envelope landed through my door. Inside were a cassette tape and a photocopied picture of James Dean, and on the cassette was a compilation of songs by The Crystals, The Shangri-Las, The Shirelles, Sandie Shaw and Marianne Faithfull. I thought it was a good sign.

Our second meeting was in my room at Shelley's. Morrissey came over in the afternoon, and we made our way up the stairs past Shelley's framed portraits of sixties stars until we got to the attic. It was another beautiful day, and through the open window we could hear the sound of the schoolkids playing. Morrissey took out some more lyrics for me to work on. As I took the pages I saw the title 'The Hand That Rocks the Cradle', and without thinking about it I started playing a chord change along the lines of the Patti Smith song 'Kimberly'. It seemed to scan right with the words and suggested a bass line, which I played at the same time. I continued to play, and then Morrissey started singing the words, and within a few minutes the tune was born. After laughing a lot and rehearsing it a couple more times, I recorded what we had on my tape machine, then I overdubbed a ringing guitar line on top, and my new partner and I had our first song. It felt like an important moment. I was thinking about the words and how the style was almost vaudevillian, although I hadn't analysed what it was all about.

I looked at the next lot of lyrics, for a song called 'Suffer Little Children', and as I sat cross-legged on the floor with my guitar and the two sheets of paper at my feet, I pressed 'record'. As I looked down at the words again, my hands started to play a tune. Something was happening; the song was coming through the ether. I kept going with the verse and Morrissey started singing along, the words and story appearing in my eyes and my mind. I followed the momentum as my guitar delivered the music under the voice, and the song was suddenly all there, a song that didn't sound like anyone else and didn't feel like anyone else, a song about the Moors murderers. I didn't know what to make of it. All I knew was how it felt, and it felt strangely true. My emotions were hanging in the air and I was just following the moment. I picked up a small musical box that was lying in the room, wound it up and went over to the window. I held the music box out of the window as it played its melody, and in the other hand I held a microphone and recorded it, along with the sound of the kids playing. Apart from the surprise of being presented with such unexpected words, there was one sentiment about coming from the north in that second song that caught my attention more than anything else, and it defined an aspect of us from that first day of us working together. It said to me, 'We do things differently.'

Morrissey and I had started our partnership, and whatever it was that we had, it was ours and was totally unique. We were two people who had already dedicated most of our young lives to becoming who we wanted to be. We'd both worked obsessively on what we were doing in a way that no one else around us could come close to, and we recognised in each other the same commitment and emotional need to follow our visions. We were different personalities and opposites in many ways, but the things that we had in common created an exclusive bond. We'd both chosen a life of total immersion in our passions, and an intense romanticism about pop culture, and when we came together we both thought that it just had to be destiny.

Our conversations seemed to naturally flow. One of us would talk about something that seemed very important, and the other would encourage it. On the second day that we got together, I recited a list of things that I thought our group should be and would do. The first thing was that our debut album should be eponymously titled; then I said that our first single should have a navy-blue label with silver writing on it and in the brackets beneath the song title it should say 'Morrissey and Marr'. I said that we should sign to Rough Trade Records, and then I predicted that even though she hadn't made a record for years, we could write a song for Sandie Shaw. We didn't have a group yet, and only had two very odd songs, but I saw all of those things for us and I knew it was just a matter of working at it.

Angie arrived and met Morrissey for the first time, and we gave him a ride to the train station in the Beetle. When he left I turned to her and said, 'What do you think?'

'Yeah,' she said, with her usual sure instinct, 'I think it could work,' and we took off to see Andrew Berry in St Anne's Square, with me practising harmonica along to the Stones and my feet up on the dashboard.

Everyone in town hung out wherever Andrew Berry was, and that usually meant that John Kennedy would be there too. John was another pied piper around town who I'd known from my schooldays at Sacred Heart, and was from one of the few other Irish families in Wythenshawe. John's hair was always tinted some shade of blue, red or green, and unusually for the times he was very 'out' as a young gay man, in a way that was brave and inspiring. Everyone called him JK, and he was a creature of the New Romantic culture that had started with Manchester's Pips nightclub, when it had essentially been all about Bowie and Roxy Music. Pips had been particularly influential as it was the place where the members of Joy Division and other bands hung out, and was also where Ian Curtis practised his dance – which, like a lot of people, he'd copped from Bowie's appearance around 1976 on the *Dinah Shore Show*. Everybody danced liked David Bowie and Bryan Ferry, including me. But now was a different time, undefined, and we all had the feeling that something was about to happen.

All of us considered Manchester to be as important as London, and this was the attitude that John Kennedy had when he tirelessly pestered national magazines like *The Face* and *i-D* to come up to do features on his friends. It didn't matter to John whether his friends were in bands, or DJs, or on the dole. What mattered was that they had a city-centre attitude, and looked striking in some way. I was interviewed for a magazine about being 'a face on the scene', and I was also on another television programme, this time about fashion, where I was interviewed by Shelley Rohde. As I was living in her attic, it was a bit odd for us both, but Shelley took advantage like a true pro, and threw me with her very first question – 'Why are you wearing that cap?', which was a good opening gambit and totally valid. JK suggested that for the TV show and the magazine I call myself 'Johnny La Mar', which I didn't, even though he was actually serious about it. Some of the names he gave people stuck though, like 'Spikey Mike', or even 'Mind of a Toy', which was a personal favourite of mine.

I started DJ'ing with Andrew on Thursdays at Exit. Some nights would be packed, especially when JK had managed to put on an event, and some nights would be just us and our mates. It didn't make any difference to us what was going on, as we used the place as our own, hanging out and drinking Harvey Wallbangers and playing whatever records we liked, which was usually a lot of James Brown and John Lee Hooker, with some new alternative stuff like Gang of Four's 'I Love a Man in Uniform', and Josef K's 'The Missionary'. After we'd locked up, a bunch of us would proceed noisily through the city centre to get the night bus to Andrew's flat on Palatine Road near Factory Records and continue our experiments in inventing ourselves and our lifestyles. I'd usually stay up all night, psyched on life, or occasionally I would squeeze on the couch with two people I vaguely knew, with four other people on the floor who I didn't know at all, and then two hours later I'd get up and race to the bus stop to get to work.

While I was supposed to be working in the shop I was starting to spend more and more time next door in Crazy Face, a situation which did not go unnoticed by my boss. I would often go over to Joe's office on Portland Street at lunchtime, play the cassettes of the new songs I was working on and get dreaming out loud. Everything was a philosophy to Joe – he would philosophise about anything, and he always had a theory about something that was terribly important and that no one else had ever thought of. He once spent days working on the idea that Jackie DeShannon had invented British guitar music because of the twelve-string motif on the song 'Needles and Pins', and trying to figure out the extent of her influence on The Beatles because they toured with her in the US. He made a cassette with a mix of her songs, followed by Beatles songs that he'd worked out were directly influenced by DeShannon, and it has to be said he made a pretty convincing case.

Joe would also talk a lot about how things really were in

Manchester in the fifties and sixties. He hated the mythology that had come to define the city – this idea that it was some kind of dark and dreary purgatory – and said that it was put about by people who were either not where it was happening at the time or who had watched 'too much *Coronation Street*'. As far as Joe was concerned, it was all just a pseudo-northern cliché. His was a youthful Manchester that exploded after the war into colourful music and film with clothes to match, and he saw that my Manchester was turning out to be the same. One day he leaned over to me in his uniquely conspiratorial way and pronounced, 'This is your city,' which made me really think it was.

Other lunchtimes I would go over to my friend Rick's second-hand shop in the alley on Back Bridge Street to borrow a polo-neck sweater and then run round the corner to Carl Twigg's antique shop on King Street West and chat with him about what had gone on in town the night before. My friend Tommy, who worked in the Virgin Records store, would order re-releases of Motown singles I couldn't get at Rare Records, and I would dart in there to pick up a copy of '(Come Round Here) I'm the One You Need' or 'Put Yourself in My Place' before running in to see Angie at Sassoon's, and then return to X-Clothes, where I would be predictably late. The best times to be working in the shops though were at the weekends in the summer. I would wander around town after work on a warm Saturday evening before the clubs opened, on my way to meet my friends, aware of what it is to be young. I would stand on a corner and look up above the buildings on King Street, and even though I only had a fiver in my pocket, I'd know it was as good a place to be at that moment as anywhere else in the world.

The Smiths It Is

S ome nights I'd spend on my own in the attic at Shelley's. I needed the solitude to think and the time to write new songs. I was finding inspiration in all sorts of music, but mostly I was listening to the girl groups. I wondered if the approach on those records could be applied to a guitar band, and I worked on eradicating any traces of traditional rock guitar that might be in my songwriting, while trying to maintain my own sound. I wanted what I was doing to be modern, and I wanted my friends to like it and think what I was doing was cool.

Morrissey and I would speak most days on the phone, and sometimes he would come into the shop and we'd make arrangements to get together at my place. Occasionally I'd go over to see him at his mother's house. It was after one of these afternoon visits, when we were standing on the pavement as

I was leaving, that he held out his hand and presented me with a small white card. On the card were three names written in blue biro: 'The Smith Family', 'The Smiths' and 'The Walking Wounded'. I took a moment to consider as I didn't know if I liked any of them, but I decided that 'The Smiths' was the one I disliked least, so I pointed to it. 'OK then,' said Morrissey with a smile and a bow of the head, 'The Smiths it is.' I said goodbye and walked down the road towards Old Trafford train station. I thought about the new band name for a minute and it sounded like a family, and I liked how simple it was, then I thought about it some more and decided that it was great. The Smiths – it fitted. The Smiths it was.

My main priority was to find other musicians and try to record a demo. I started to look more seriously for a drummer and a bass player from the people who were coming into the shop. I considered a couple of the rockabilly guys who were around, but they were too out of town and too deep into the retro fifties thing to be an option. I got Pommy over to mine a couple of nights to try him out, but even though we got along really well it was obvious that he was never really going to make it as a guitar player. We kicked around some ideas, but he ended up saying, 'I can't play these chords, this is torture.'

Simon Wolstencroft was the obvious person to get in on drums. We'd already been in a band together and he was a good drummer. There was, however, the problem of Si's new-found enthusiasm for hard drugs, though I figured that somehow it could be worked out. I called Si at his parents' house to tell him about the new band and to ask him if he'd play with us.

'What's it called?' enquired Si.

'The Smiths,' I said.

'The Smiths?' he replied. 'Haha haha ha ha . . . ha haha ha haha . . . haha ha haha.' It wasn't exactly a vote of confidence.

'Thanks, Si,' I said, 'you'll get it when you hear us.'

After more amused incredulity at my new band's moniker, Si agreed to come and check us out. Now all I needed was to find somewhere to make it happen, and the only place I knew of was Decibel Studios, the scene of the crime.

Going back to Decibel after what had happened with the cops was an uneasy prospect for me, but the excitement of getting our songs down on tape made up for it, and so I managed to convince the owner, Philippe, to give me some free studio time on the condition that I wouldn't have the SAS or Special Flying Squad kick in the doors and smash the place up.

Another condition of using Decibel was that the studio engineer, Dale Hibbert, would be around to watch us and essentially make sure nothing terrible happened as a result of my being there. Dale was a likeable fella who'd once helped me engineer a Freak Party demo. I didn't know him very well, but we'd talked about The Velvet Underground, which gave us some common ground and which I always took as a sign of someone I could relate to.

When I'd first met Dale he was playing bass in a band, and although he didn't look the part I asked him if he'd be up for playing on the demo for The Smiths, as not only was it the obvious thing but it would also give me a chance to play with

129

a different bass player than Andy and see how it worked. Things seemed to be looking good for us until I got a call from Si to tell me that he was having second thoughts about playing with us and didn't want to leave his job. It was a blow, and I couldn't understand why it was so hard for other people to get on board, as I had such a strong sense that I was on the right track. I couldn't let us fall at the very first hurdle, so I tracked down Bill Anstee from Sister Ray and asked him to play drums on the demo instead. He was sceptical at first, and then he agreed to come down to a rehearsal. I was relieved when he showed up, but I knew immediately that it wasn't going to work and that he didn't like my new band. Maybe it was because we were singing about the Moors murderers, but he was so nice about it I actually felt bad for him. There was no way I was going to let the chance of a free night in the studio disappear though, so I went back to Si with the biggest bag of weed I could get and he finally agreed to come down to play on the demo the following week.

All the while I was wondering about whether I was going to be able to find anyone as good as Andy on bass. I ran through the songs with Dale, but it didn't sound right. I even packed him off to Andrew to get a decent haircut, but no, it still didn't sound right. When the night came to finally make the demo, Si showed up with his kit and we ran both the songs down. We did 'Suffer Little Children' first and it went surprisingly well for our maiden voyage. I was pleased with how quickly it came together, and to hear ourselves in a studio for the first time felt like validation and a massive step. When we came to record 'The Hand That Rocks the Cradle' though, my doubts about Dale were there for all of us to hear. I had written the bass line, and even though it was just six notes repeated over and over, he just couldn't get it. We tried a few times and were as supportive as we could be, but in the end I had to play the bass on the demo myself.

From the minute I got the cassette of the two songs we'd recorded I was off around town on the rampage. I went from shop to shop, playing it to everyone I knew, and if you were in town and you had ears and didn't see me coming you were going to hear it. Such was my enthusiasm for my new band that even though the tape was two really downbeat songs which I was starting to realise had been very badly recorded, you would have to put up with hearing it just to get rid of me. I would play the tape in X-Clothes four or five times a day, and when my workmates informed me that they'd heard it enough, I would nip in next door to make sure the girls in Crazy Face had heard it that day. Once I played it really loud in the shop at three o'clock on a Saturday afternoon when the place was totally packed, and when most of the customers left it didn't deter me one bit. I was probably quite annoying.

Morrissey was doing some band promotion himself, and decided to take the tape to Factory boss Tony Wilson. Tony later went round saying that he turned down an opportunity to sign The Smiths to Factory, but he knew I would never have signed The Smiths to Factory, even then. I liked Tony, but I'd already refused invitations to join a couple of his bands and I wouldn't have had my own band dressed up in khaki shorts for anyone. I was sure that if we were to be on an indie label it should be Rough Trade, and definitely not Factory.

After he met with Morrissey, Tony came into the shop to tell me that he thought we were 'special', and that the press would love us because 'your singer was a journalist', which I took as a snide remark and to which I gave him my usual reply of 'Fuck off, Tony'.

One person who didn't like the tape was Si, and that was a problem. Morrissey and I had thought we'd found our drummer, and we even had Angie take some photos of him as a band member, but Si didn't want to join and he didn't like what we were doing. He also thought we had no prospect of making money. I told him he was making a big mistake, and I suspected his judgement, but I respected him for being honest with me and so I resigned myself to looking for someone else.

We needed to find someone and find them quickly, as I'd got us our first gig on a night that JK was putting on at the Ritz in town. He and Andrew had devised a fashion show that was meant to showcase a couple of designers and the scene we had going in Manchester. The main headliners were a band of London salsa scenesters called Blue Rondo a la Turk, whose act was to groove around energetically in zoot suits and blow whistles. We would be fifth on the bill, before the fashion show and the drag act, and the semi-naked dance troupe.

It was exciting that we had a gig. I'd been busy working on new songs, and I'd make tapes and give them to Morrissey to write his lyrics. We'd decided that at the Ritz we'd play 'Suffer Little Children', 'The Hand That Rocks the Cradle' and a new one we'd written, called 'Handsome Devil'. We also planned to do a song by the girl group The Cookies, called 'I Want a Boy for My Birthday', which I realised would send out a message that not only didn't bother me but which I was fairly amused by and quite excited about.

We met with a couple of drummers through word of mouth but none of them struck me as lifers or prospects, until one day Pete Hunt came to tell me about a guy he knew who lived in Chorlton called Mike Joyce. Pete seemed quite serious about his friend being considered, and at that stage serious was what I needed. I'd had enough of people who were casual; I wasn't expecting the same level of dedication as myself and Morrissey, because we were obsessed and were sailing the ship, but I felt that whoever was going to be in the band had to be committed. Pete assured me that Mike and I would get along and that he had been in a band called The Hoax, who I knew nothing about, but I trusted Pete and he suggested that Mike should meet me at Legends that night. It sounded good, so I made my way over there later on.

Legends catered for a slightly more cider and goth crowd than the hip hairdressing set at Exit, and the lights and sound system meant it was a good place to derail your senses. At some point early in the evening Pete came over with Mike Joyce. He was friendly and confident, with an edge to him that I couldn't quite put my finger on, and his look was a kind of spiky punk, which wasn't my thing but which he managed to pull off. He asked me about the band and what we had going on, and I told him about the gig and what I was into, and before I knew it we were getting drunk and joking like we knew each other. We got along on a few levels, the first one being sense of humour. Mike liked a laugh, and I found him very funny and irreverent. He was quick and in your face, and he was looking for something good to do while having fun doing it. When I asked him about his interest in my band and the possibility of him coming down to a rehearsal, he was vague and said he was already in a band called Victim. I couldn't quite make out the situation, as they were originally from Belfast but might be going back home. I didn't know if he was saying that they were splitting up or that he was going to Belfast with them; it sounded like both. Whatever was happening, it didn't seem like they were doing very much, and I left Legends hoping that Mike was a decent drummer and that maybe he could play with us at the Ritz.

A couple of days later Mike turned up in the shop, and after some small talk he agreed to come down to a rehearsal so we could check him out. He'd been listening to the tape, and although he wasn't sure about the band, his flatmate had liked it and thought it was worth giving it a go. I went to help him pick up his drums from a dodgy dive in Manchester, and we got together in Spirit Studios for an audition with Morrissey and Dale.

The four of us gathered in the dusty, cold, half-built concrete bunker, a couple of feeble light bulbs making it particularly dreary, as though we were underground captives. I introduced Mike to the others, and he appeared to be nervous. I made an effort to get everyone acquainted, but there seemed to be some tension in the room. I wondered if Morrissey wasn't keen on Mike and was thinking that Si was more right for us, but I elected to get going with what would be easiest by playing 'The Hand That Rocks the Cradle'. Mike picked up the song pretty quickly, and I tried not to make it obvious that I was examining his playing. He was doing fine, but there was something off about what I was hearing and I wasn't sure what it was. I knew I was playing the guitar correctly and it wasn't Morrissey's singing, so either the drumming wasn't good enough or the bass wasn't right. At this point Dale's shortcomings as a musician were back on my radar, and I couldn't ignore it. Things got more relaxed when we started the new song 'Handsome Devil'. I'd built it from a riff that I had come up with when I was in the Valentinos, and I was thrilled to be playing the first rock 'n' roll song in The Smiths' repertoire. We played 'Handsome Devil' a couple of times and I made a mental note to myself to 'write more of these'. After going through the other songs, things wound down, and as I was accompanying Mike up some half-finished breeze-block steps on the way out, he turned to me and asked if I thought he'd done all right.

'Yeah,' I assured him, 'it went well.'

'Oh good,' he replied, 'because I took some mushrooms earlier and I can't tell.'

With that admission I suspected that Mike was either really unprofessional and not a serious musician, or really ballsy and worth a shot. I decided he was worth a shot.

The Ritz

The immediate future was all about the upcoming debut at the Ritz. I'd told my family about our first show, and Claire was impressed that I was playing her favourite venue. Joe, Angie, Morrissey and I were getting busy, rallying as many people as we could to come down, and JK and Andrew had made posters that had gone up everywhere around town. It was really good to see the name 'The Smiths' for the first time in public. Morrissey had suggested that for the gig we invite his friend James Maker to introduce us. I didn't know James, but I thought that being introduced for our first show sounded good, and when I discovered that he would be wearing high-heeled stiletto shoes while he did it, I liked the idea even more.

Mike was going back and forth about whether he was going to join the group permanently or not, and he wasn't certain he could do the Ritz gig. It was difficult as we were quickly becoming friends, hanging out in the shop or on nights out together, and it was a big dilemma for me. Morrissey hadn't written off Si, and one day Mike would be up for playing with us and the next day he was staying with Victim. I was never impolite, but I felt that we were the best thing he had going as Victim hadn't done anything and were thinking of packing it in anyway. There came a point a few days before the show when I reasoned with him to just do it so the band could at least get our start; I'd deal with the future later.

The day of the first Smiths show finally arrived – 4 October 1982 – and it happened to be a Monday, which meant I had the day off from the shop and was able to get to the Ritz early to hang around and watch all the fuss. John Kennedy was sashaying around the gilded ballroom, busily directing all the members of the dance troupe who, though still fully dressed, were a total camp carnival, even at two in the afternoon. Andrew Berry was cutting and fixing the hair of all the models in his much-coveted Fiorucci shirt and impeccably placed trilby, while being one of the only people on earth who could get away with wearing jodhpurs without looking a total idiot. I flitted about the place nervously with my Gretsch in its case, smoking a lot of cigarettes while I waited for the other Smiths to arrive. Everywhere I looked, there were girls half-dressed and girls undressed and boys in vests and men in togas. Eventually the band showed up and we located ourselves on the left-hand side of the famous sprung dance floor to get our equipment ready. Mike still hadn't made his mind up about whether he was going to leave Victim, which caused me some concern, but I'd persuaded him to take part nonetheless. Suddenly Blue Rondo a la Turk arrived, jiving through the ballroom in a huge whoosh of zoot-suited magnificence, and we watched in awe as the headliners unloaded their trumpets, timbales and congas. Some of them had pencil moustaches. When they finished their soundcheck, we gamely made our way on to the packed stage to set our gear up, and a burly roadie came up to me and Pete Hope and said, 'You better not even think about touching any of our fucking equipment.'

'What was that?' I asked him.

'You move any of our mics and you're dead.'

Pete and I nodded, but the confrontation sent me into an attitude overhaul of indignation that quickly spread to the others, and cured our nerves. We were ready now for whatever was going to come our way.

Just as we were about to go on, Morrissey informed me that James Maker was going to be dancing next to us go-go style, which I thought was unnecessary but not a big deal, and after some impressive-sounding words of introduction from James in French I ascended the stairs to the stage for the very first show by The Smiths and my first official engagement as a professional musician. *Thwang!* What the . . . ? A wave of cold dread rushed through me as I realised I'd banged the headstock of my guitar against the wall. It was a sign, it had to be, the moment was too significant; it meant that either all my dreams and life's work thus far were about to expire in the next critical minute, or I had just exorcised all the bad luck I had accrued over my eighteen years with one divine bang of my Gretsch. I held the pick and looked out into the spotlight. My left hand formed the G6 chord that opened the first song and . . . *strum* . . . *strum* . . . it was . . . half and half – not totally perfect and glorious, but not too imperfect and disastrous for me not to be able to guide it and live with. Maybe it *was* symbolic. We got through the first couple of songs just fine, and then Mike had an issue with his snare. The interest in the audience picked up when we got to 'Handsome Devil' though, and in a moment of assuredness I looked over to my right and caught sight of the bass player dancing around like a four-year-old at a toddlers' disco. Uh-oh. 'What the fuck are you doing?' I thought, and I really hoped he would stop, but no, Dale was grooving and what's more he looked like he was really enjoying it. At that precise moment I knew we'd have to part company, and between James go-go dancing in stilettos on my left and Dale getting on down with his bad self on my right, our first ever gig was turning out to be a more lively affair than I could possibly have dreamt up. Luckily for Morrissey he was stuck out front and was unaware of the business that was going on behind him. The Smiths finished off our tentative and bizarre debut with 'I Want a Boy for My Birthday', to total bemusement from the crowd, and with that we descended the steps to make way for the avant-garde dance troupe. Thank you and goodnight.

Joe came up to me immediately and was absolutely jubilant, saying that he'd never heard a guitar played that way before and that he thought Morrissey was great. I'd not seen him so excited and his reaction was exactly what I needed. I said to him, 'We're going to need a manager, Joe. Do you fancy being our manager?'

After pausing for a few seconds he answered, 'Yeah . . . sure. I've never been a manager but I'll give it a go.'

I instinctively knew he would say yes. I was the right person asking the right question to the right person. As far as The Smiths and management went, that would be the only time that would ever happen.

I now knew that Dale was not right for the band. We met up at the rehearsal room a couple of nights later and I told him it wasn't working out. He took it very well and didn't seem particularly surprised, and then he wished me all the best, which I thought was very gracious. I also had to work out what we were going to do about the drums situation, as Mike was still not sure that he wanted to join. I had gone along with the Ritz being a temporary thing to see how it went, but then I had expected him to jump in enthusiastically. I needed to move on and find someone permanent as I'd got us another gig, this time at Manhattan Sound, and with an ultimatum of 'now or never' and some persuasion from his friends, Mike told us that he was in.

We had acquitted ourselves well enough at the Ritz that people around town were suitably impressed. So much so that my friend Tony O'Connor from the students' union at West Wythy came into the shop and asked me if I had a tape he could take to his boss at his new job at EMI. It all sounded a bit too easy but I wasn't going to say no, and the following day Tony and Morrissey went with our demo to the home of The Beatles in London while I waited expectantly by the payphone in the shop. Tony's boss wasn't exactly blown away with our tape, but he liked what he'd heard enough to give us £200 to make another demo. It wasn't *A Hard Day's Night*, but it was better than nothing and we had some new songs I couldn't wait to record.

I knew I was going to have to get Andy Rourke in on bass. I had no inclination or desire to audition any more strangers, who I knew wouldn't be as good. I was excited about the prospect of getting Andy in the band, but I was still angry about the heroin and I was unsure about how things were going to be resolved. I went round to his house, where I'd spent so much of my time and where I knew some of my old friends were, and they were all there in the front room, exactly where I'd left them a year before, except now they were looking several years worse. There was a bleak stillness and a dead air to the place. One former friend jumped up confrontationally to demand why I was back while the others skulked in embarrassment and smug, junked-up dumbness. I wasn't planning on staying for long, and I went into the back room where Andy was to speak to him alone. It was good to see him, and he was surprised I'd come round. He looked the same as always and told me about the job he had in a timber yard and how he hated it, but at least it meant he was working every day and I was glad he wasn't in the same pit as the zombies in the next room. I stuck to the matter at hand and told him about the new band I was putting together, and asked if he wanted to join. I told him that it was on the condition that there wouldn't be any heroin. I played him a tape of the gig at the Ritz, and he liked what he heard and said he would come and play on the EMI demo. I left Andy's for the last time and I wondered if it was all going to work out, and if

The Smiths was now a band. It could be perfect. I put all my faith in it, and I just hoped we wouldn't have any problems.

The Smiths first got together in a tiny basement with no windows and dark blue denim on the walls at a place called Drone Studios in Chorlton. Morrissey and I had been writing with a passion, and we had enough money from EMI to record three songs: 'Handsome Devil', 'Miserable Lie' and a new one called 'What Difference Does It Make?'. There are numerous accounts from bands of how they knew things were absolutely right from the moment they started to play together, and it's the same for The Smiths, except that in our case I knew it was right from the moment I introduced everyone to each other on the street in Chorlton that December morning. We even looked like a band.

When we started playing the first song, which was 'Handsome Devil', it sounded so good to us that we did what every other band does in that situation: we started to laugh. It's a fantastic truth and a profound irony that the very first thing The Smiths did when they got together was to start laughing uncontrollably.

We got into things quickly and Andy was great on bass. He and I picked up where we'd left off in the last band, playing off each other, and we all knew he was the right man for the job. The day then got a little strange when Mike informed us that he could see Dale looking in through the window in the kitchen upstairs. I assumed our drummer had been taking mushrooms again, but when I went to check it out I saw Dale myself, loitering in the garden and peering in through the window. I went out to say hello and see why he was there, and he went to great lengths to convince me that he just happened to be taking an impromptu look at the studio on the day we were in there recording. I was curious about why he wanted to check out a studio from the garden, but I gave him my best and left him to it.

The rest of the session went smoothly and things got really good when we heard 'What Difference Does It Make?' coming back through the monitors. It's a good sign when your best song is also your most recent; you feel like you've taken a step up. We tried out a saxophone on 'Handsome Devil', because I was listening to a lot of Little Richard, and a nice man came in and tried his best, but The Smiths and the saxophone were never meant to be and I was OK with that. When the three songs were finished, we gave a copy to Tony O'Connor to bring to EMI. I didn't have too much expectancy that they would go for it, and when they came back to us to say that they 'couldn't hear anything in it', neither Morrissey nor I were particularly surprised or crestfallen. I focused on trying to get us more shows and writing another song as good as 'What Difference Does It Make?'.

My job at X-Clothes was starting to get difficult. I loved being in town every day, but I wanted to spend all my waking hours on the band, a fact that was duly noted by my boss. I was meeting up with Joe at Crazy Face more often and was getting back from lunch later and Lee didn't like it at all. He also disliked the fact that I seemed to be just hanging about, talking to everyone about my band and treating the place like a nightclub when I was supposed to be working, and it espe-cially irked him that I did that while being able to sell more clothes than anyone else. It wasn't my fault, I just had the knack. I was musing on this predicament with Joe one afternoon when he made a suggestion: 'You should come and work here,' he said. 'You can open a shop in the basement.' I knew that Joe only made decisions after very careful consideration. There wasn't too much to think about, except to be very excited and a bit nervous about the responsibility of opening a shop, but if Joe thought I could do it then I would, and I ran through town and over to Sassoon's to tell Angie, my head spinning with it all.

Portland Street

The Smiths had our second show coming up at Manhattan Sound in January 1983. I was in my room at Shelley's a few nights before and was thinking that I had to find the band a roadie. The fact that we wouldn't be getting paid meant I'd have to rely on the kindness of someone who wasn't a stranger, but where could I find such a friend? After musing for a while I walked across the landing to where my housemate Ollie was busy with his continued experiments in all the different ways to apply a bong. The hyper twang of his favourite funkers was blaring from his record deck.

'Ollie? . . . Ollie!' I yelled.

'Yeah?' he shouted back, a bit narked at being interrupted from the jazz-funk reverie.

I went into his room and asked the giant favour through the fog: 'The band needs a roadie, do you fancy doing it?'

He thought about it for quite a while before answering. 'Will I be getting paid?' he asked.

'No,' I replied, 'but it'll be a laugh.'

He thought for a moment longer before giving me his verdict. 'OK then,' he replied, and that was that, we had a roadie. Ollie was a mate.

There was a buzz around town about our second show. This time we would be headlining, and we'd play on the dance floor while a film of the drag queen Divine was projected on the wall next to us. Once again flyers went up around town, and we heard that the place was sold out, which was heady stuff for us and something I hadn't really expected. There was a lot riding on the second show as not only were all the fashionistas there who knew me and Angie, but we had piqued the interest of the Manchester old guard, who had known of Morrissey from being around gigs during the punk days. I had been given the impression from different sources that my new partner was a serial hermit with absolutely no friends, but he introduced me to quite a few people, one being Linder Sterling, who I knew of from seeing her band Ludus and who was always interesting, and another being Buzzcocks' manager Richard Boon. I liked Morrissey's friends, and he never introduced me to anyone that wasn't really supportive of the band. Meanwhile, our friend Tony Wilson offered to introduce us onstage, and New Order manager Rob Gretton and the rest of the Factory crowd were coming too. It seemed that people were starting to notice us.

We played the same set as we had at the Ritz, but added 'What Difference Does It Make?' and a couple of other new ones, including the first of our sad and pretty compositions, called 'What Do You See in Him?', which I loved. We were still playing 'I Want a Boy for My Birthday', but in the light of the songs Morrissey and I were now writing the song felt redundant and a bit contrived. Having the right line-up made it very obvious that we really didn't need a go-go dancer, so it would be our last with James Maker, and it may have been the new songs or the sense of occasion, but it was at the Manhattan Sound that I first recognised that we were a band with a singer who was not only a unique lyricist but a unique presence onstage. He was made for his audience, and we were made for our audience. Now we just had to get them to find us.

I was hanging out at the Haçienda on the nights when there was nothing better to do in town, which meant most nights during the week. It was an industrial-looking space so echoey and vast that on the rare occasion when there was a crowd it still seemed like it was empty. I would often go on a weeknight with Angie and the two Petes, and just about the only other soul in the club besides us would be the DJ, playing electro music to the very bored bar staff. We would stand around on the balcony, looking down on the empty dance floor, and watch the stragglers wandering round while two huge video screens opposite played *Eraserhead*, a film everyone was talking about by the weird new director David Lynch. I was happy enough to be there – it was somewhere to go where you wouldn't get any hassle, and I could wander in and get free drinks at the bar. Andrew Berry had a job as a DJ, and I could hang out in the booth playing whatever records I liked, such as 'Ghost on the Highway' by The Gun Club and 'Shack Up' by A Certain Ratio.

In spite of the complaints about the sound and the gripes by the members of some of the Factory bands, there was a feeling in the early days of the Haçienda of being right on the cutting edge. It may have been overambitious and a commercially naive venture, but it was fantastically idealistic and it gave alternative people in Manchester the most modern place to go in the world. New Order were the undisputed centre of the whole scene. There were always rumours about how much money the club was costing the band, and they appeared to be playing there every week to keep it going. I knew a lot of people at Factory Records, and even though we weren't working together we were of the same mindset, which was to escape the constraints of the straight world and try to get on doing something creative. No one was chasing commercialism, it was too boring and too uncool, and obtaining it didn't seem like an option for any of us anyway. I respected New Order, not just because they were successful, but because they were successful on their own terms.

The person I knew best at Factory was Mike Pickering. He was a real music expert and was usually with New Order's manager Rob Gretton. Mike was a catalyst on the Manchester scene, and it was through him that we got our first show at the Haçienda supporting the Factory band 52nd Street. It would definitely be a step forward for us, and when I saw the posters around town for the show I decided that it was time to take Joe up on his offer to open a new shop. I handed in my notice at X-Clothes, and on the last day I got my leaving pay and treated myself to a pair of black Ray-Ban Wayfarer sunglasses.

Joe cleared out the basement of the Portland Street building to make room for the new shop. At first I was going to stock it with the current Crazy Face items, but then I put in second-hand clothes from my friends' shops that they thought I could sell. We decorated the place with film posters and some original black-and-white framed press shots of Marlon Brando and Bo Diddley that Joe had bought from Paris in the seventies, and I painted the musical notation to the Stones' version of 'Not Fade Away' along the top of the walls, as it was one of my many obsessions at the time. Joe was very serious about his role as 'The Smiths' manager. Now that we were working together, we were able to spend more time discussing things and getting more ideas, and he moved his office into the adjacent room so he and I were in close proximity.

We were in the Manhattan after work one night when he brought up the idea that we should do something at the Haçienda to change the sterile atmosphere of the place. 'We could bring in a lot of flowers, cheer the place up and get away from the Factory vibe, make it our own.' It sounded like a nice enough idea, but I didn't give it much more thought. I was more excited about the fact that working in Crazy Face meant I was able to get my own bespoke jeans made up for me. Up until then I would beg a black pair from Kate in the wholesale department, and because I was so small I'd get a size eight from the children's range. Then I'd customise them by taking a pin and fraying the end of the seams, or sewing a strip of blue suede around the bottoms as turn-ups. A very big thing for me was discovering the photos of Stuart Sutcliffe with The Beatles in Hamburg. I thought he was the hippest thing I'd ever seen, and the fact that his look was post-1950s rock 'n' roll but pre-Beat Boom beatnik said something to me at the time. I scoured the second-hand shops and found an old pair of white Johnson's shoes that I dyed navy blue, and then added a white polo-neck sweater and a low V-neck that I bought from Marks and Spencer. I showed the Stu Sutcliffe pics to Kate in the factory and asked if she could make me some black jeans with a V cut into the side of the leg, and when I had all of that down I dug out my Ray-Ban Wayfarers from X-Clothes.

My days would go like this: I'd wake up in my room at Shelley's at nine forty-five after staying up writing songs or hanging out with Ollie. I'd get dressed in a hurry and dash down three flights of stairs and out the door to run to the train in time for work. I'd keep hurtling down the street until I got to the girls' school, then I'd slow right down and try to look cool and not totally flustered as I sauntered past nonchalantly. Once past the school, I'd pick up speed, career into Altrincham train station and buy a Cadbury's Caramel chocolate bar and a small bottle of Schweppes lemonade for breakfast from the waiting vendor, before jumping on the train just as it left at five past ten. I'd get into Manchester with about three minutes to get to the shop, which was ten minutes away. I always arrived around ten forty-five, when Joe would be sat at his desk on the phone. He'd finish his call and roll a joint and put on a cassette of John Lee Hooker or something relating to whatever music we were talking about the day before, and then we'd talk about what was happening with the band. When it got to around eleven thirty I would wait for an appropriate pause in Joe's thinking, then suggest taking down the shutters from the door and opening the shop. Every day went this way, unless I'd slept on the floor of Mike's flat, which was closer to town and in which case I would get the bus, but I would still manage to be ten minutes late. The rest of the day would proceed in a similar fashion, with friends dropping by and me pretending to be selling clothes. When it got to around five in the afternoon, Morrissey, Mike and Andy would arrive and we'd get into the service elevator and take it to the giant factory floor at the top of the building where the machines cut the Crazy Face fabrics, and we'd rehearse the set or learn a new song.

It was important that the band were tight. We wanted to be good, and we were fine with going over the songs until we felt it was right. It was often very cold on the top floor, and my guitar strings would be freezing wires. But we never slacked off, we were into it and had a work ethic, and besides there was nothing better to do. The Smiths never went to the pub, not as a band or as individuals. There had been a tradition going back years of British musicians getting together in pubs, before rehearsals, after rehearsals, before gigs and after gigs. Bands formed in pubs and bands split up in pubs, but it wasn't our scene. We became a band through playing together. Andy taught Mike the art of locking in with the bass. It took a while to gel properly, but they persevered and worked at it until we all started to get on the same musical wavelength. A guitar string would snap and I would have to stick a safety pin on the end of it to keep it in place. We'd finish around ten, going as long as we could, and I'd take a dreary train ride back to Shelley's and Mike would catch a bus to Chorlton. Morrissey and Andy would travel together on the bus back through Stretford and Sale. It was through these experiences that the members of The Smiths got to know each other. Most bands start out at school or in the neighbourhood. They grow up as friends and want to do something together. They have a shared history and experience of each other's lives and backgrounds, but it wasn't like that for The Smiths. The other three members didn't know each other before joining the band, they became friends through being in The Smiths, which happened through me, and for this reason my role, besides playing the guitar and writing the music, was like the centre of the wheel; the band viewed me as the one who pulled things together and was resourceful. Apart from going back to Shelley's to write and sleep, I spent most of my time in the Portland Street building. Everyone could find me at the band's HQ. It was a good job and I was loving it.

Hand in Glove

The upcoming Haçienda show was a big deal. It was the most prestigious place we'd played and it was only our third appearance. Joe was saying, 'We'll have to get a gig in London when you're ready,' which I knew meant, 'I'm listening and you're not ready yet.' As well as the Haçienda show we'd also managed to get ourselves on to the bill supporting Richard Hell at Rafters, which to me was really big time, and we had a few new songs to play and one new song in particular.

I'd been around at my parents' house with Angie, absent-mindedly strumming an old acoustic guitar that I'd left there. At first I thought the riff I was playing was something like Nile Rodgers might do with Chic, but then it quickly developed into my own style, until I hit what felt like pure inspiration. There wasn't anything at the house to record the tune on to, and the only thing I could do so Morrissey could hear it was to drive to his house with the guitar and play it to him before I forgot it. I made a desperate plea to Angie to drive me in the Beetle and we set off fast, with me playing the tune around and around on the guitar while I tried my best not to change it or lose it. On the journey Angie made what was for her a rare suggestion. 'Make it sound like Iggy,' she said.

'What?' I asked.

'Make it sound like Iggy,' she repeated, now sounding more like an order than a request.

I adapted the clipped, rhythmic approach I was using and changed the riff to a big open chord strum that I thought would be more like something from *Raw Power*, and within seconds it sounded really good. I kept the riff going, and when I got to Morrissey's I prayed it wouldn't be one of the rare occasions when he'd left the house. He opened the door to find me strumming and stuttering about a new song, and as I serenaded him on the doorstep he scampered away quickly to get his tape recorder so we could record the tune. When we got together to rehearse a couple of days later, I was eager to show Mike and Andy the new song and we had it sounding good straight away. Morrissey then took the mic and held a sheet of paper, we all went into the song for the first time together, and *bang!* It was called 'Hand in Glove' and it was the best thing we'd done. The spirit in the singing was the same as the spirit in the guitar. The song defined us and described the devotion and solidarity of a powerful friendship. It was a declaration and our manifesto. The words were perfect, the music was perfect, my life was perfect.

The night of the Haçienda show finally came. Andrew was the DJ, and Ollie was dispatched to get some flowers for the night as Joe had planned. The place was so cavernous and boomy it felt like we were playing to just a handful of our friends in a big concrete room, which turned out to be exactly what it was. We made the best of it and I hoped that people liked it. Later on, Morrissey's sister Jackie came into the dressing room to say that she thought the band was great. The Smiths had taken a necessary step on the road to recognition in Manchester and we had acquitted ourselves well enough.

As always, Joe was working on the next move, which he thought was to play in London and to find a record company. The two of us and Morrissey were trying on a daily basis to make things happen, and Morrissey and I were even daring to dream about the possibility of making a single. We had the demos from Decibel and Drone to send to the record companies, but we were evolving so fast as writers that we'd moved on from those early tapes. I'd announced that we should be on Rough Trade, and the thought of taking the conventional major company route seemed redundant and most probably ineffectual. I still liked the idea of Rough Trade, and then Joe stepped in once again and offered to put up £225 to record 'Hand in Glove' in Strawberry Studios. It was beyond exciting and I was ready to go.

Joe and I had already been discussing the possibility of me moving out of Shelley's and into his house with his family in Heaton Mersey. It meant that we could spend more time working on the band and drive to and from the shop together every day. I would live with Andrew Berry in the two-room flat above Joe and his wife Janet and their two-year-old son, Ivan. I took to my new digs by writing the music for a new song called 'Accept Yourself' and we added it to the set opening for Richard Hell. It was cool to be playing with someone whose records I'd admired, and I considered the show to be our first real test in front of a non-partisan crowd. We had to stop the set as I broke a string, and because I didn't have a back-up guitar I had to go through what seemed like a lifetime changing the string onstage while the band waited. When we finished playing, a very wasted Richard Hell appeared from backstage, put his arm around me and said, 'You're a great guitar player.' I didn't know at the time if he was serious or just being kind because he saw me struggling with the broken string, but either way, and in spite of him breathing lethal toxic fumes over me, it was a nice gesture and it really meant a lot.

It was good to be living with Joe's family. Being around Janet and their son Ivan gave me a sense of domesticity and order that helped to keep me grounded. Janet was dynamic and always very busy, looking after the family and running a couple of shops herself. She understood that Joe and I were on a mission, and she adapted her family's home life in support of it. I loved having a little kid running around. Ivan would wait for me at the bottom of the stairs if he thought I was home, and I would try to get back early some nights so he and I could play together with his toys. As tolerant as Janet was, she was also formidable, especially when it came to her family. I could get away with playing loud music and even have a cigarette now and then, but when I surrendered one night to Ivan's request for the can of Coke I was holding she hit the roof and all I could do was hide. I wasn't aware of exactly how much sugar and caffeine was bad for toddlers, but I knew by the time she had finished kicking off, and it didn't help that Ivan followed me around for days afterwards asking me for a Coca-Cola.

Living with Andrew was great. Even though I had a lot of different friendships with different people, if you asked anyone who they thought my closest friend was at the time they would've said Andrew. I've always had a best mate, even from the days of Sacred Heart with Chris Milne. It sometimes worked out that because my focus was on being a musician, whoever I was close with would end up being enlisted in my band, which was how it was with Andy Rourke at school. Sometimes my relationship with a bandmate takes on a different dynamic because of the roles and chemistry in the band. We can be good friends, but it's also work. One of the reasons why Andrew Berry and I were such good mates was because we weren't in a band together, and as significant as my relationship with Morrissey was, having a best friend that I could confide in outside of the band was always helpful, especially when I was in The Smiths.

The other thing about living with Andrew was that we had all the records from the DJ booth at the Haçienda. In the front room were boxes of albums by Suicide, Material, James White and the Blacks, and everyone on the ZE label, as well as a whole stack of electro 12-inch singles. Andrew introduced me to a lot of club music, mostly from New York, that was brand new and completely different from the post-punk guitar music I was investigating, and it gave me an appreciation of club music that would endure. Between his knowledge of club records, Joe's love of sixties soul singers, and my own quest for modern guitar music, the whole house was an extraordinary mix of disparate influences that somehow made total sense to me.

When the moment finally came to make my first record, it was like stepping up to destiny. I had fantasised for so long about what it would be like to actually make a record, and now that it was about to happen I was not going to get it wrong. The band and Joe made our way into Strawberry Studios in Stockport on a drizzly Sunday morning, and as we started setting up I realised that it was my responsibility to direct the recording. I was secretly nervous and when we met the house engineer, who acted as if we were a huge inconvenience, I just crossed my fingers and hoped the spirit of Phil Spector and Andrew Loog Oldham was with us.

We didn't waste any time. After a perfunctory twenty minutes or so of getting an adequate drum sound, the band went through the song a couple of times to make sure the levels would be correct on the tape and in our headphones. We saw the red light and dived into the first take, and then did a second, more confident take. It was sounding good to us already and we were enjoying the experience. By the third take, we had upped the feeling even more. Our nervousness meant that we'd played the song slightly fast, but it turned out to be a good thing as it gave the performance an impatience and enthusiasm. We captured a rush: take three could be the record. We took off the headphones and wondered what was going to transpire as we followed each other back into the control room. One of the greatest things in the world for a band is when you all stand together behind the mixing desk to listen to a performance of a song that you've captured in the studio. There's an elation that's barely contained until the end of the playback, just in case you jinx it, then a wave of joy that you all feel together in the same moment. If you multiply that by the fact that it was our first record, then you can imagine what it meant for The Smiths to hear take three of 'Hand in Glove'. I set about finishing the track by doubling the electric guitar and then overdubbing an acoustic twice on the right-hand side. Mike played a tambourine part and then Morrissey recorded a ghostly backing vocal. It was inspired. As we were mixing the song, I wondered if there was something we needed to announce the start of the record, a kind of finishing touch. I took out the harmonica, asked everyone to bear with me in case it didn't work, and I came up with a phrase in the corridor on my way into the live room. I recorded the harmonica and I'd made my first record.

When it was done, I went outside and the mood of the record was all there in the street. It sounded like it was from the mist of the north and from somewhere in the past. It sounded like the future too. It could even have a navy-blue and silver label.

London

None of us knew exactly how we would get a gig in London, but scouring the back pages of the weekly music press it looked like the Rock Garden in Covent Garden was the place where new bands played. Pete Hope was about to take a trip south, and after offering to go into the venue to try to get us the gig, he managed to secure us our first London appearance. We would even be paid £25 for our trouble. Joe had proposed to me and Morrissey that the band should get a van in order to play gigs, and he put down a deposit on a Renault Cavalier that, once we threw in a mattress, would become our new home. Heading down to London to play for the first time made me acutely aware of just how Mancunian we were, and I had no idea if the aliens in the capital would get it.

The Rock Garden was a little brick basement that sounded

like a tin can and had the appropriate no-frills ambience referred to as 'throw and go'. We clambered up to the tiny high stage and played a spirited set to not many people, which because we felt on trial brought out a defiance in us that we would learn to call upon in the future. The audience liked us enough to call us back for an encore, which was a first for us and made the gig feel like a victory, and then we took our victory back up the motorway, in our new home, to planet Manchester.

The activity at 70 Portland Street increased even more after we'd been in Strawberry Studios. Joe's life was now all about the band, and everyone in the building was living with our own soundtrack, 'Hand in Glove'. We wracked our brains for ideas about how best to get our song out on vinyl and decided that if we were unable to find a suitable record company then we would form our own label and put the song out ourselves. I liked the plan, as at least it meant a guaranteed release, but I still had my mind set on Rough Trade. There was only one thing left to do: I had to go there and ask them to sign us.

I'd stayed in touch with Matt Johnson since we'd met the year before, and I called him and asked if he could put me up when I got to London. Matt offered to let me stay on his couch, and I made my way to Rough Trade and took Andy with me for moral support. When we got to the Rough Trade offices I had no plan or strategy; it was just a matter of winging it. I asked at reception if there was someone we could see about playing our tape, but we were given the brush-off as everyone was either too busy or out of the office. We hung around conspicuously for a while and made more enquiries about when to come back, until the young guy at the desk finally gave in and allowed us to wait while he got a message to Simon Edwards, who I assumed was a Rough Trade boss. After a long wait we were eventually seen by a courteous and businesslike man who asked us the name of the band, then took the tape into a small office down the corridor, presumably to play it.

Andy and I waited anxiously, and I was hoping that the gentleman was grooving irresistibly to 'Hand in Glove' at full volume in a state of euphoria, punching the air with the realisation that he'd discovered the biggest new guitar band in England. He came back quickly and coolly handed the tape to me.

'Yes, it's good,' he said, 'but I can't really do anything. You'd have to let Geoff hear it.'

'Good,' I thought, 'he said it was good, he didn't say "go away".' But still, it wasn't exactly the reaction I was hoping for. I thought he'd at least be out of breath after all that grooving. 'Who's this Geoff?' I thought. 'Who's Geoff?' I said.

'Geoff's the head of the label, and he decides what we put out,' said Simon. 'Perhaps you could send it to him?'

'Send it' – that definitely sounded like a brush-off, and my heart rate quickened as I feared my opportunity was slipping away. 'Can I see him?' I asked. 'We've come all the way from Manchester.' I was getting a bit desperate; I knew how good the song was and that all they had to do was hear it and they'd love it.

'Geoff's in a meeting all afternoon. I can't disturb him now,' said Simon politely, and then gestured over to an office where a tall man was stood talking by a window.

It was clear that this was as close as we were going to get for the moment. I wasn't about to badger the man or prostrate myself before him, but my instinct also told me that I was on the brink of a crucial moment. As we turned to walk out of the building, I nodded to Andy to follow me into the ware-house, where there was a loading bay filled with hundreds of boxes. I started to act like I was stacking records. So far, so good. There was so much activity in the loading bay with people coming and going that no one noticed any interlopers, even if one of them did look like Stuart Sutcliffe. I kept watching the office where I'd seen Geoff, waiting for him to come out. An hour or so passed, and then I saw him come out of the door and make his way down the corridor, looking very busy. Here was my chance. I walked up to him and took out our tape, and as he went past me I grabbed his arm and said, 'Geoff . . . hi.' He stopped, and I was surprised myself at how unexpected the moment was. 'I'm in a band from Manchester, we're called The Smiths, and we've done a song we'd really like to put out on Rough Trade.' I needed to let him know about our commitment to it coming out, so I said, 'If you don't want to put it on the label, we could put it out on our own label and you could distribute it.' Geoff was calm and seem-ingly unconcerned at being accosted by a tiny northerner.

'I'll listen to it over the weekend,' he said.

I believed him, and in my happiness and enthusiasm I blurted out, 'You won't have heard anything like it before.'

Mission accomplished. As I walked out of the Rough Trade

building and carried on down the street, it felt like I was living in a movie. I was imagining things and scenarios for me and my band, and they were actually coming true. I left Notting Hill to go and stay with Matt Johnson in Highbury while Andy went back to Manchester.

Since I'd last seen him, Matt had been busy putting together his own situation, which wasn't a band in the traditional sense and had been christened The The. Still only twenty-one, he had signed a five-album deal with CBS Records and had recently put out two great singles called 'Uncertain Smile' and 'Perfect'. When I got to his house, a very beautiful girl answered the door who I recognised from the cover of *i-D* magazine, which we'd sold in X-Clothes. She introduced herself as Fiona, and she was Matt's girlfriend. She showed me into the flat where Matt was crouched on the floor, wearing headphones and surrounded by equipment that was strewn all over the carpet. A Casio keyboard and a black Fender Strat and drum machine were all plugged into a little four-track cassette recorder, and there was an electronic autoharp lying around and some microphones, one of which was plugged into an echo pedal. I hadn't seen anyone working this way before. It struck me as incredibly modern and inventive; he was totally self-sufficient. When he'd finished what he was doing, he played me his new track. It was built around the electric auto-harp lying on the floor, and it was a sublime song called 'This Is the Day'.

Matt and I went out to celebrate seeing each other again. Driving through London's West End in his old Rover, we caught up on everything from synths and recording techniques to the film music of Bernard Herrmann and our mutual fondness for glam rock. He told me about his recent acquaintance with the New York underground scene, and he quizzed me about my band and what was going on in Manchester. It was great to get together with Matt again. He was curious about everything and seemed to always be on some kind of quest. We stayed up and talked again about how we should do something together sometime, but for now we had our own missions. When I left Matt's place the next day, he was back on the floor, surrounded by his equipment. He was about to embark on a serious creative roll, producing an album called *Soul Mining* that would become much loved and hugely influential. I went back on the train to Manchester, about to discover that The Smiths had just landed a record deal.

I got into Joe's office on Monday morning to hear that Geoff Travis had called to say he loved 'Hand in Glove' and wanted to release it on Rough Trade. We called the rest of the band and Angie came over and the whole building was buzzing like it was happening for everyone.

Up until that point, releasing a record with my own band had been the height of my ambition. I had imagined it since I was very young, and had pursued it purely on instinct and desire, not knowing how it might actually transpire. For all my proclamations to friends, and my clear predictions for the band, I was still trying to will my desire into destiny, but now it appeared that it was actually about to happen. It took about twelve days for Rough Trade to manufacture 'Hand in Glove'. Morrissey had supplied them with the cover design. I was impressed and also relieved to have someone in the band with a strong vision for our aesthetic, and the B-side of the single was a recording we'd made of 'Handsome Devil' from the mixing desk at the Haçienda show.

Joe had told me that a box with twenty-five records would be arriving at the train station, and I walked across town and through Piccadilly Gardens to pick it up like I was in a dream. I collected the box, stood on the station approach and ripped open the packaging. The record sleeve was a metallic silver, with a blue photograph and the name of the band on the front. I took the record out of the sleeve and stared at it. There it was: the blue-and-silver label with the band's name, and below the song title the names 'Morrissey and Marr' in brackets. I stared at it as swarms of people hurried by, and I took the moment in. I'd finally done it, and with a great song and the right sound. 'Hand in Glove' was beautiful, and from then on I'd just have to take everything as it came and see what happened next.

Because we were now on Rough Trade, it meant that not only would the band have a record out but we also had a new home with new people to get to know. Joe was busy planning things with the label boss Geoff Travis, and an engaging American record plugger called Scott Piering, who would play a major part in the band's development. The three of them immediately started booking us gigs in London and at small venues around the country, and everyone at Rough Trade was swept along on a wave of anticipation. Our new record company acted like they thought we were going to be successful and were special, and because they did we believed even more that we could be.

The Heatwave

'Hand in Glove' came out on 13 May 1983, within a month of me bringing the tape to the record company. Our first public airing was on *The John Peel Show* on BBC Radio 1, and Angie and Andrew gathered around with me and Joe in his kitchen to hear it. It was important that it sounded really good. *The John Peel Show* was the only radio programme that anyone I knew bothered to listen to, and it was a beacon for my generation. Getting played by John Peel didn't mean that we were automatically about to become pop stars, that was not the point, but it did mean that as far as the alternative music world was concerned we were getting in the game. When I heard our single on the radio for the first time it sounded right and it proved to me that we belonged. It sounded good to Peel and his producer John Walters too, and we were invited to the BBC studios in Maida Vale to record a session for the show. Scott Piering had assumed the role of our de facto custodian at the record company as well as our radio plugger, a role that the band and Joe were grateful for, as he showed us the ropes at Rough Trade and the BBC and steered us towards people and situations that would be good for us and away from some people who weren't.

Walking around the maze of corridors at the BBC, I felt simultaneously like a card-carrying professional musician and a schoolboy required to show due deference around the establishment. We had left Manchester in the van at 7 a.m., and four hours of bouncing around on a mattress and talking excitedly in a fog of hash smoke had left me fairly frazzled, but once I was directed to the BBC cafeteria and got loaded up on chocolate and lemonade I was ready to go. The producer who had been assigned our session surveyed the scene without acknowledging us, and it was apparent that his demeanour for the day would be that of a disapproving Latin professor on a wet afternoon. I wondered how he would accomplish the task of capturing our blistering sound and maverick spirit while seemingly being so fed up, and I was drained just looking at him. But the band got up to speed from the very first song, and we managed to rise above his mood with our growing professionalism and our enthusiasm for what we were doing. There was always a really strong and positive atmosphere when we were in the studio, no matter where we were. We were excited about what we were doing and we couldn't get our ideas down quickly enough.

Once we had recorded the main take of a song to our satisfaction with the basic guitar, bass, drums and vocal tracks,

Morrissey would then re-record his vocal quite quickly, and when that was done I would go through the drum track to make sure it was right, so Andy could then work on the bass if we wanted to change or refine anything. After this, the recording became fun for me. We knew we had the foundations of the music right, so I could then devise whatever guitar overdubs were needed and experiment with ideas, using the different techniques I was learning along the way. The other band members encouraged me to do whatever I wanted, and trusted me to deliver something good. As the day went on in Maida Vale, our work ethic and endeavour was noticed by the producer, who started to involve himself more. At one stage he even made a joke, something about us being miserable because we came from the north. It seemed we had brought out his sense of humour, even if it was patronising, and to be fair we were singing a song called 'Miserable Lie'.

The producer's reaction to our songs was something that I would very much have to get used to in the future. Our lyrics and some of the comments Morrissey was making in the music press were starting to get us attention. From the off I knew it was best to let Morrissey do all the talking to the media. He had his agenda and world view, partly because he was older, but mostly because he was just so good at it. As far as the band's relationship with the media went, I could see that our frontman was an expert with the press and could do a better job of it than me and almost everybody who sat down to interview us. I thought his interviews were often very funny, and the controversies over the early lyrics came as a surprise. I considered it all part of being in a band that was thought-provoking, and whenever Morrissey got criticised or pressured about anything I was supportive and went into back-up mode, both in public and in private.

We'd been put on a bill in Camden before The Fall, who were the current reigning kings of Rough Trade – or more accurately the band run by the reigning king of Rough Trade, Mark E. Smith – and I'd been told by a Rough Trade employee that Mr Smith had complained to the label about all the time they were putting into us. It was a big show for us and we were nervous. Luckily the guy doing sound was someone I'd met at my very first show with Sister Ray in Wythenshawe, and he did his best to make us feel like we belonged and got a fair shake. As the night went on it was apparent that it would be an important one for the band. We were being talked about a lot, and it was a London show on a Saturday night to a sell-out crowd. As we were about to go on, Scott Piering stopped us to get a photo of the band. We leaned against the wall and in a second we got the shot that would become the first famous Smiths image: Morrissey stood at the front with his flowers, Mike and Andy were in white T-shirts, and I stood at the back in the black leather coat I'd got when I worked at Ivor's and the Ray-Bans I got from X-Clothes.

The summer of 1983 was an incredible time for me. I was nineteen and playing with my band in London. I had my first single on the radio and there was a heatwave. The Smiths had been lined up to play a few shows opening for The Sisters of Mercy. I knew of their music and I thought they were good. They had an admirable attitude towards their audience, who they seemed to regard more like guests at a communal gathering than fans; their attitude towards their support acts was admirable too. When you're the opening band you get used to being ignored by the headliners, and the road crews of headliners can sometimes act like you're an intrusion on their turf. Throw into the mix the fact that you're from out of town, and your day can be a struggle. The Sisters and their crew went out of their way to make sure we were looked after, and I would occasionally spend time before we went on with their singer, Andrew Eldritch, who was very cool. If you're decent to begin with you should be hospitable to a new band, especially when they're young. You need help when you're starting out, and whenever I received some kindness in those situations I appreciated it and never forgot it.

It was at the shows with The Sisters of Mercy that I started getting pre-gig nerves. Anyone would think that receiving sudden praise for being the next big thing would give you more confidence, but I had to adjust to the acclaim that was coming on like a tidal wave from every angle. It wasn't that I thought we weren't worthy; it was because I had my own guitar style with no flash solos, and I didn't know what this new world was expecting from me. The band had gone from trying to convert a few people standing at the bar and not really getting it to stepping out as the next big thing, and my attitude of 'you won't have heard anything like this before' had suddenly disappeared. I would be back to normal as soon as the first song started, but I missed how it had been when our backs were against the wall and so I had to recalibrate a new attitude. One night in the dressing room at Dingwalls I came up with the logic that having some money in my pocket would make me feel lucky, and because I didn't have any I asked Joe if he could loan me some. He gave me a £10 note, telling me he needed it back afterwards. We walked onstage and played a dazzling show to an adoring crowd which finished with our first stage invasion. After that I never went onstage again without putting a £10 note in my pocket.

After every gig the band would drive back to Manchester with Ollie and Joe in the van. There were no windows, and the four of us would sprawl on the mattress, not listening to music but just talking and joking the whole journey. We went back to play the Rock Garden after only a few months since our first gig there, and as we poured out of the van and on to the pavement in Covent Garden we met the first ever Smiths fans, called Josh and Anna, holding flowers in the sunshine. It was a new thing to see people dressed in imitation of us, and I looked around and noticed that all of the band were wearing different variations of bespoke black Crazy Face jeans. Morrissey's were baggy with a low seam at the back, Mike and Andy's were drainpipes, and mine were the kids' ones with the fraying at the bottom. Morrissey and I had beaded necklaces and we were wearing the same brown corduroy shoes. We all had the same kind of clothes with slight variations, and we looked nothing like anybody else.

It was around this time that we added another important member to the entourage. Grant Showbiz had been the soundman for The Fall and Alternative TV, and amazingly enough had been someone Andy had told me about in school after seeing him at a concert by the band Here & Now. Grant was an unusual and outgoing figure on the London live circuit, and as with Scott Piering, we were lucky to find someone who had some experience. Grant believed in us and was totally dedicated to doing a good job for the band.

Our agreement with Rough Trade had been for only one single, and they were eager for us to do a longer deal with them and record our first album. We were being courted by the major record companies, and Joe had been getting requests from Virgin, Warners and Polydor, among others. CBS were making the most serious noises, and a couple of suits came backstage to meet us a few times and were nice enough. Morrissey and I went to some meetings as much out of professional curiosity as anything else, and it was interesting to compare the major scene with our independent label. What struck me most about the majors was that I didn't see any records anywhere in the offices, whereas at Rough Trade and Factory there were boxes all over the place. I didn't consider that there might be a warehouse somewhere with millions of records in them, but even so I expected to see some records around the place. The other thing that I noticed was the huge pictures of shiny pop stars I didn't like, which confronted me from the moment I entered the building. It's funny how important little things like that can be when you're meeting big business – it was important to me anyway – and in the end both Morrissey and I knew that we'd be better off sticking with Rough Trade.

Geoff Travis came to Joe's office in Manchester with the Rough Trade contract for Morrissey and I to sign. For the two of us it felt like we'd reached the summit of the mountain we'd been climbing since the first day we met. Mike and

Andy were there, and although they weren't asked to sign the contract, Mike signed it as a witness. The advance payment would be £4,000. We were all really happy. We were going to make an album, and another and another, and more singles. That was everything I wanted. When Geoff took off back to London, Angie and I went out with Mike and Andy to the Haçienda to celebrate. The two Petes came with us, and we hung out with Andrew in the DJ booth, playing records and drinking cocktails.

The heatwave continued, and every day we made our way into a little studio called the Elephant in London's dilapidated Wapping wharf to record our first album. Troy Tate had been assigned as the producer. I liked Troy. He was a talented musician who was mostly known for being the guitar player in The Teardrop Explodes, and he was passionate and had a vision for what he thought our first album should be. The sessions were conducted in a sweltering heat as the basement studio had no air conditioning, which was particularly arduous when we were working at 3 a.m. Not only was it energy-sapping but the baking temperature meant that the guitars were difficult to tune. I'd spend twenty minutes tuning my guitar to the piano, only to find out the next morning that the heat had also put the piano out, so I'd have to record the whole night's work all over again. I did enjoy the process of making our first album though, and it was good to work for the first time with a producer. Troy's vision was to capture the way the band sounded live. He thought it was important that the record represented the way we were in the clubs and was an authentic document. He worked pretty tirelessly to get passion from a performance and was very nurturing with me, something I later discovered had alienated him from other members of the band who thought he wasn't spending enough time on them. I was oblivious to any such problem, as by the very nature of what I did in the studio I had to spend more time recording with the producer than the others. Either way it didn't work out, and when the band and Joe finally gathered to hear the finished work Morrissey didn't like the album. It was excruciating for everyone, but I could hear myself that the mixes sounded underproduced and were not the finished article that we needed as our introduction to the world. Why it was deemed necessary to scrap the album entirely rather than just mix it again I didn't know, but I wasn't going to make too much of it or spend too much time thinking about it. It was a document of how the band really were at that point though, and it was the last time I saw Troy. He dropped out of the music business shortly after.

Marple Bridge

Andrew Berry and I had continued to live with Joe and his family. I'd stopped running the Crazy Face shop and spent my time either with Angie or working on songs. Joe's wife, Janet, had suggested that I might want to use a cottage she had in Marple Bridge, a picturesque little village about twelve miles out of town. It was good of her to furnish me with somewhere to write songs, and with all the coming and going and my nocturnal activity she probably needed me and Andrew out of her house so she could get on with the business of bringing up a family. It was odd living in a rural environment. I still got the train into town most days for rehearsals, but if I wanted to stay out at night in town I'd either have to head back before the trains stopped, or crash on Mike's floor, which is what I usually did. Some nights Angie and I would stay in the cottage and she'd drive back late to her parents' house, and other times I'd stay in listening to records with Andrew and get into my new favourite pastime of taking acid. I'd already done acid a few times in my early years. It was full-on but always interesting, and I considered it to be a recreational and creative thing and not heavy. The cottage was perfect for tripping. It was quiet and you could take walks by the canal and go wandering around. At night we could play music as loud as we wanted, and as we lived so far out of town we wouldn't have any unexpected visitors. In some of The Smiths' early reviews my guitar style had been compared to Roger McGuinn from The Byrds. I knew a little bit about The Byrds, but I wasn't familiar with them to the extent that everyone had assumed. I'd come to my sound through different early influences like glam rock and new wave, and besides the influence of folk music it was a coincidence that my and Roger McGuinn's sound came out sounding similar. Getting this comparison made me investigate The Byrds more, and the combination of the acid and living out in a village in the summertime made me appreciate The Byrds, Buffalo Springfield and The Lovin' Spoonful all the more; the music went with how life was.

Andrew had given Morrissey his quiff when the band formed, and Mike and Andy theirs too; he also cut Bernard Sumner from New Order's hair. I had been sporting a quiff of varying colours and trajectory for the previous couple of years and it was time for a change. When people first saw the band we all had our quiffs, and while it was all right to be inspired by Johnson's or the Beatniks, I didn't ever want the band to be thought of as rockabillies. I was bored and wanted something original, and living with my best mate who was a hairdresser meant I could get creative. I started thinking about how the Perrys had looked around town a few years earlier, especially the girls. My sister had been a Perry girl and I had copied the frayed jeans and corduroy shoes that she and her mates used to wear. A big Perry thing was the bowl haircuts and if you happened to be playing the guitar you looked the same as Brian Jones or The Byrds or Sterling Morrison from Velvet Underground. I got Andrew to give me a bowl cut and I started wearing suede moccasins, with a necklace over a crew-neck sweater. I borrowed Andy's sheepskin coat, which was another Perry item, and with a bit of lateral thinking I worked out that it was Stuart Sutcliffe who first changed his haircut to create the Beatles mop style. It all made sense. I would take the ethos of the band further in looking more feminine, and working class, and definitely more Mancunian, and as our audience grew, some of the fans started to appear with bowl cuts and moccasins, with sweaters tied around their waists.

The first real money I made was when I got my first publishing deal. I had no idea what publishing meant, but it was amazing to have a few thousand pounds and I asked Angie if she would come with me to get an engagement ring. We took the train to London and went to a jeweller's on Regent Street. It was an exclusive place, and the staff all clucked around us, inspecting the teenagers that had come from the north to buy a ring. They were amused that I was wearing eye make-up and a poncho with beads, and it was good that Angie had something nice to celebrate after everything we'd been through to get where we were. I spent the rest of my money on a bass stack for Andy and a drum kit for Mike, and I got myself a black Rickenbacker 330 six-string. I bought the Rickenbacker because I loved the look of it and also because I knew it would make me play in a way that would be good for my writing. Some guitars are designed to be as easy to play as possible and are great for a rock approach, but as much as I liked the Gibson Les Paul I was aware that it might influence my style in the wrong way. The Rickenbacker would make it more difficult to fall into an automatic rock technique, and from a sound point of view it wouldn't be bluesy. It suited me perfectly and it steered me towards writing new songs like 'You've Got Everything Now' and 'Still Ill'.

New songs usually started with me recording the music on to a cassette and then giving it to Morrissey to write his lyrics and vocal lines, which he would complete within a day or two. Other times we would get together at my place and sit face to face, about three feet away from each other, while I played my new tune into a tape recorder that was balanced between my knees. Angie would sometimes be in the room with us; and once Andrew was with us, when we wrote 'Reel Around the Fountain'. There was nothing that could compare to having a new song; it was always the best thing. But we were pragmatic and well aware that we had to keep them coming and make them better, not only for the band's career but to prove something to ourselves as writers.

We'd done a couple more Maida Vale sessions since the first one for John Peel, and I'd got the hang of recording four songs under strict time restrictions. Having the sessions booked also gave me an impetus to come up with songs quickly, and one morning I woke up with an idea to do something that sounded optimistic. I'd noticed that our label mates Aztec Camera were getting a lot of radio airplay, and I wondered if it might be because their songs were more breezy and upbeat. The sun was coming through the window, and I picked up my guitar and strummed a chord sequence that conjured the feeling I was trying to evoke. After a minute of playing, another sequence appeared under my fingers from nowhere, and after following that for a while I had what I thought was a song. Without needing to refine it, I recorded what I had on to my machine and then I overdubbed the first thing that came to me. Listening back, I thought the tune had a good feeling that seemed to come from out of the air, and I brought the cassette into Joe's office and gave it to Morrissey. We rehearsed it a few days later and it was immediately great fun to play, and then Morrissey sang his vocal line and the song became 'This Charming Man'. When music is effortless, no matter how complex or emotional, there's something so right when you're making it. When a group of individuals are working instinctively and intricately, thinking within milliseconds of each other, it's as close to real magic as you can get. We knew we had to do it for the John Peel session the following week, and when Geoff Travis came into the BBC studio he declared it a hit single before he'd even finished hearing it.

On the day of the session I struck up a conversation in the BBC cafeteria with an interesting-looking guy who was working in one of the studios. I found out he was John Porter, who had been a member of Roxy Music and who'd produced Bryan Ferry. After persuading him to work on one of our sessions, we all thought John would be the right person to produce our first album after the Troy Tate sessions hadn't worked out, and we set about recording 'This Charming Man' as our second single.

Before we started on the single and the album, Morrissey and I were approached by Rough Trade because they and John Porter had reservations about Mike's playing. Often with young bands the producer and the record company will say that someone needs to be replaced, and it's usually the bass player or drummer. John and the label put quite a bit of pressure on us to use another drummer, but Morrissey and I weren't having it. We thought the personnel of the band was just fine. We chose to show our solidarity, and if anything the episode spurred Mike on to prove to the producer and everyone else that he was more than capable of doing a good job.

Working with John immediately got us results. He'd been involved behind the scenes on a lot of records in the seventies and was an accomplished musician. He and I formed a musical and personal relationship that was inspiring, and with his knowledge of recording techniques and my energy and ideas, we started to explore a lot of things. John was a proper, old-school producer. He considered all the aspects of the record-making process, from what key the song was in to the tempo and arrangement, and he nurtured not just me but all the band.

'This Charming Man' starts with the guitar riff, double-tracked by a Telecaster and the Rickenbacker, which creates

the chiming sound that was most people's introduction to
The Smiths. When the vocal comes in with the first line, there's
an abrupt stop to introduce the singer and the story, which is
a device used on a lot of the old fifties rock 'n' roll records.
The song then takes off for a second time as all the band kick
in and the story unfolds and quotes the song's title after the
third line. Underpinning it all is the hyperactive bass line and
a punchy drumbeat, with crashing chords played on two electric and two acoustics guitars that add excitement but are set
back enough not to draw attention to themselves. As the first
chorus hits, everyone ramps up the intensity as the bass plays
double time and the drums become even more animated. We
then overdubbed a counter melody on a twelve-string Rickenbacker, which we recorded backwards to give it a ghostly effect,
and put some high ringing guitar harmonics at the end of each
chorus. When we'd done all that, I put the guitar in a drone
tuning and dropped a metal knife on to the strings through a
loud amplifier with tremolo on to make a percussive, bell-like
sound effect.

When the sessions for 'This Charming Man' were finally
being completed, I sat behind the console and listened to our
new single in awe. I was impressed by what we'd done, but
more than that I was really impressed by the band. The vocal
was fantastic, the bass playing was completely original, and
the drumming kept it all together perfectly and was right on
the money. The approach to the guitars was really innovative,
and I dubbed it the Guitarchestra. With 'This Charming Man',
John Porter had taken what I could only dream of in my
bedroom and made it a reality. I thought my band were the

Above: Joe Moss totally believed in me and the band.

Left: 'We had the same obsession and dedication.'

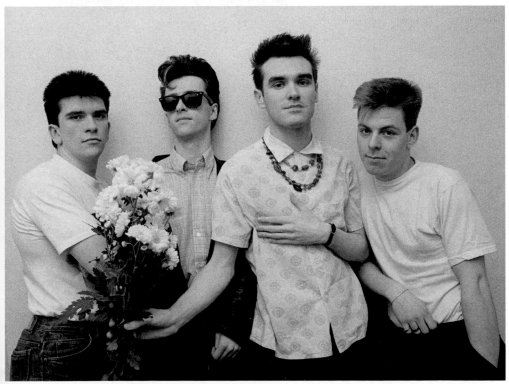

The first famous Smiths image. In the black leather coat
I'd got when I worked at Ivor's and the Ray-Bans I got from X-Clothes.

'I started thinking about how the Perry Girls looked around town.'

Top left: With Andrew Berry in Earls Court. 'I've always had a best mate.'

Above: The Ronettes inspired me to take things to a whole new level.

Left: Earls Court, 1984.

Below: Just about to go onstage with the Gibson 335. Belgium, 1984.

Above: 'A young fan took it upon himself to scale the iron barrier. Before anyone could do anything about it there was a whole mob dancing with us.'

Opposite: 'I loved the 1985 US tour.'

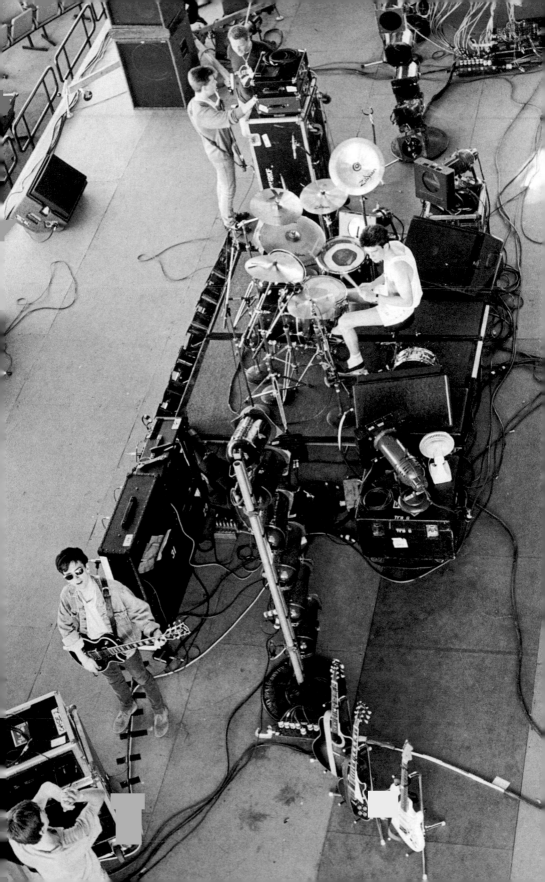

Above and right: Oxford, 1985, aged twenty-one.
'I took my role as the band's producer seriously.'

Above: On the road, 1984.

Right: 'I had an intimate relationship with my songwriting partner, who I loved, I had a girlfriend who was the love of my life, and I thought my band was the best in the world.'

Over: Red Les Paul. Soundcheck, Paris.

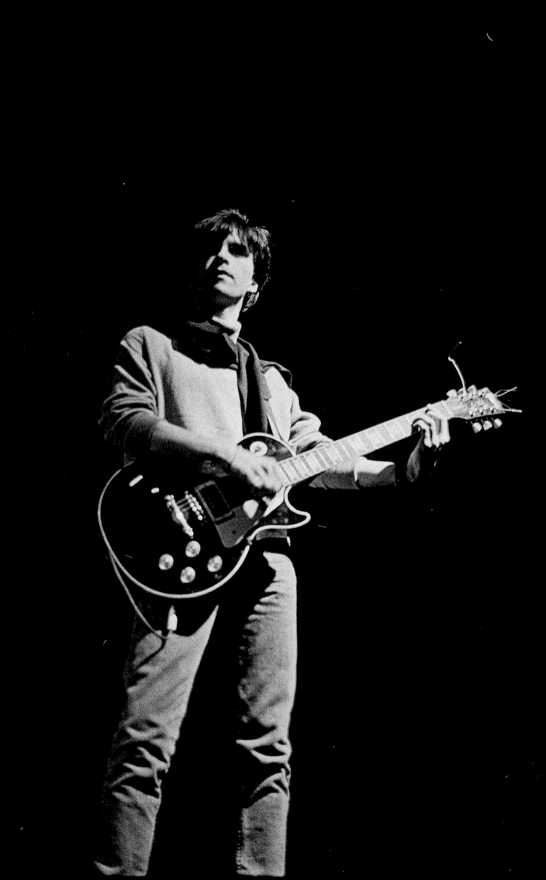

best. We were eccentric and subversive, and we were about to gatecrash the mainstream.

We were invited to make our television debut on a programme called *The Tube* as part of a segment about new bands. The filming was being done in Newcastle, which meant that as usual the band had to leave Manchester at hell o'clock in the morning. I'd been up all night buzzing, and when filming got under way I had the distinct impression that the director had instructed the cameraman to avoid me at all costs, as every time we did a take he filmed everyone else but me. I figured I must be mistaken, and that our first appearance on the telly had turned me into a paranoid egomaniac, but still it did seem like I was being cut out a bit. When the moment came for The Smiths to make their TV debut and our families and friends all gathered round to watch, every single shot of me was from the neck down, and the camera moved away any time it got anywhere near my face. It was strange, no matter how many times it was shown it was always the same, even Joe was stuck for a theory.

After some conjecture I concluded that either the director must have had some weird personal vendetta against me, or maybe, just maybe, I was considered too weird or dangerous to be on the screen. Nineteen-year-old me? Surely that was crazy. It was only years later that the mystery was finally solved, when the director admitted to a biographer that he had in fact deemed me too risqué to transmit. Apparently he thought I'd looked too drop-dead decadent for the nation's youth to be able to cope with. I thought I looked all right. The irony is that this was for a television programme that was supposed to be cutting-edge.

Top of the Pops

We continued working on the album in Manchester's Pluto Studios. Morrissey and I would meet up in the morning in Piccadilly, walk to the studio and plan what was happening next. We were on our way to record 'What Difference Does It Make?' when the subject of financial arrangements came up. I wasn't thinking that we would actually make much money at that point, playing the weird songs that we did on an indie label, but we decided that we would split the income for the group with 40 per cent each for me and Morrissey, and 10 per cent each to the other band members, seeing as we ran the band. However much I'd have liked to have thought that The Smiths were made up of equals, we weren't, and unlike some bands The Smiths didn't fall into being a band together. Everyone had been recruited to do a specific job, and there wasn't an equal division of responsibility. Morrissey and I dealt with the management and the record companies, and as far as Rough Trade were concerned The Smiths were me and Morrissey.

Like all bands starting out, none of us liked discussing the financial arrangements. I wanted to continue making the record, and I didn't want to deal with it so I put it off. Morrissey didn't want to deal with it either, and halfway through the session he took off to London to get Geoff Travis to handle it. That night I got a call in the studio from Geoff. He told me that the sessions would not be resuming until I resolved the issue. It was stressful. I was in the middle of making our next single, and the recording had been stopped to sort out finances that we didn't even have. I was twenty years old, I didn't know how to deal with it, and I was pissed off to be put in that position. It would've been wise and prudent to have taken some advice. Joe was confused that as the band's manager he hadn't been called upon to take care of it. Morrissey had gone to Geoff instead, and all Geoff had done was inform me that we weren't able to continue as a band until I sorted it out. I wasn't happy either that it had been taken out of Joe's hands, and I decided that if it all fell to pieces he and I would just have to start again. Joe talked me round and said he'd straighten it out, and then he called a meeting between me, Mike and Andy the next day. I told them the situation had to be resolved and said that if they didn't want to go ahead, I understood, and, as disastrous as it was, I'd go and do something else with Joe. We all talked about it and the next day we were back to normal and it was like nothing had happened. We didn't even think to put it in writing. It would've been a good idea if we had as the uneven split of

The Smiths' royalties would eventually boil over into a court case, in which Mike and Andy denied they had ever agreed to an unequal split.

The release of 'This Charming Man' in October changed my life and the life of everybody else in The Smiths. The record quickly went into the national charts, and suddenly we were known not just in the music press but in the suburbs and schools. It felt like we had arrived from a different dimension to take over the pop scene, and because we were so different and very distinctive we got the country's attention and everyone had an opinion about us, whether they liked us or not.

'This Charming Man' changed the lives of our families too, as suddenly they all had a famous brother or son. My family came to shows when we played in Manchester, and I would usually call them from wherever I was to let them know how I was doing. I'd make a point of seeing them whenever I could. Claire had moved out of the family home and was busy with her own life, but we never let too much time go by without checking in with each other, and we would always stay in touch.

We were booked to play *Top of the Pops*, an absolute British institution and the holy grail of music television. It had been spurned by some of the figures on the punk scene but for my generation, who grew up watching all the artists of the seventies, us getting on the show was a big deal and meant that we'd be up there weirding it out with the nation's favourites. I'd learned from pop culture that it's a great thing when interesting personalities infiltrated the establishment. When I'd seen bands like T.Rex, Blondie and Bowie on *Top of the Pops*, it was like the naughty kids had invaded the straight world right where it lived and were subverting it with good ideas. Entering the hallowed TV studio for camera rehearsals at ten o'clock in the morning, however, was quite an underwhelming experience for all of us. I had grown up watching the glitz and glamour of a fantasy pop world, but I now stood in a deserted black box with zero atmosphere while we waited for the party to start. We kept ourselves amused all day by cracking jokes and critiquing the other acts in their swanky eighties finery, and stressed-looking people with clipboards kept giving us instructions while talking simultaneously into their headsets.

The band's attire for the show was the kind of thing we always wore: Mike, Andy and me were in crew-neck sweaters, Morrissey was wearing a blouse, and we all wore Crazy Face jeans. At seven o'clock, just before the show started, we were sent to make-up, and when Mike and I walked in, a woman inspected us, nonplussed, and asked, 'Who are you?'

'The Smiths,' I said to a totally blank reaction.

'Is that what you're wearing?' she asked.

'Yeah,' I said boldly and a little put-out.

'Yeah,' Mike reiterated.

'On the show?' she asked.

'Yeah,' I repeated.

We were aware that we were different from the rest of the acts on the show, and we were proud of it. We looked the same on the television as we did on the street because we looked like a band all the time; we didn't need to change into anything different. Everybody else looked like they were from the circus.

The broadcast started to a lot of noise and flashing lights, with people dancing vigorously all over the place. We waited behind a curtain while one or two bands were on, and then a couple of videos were played. I stood with Marilyn, the so-called gender-bending pop prince, who was on before us. I couldn't work out if he was nervous or aloof; he seemed to be both. We were looking at each other, but we didn't speak. Maybe he thought we were provincial nobodies. I couldn't tell. What I did know was that his record wasn't very good but he looked totally gorgeous.

The time came for us to meet the nation. Someone introduced us the way I'd heard bands introduced on *Top of the Pops* so many times before, and off we went. The first thing I noticed was that our record sounded exciting, and then I was aware of how we must be coming over to people seeing us for the first time. It was curious: The Smiths, coming down the cathode ray tube. I was enjoying strumming Roger McGuinn's Rickenbacker twelve-string that John Porter had borrowed for me from Phil Manzanera, when I noticed how vigorously Morrissey was swinging his gladioli and I remembered just how slippery the stages got at our shows. Every instinct I had yelled at me to stand as still as possible and not move a muscle, as all I could think about was sliding off the stage on live national television. Luckily 'This Charming Man' is a short song and I survived, but the stage was very slippery and I worried for The Thompson Twins, who were on after us.

It was a significant day for the band, and a busy one too because we were also booked to play a show at the Haçienda the same night and had to get back up to Manchester for what turned out to be a homecoming celebration. We sped to Euston train station from the BBC with minutes to spare, and

I called Angie from a payphone to ask her how we'd done on *Top of the Pops*. She sounded as bewildered as me and said, 'I think you've blown some minds.' Then I called my mother, who was impressed but relaxed about the whole thing and said, 'You were very good,' which I took to be a loving way to say it was great while keeping my feet on the ground.

The band, Joe and Scott spent the train journey to Manchester standing in the aisles, joking and yapping excitably. I had no idea of the significance of our performance, and I couldn't switch off my energy as we still had a show to do. When we arrived in Manchester after what seemed to be only minutes, Rob Gretton, New Order's manager, was there to meet us with Mike Pickering. They were both stunned about the scene that awaited us at the Haçienda, and as Mike approached me he said, 'There's 2,300 people in there, and the place only holds 1,800 . . . plus there's a thousand people outside on the street who can't get in.' We were bundled into two cars, and when we got to Whitworth Street I saw the whole area around the Haçienda was overrun with people. We couldn't get the cars near the building, and when we stopped to get out, swarms of fans rushed at us, screaming and grabbing. Rob picked me up and carried me through the mob and into the dressing room, which was packed with friends and relatives who were all delighted about seeing us on *Top of the Pops* just a couple of hours before. I found Angie, and we snuck under the stairwell for a minute before I went on, then Tony Wilson led us to the stage with a camera broadcasting our arrival on to the video screens while the audience welcomed us as homecoming heroes. The place was totally heaving with bodies, some around the amps and some lying across the stage monitors. It was all such an incredible contrast to the scene only ten months before, when we'd walked on to the stage to a smattering of applause from a handful of our friends. Now everyone in the country knew about the band. Our *Top of the Pops* appearance had made a big impression, and would be more far-reaching than we would ever imagine, with many people citing it as momentous. In the space of two minutes and forty-five seconds, kids all over the country had seen us for themselves and suddenly decided they wanted quiffs, and guitars, and bowl cuts, and were raiding their mothers' and sisters' wardrobes for blouses and necklaces.

I tried to make something of the Haçienda show, but halfway through the set I was spent. The day had finished me off, and all the people clamouring on the stage and my equipment made it impossible to play properly, so I just tried to sound as good as I could under the circumstances. A fan was screaming at me from about five feet away for most of the show. He was euphoric and had his shirt off, and I eventually realised he had been one of my friends from school. I couldn't fathom it, it was too odd. At the end of the show I looked up and saw my dad surveying the hysteria. He was standing next to Grant Showbiz behind the mixing desk, who was cavorting merrily and smoking an enormous Peter Tosh spliff: 'Look, folks! I'm in rock 'n' roll!' When we'd finished the encores, Angie and I escaped through the basement and we met Joe at the back of the building. He was jubilant, and his face told the whole story. He hugged us both and said, 'It's too late to stop now, Johnny, it's too late to stop now.'

New York

Like every British musician, it was my dream to go to America. As well as my discovery of The Velvet Underground, The Stooges and the CBGB's scene, my parents had been obsessed with American imagery through their love of rock 'n' roll and country music, and they'd shared it with me since I was little. I was brought up on a television diet of seventies movies and TV shows that introduced me to the skylines and crimes of Chicago and New York City, and the expanse and freedom of San Francisco and LA. So when it was announced that I was going to the States to play some shows, it couldn't come quickly enough.

One day, after I'd been in the office with Joe, making plans for the US trip, we drove back to his place, listening to music as usual. When we got to the house he switched off the engine and stayed in the car. Joe always imparted concepts he'd been thinking about carefully and precisely, so I sat and waited. 'I won't be going with you to New York,' he said. I tried to comprehend this very bad news. I thought he was going to say that there was some serious business that he had to stay to take care of, but then he continued with, 'I'm going to be leaving. I can't manage the band any more.'

I tried to grasp what he was saying but I couldn't. I stared ahead blankly at the cars in the street and resisted from fully engaging with what was happening. I was aware that Joe and Janet were expecting their second child, but things wouldn't have to change that much because of it. Everything was going so well and he loved the band, why would he leave if he didn't need to? I couldn't conceive of going forward without Joe. He'd believed in me before there were even any other band members. He'd given me somewhere to live and somewhere to work, and he'd put The Smiths before his business and personal life. He'd supported the band and given us a place to rehearse, got us a van and a PA, and he'd financed our first single. Joe didn't just look after me, he looked after all the band.

When he resigned, most people around the band felt that it was because of a conflict between him and Morrissey, but neither Joe nor Morrissey expressed that to me at the time. I resisted any speculation for everyone's sake, but there was something about Joe's resignation that felt unresolved to me. He informed the rest of the band of his decision, and he came with us to the airport when we were going to New York. Angie and I had had a stupid argument the day before, which meant she wasn't there to see us off, and it all felt like a lousy start to my first American tour. Joe checked us on to the plane and supervised us like he always did. I tried to act like everything was normal, but I was in complete denial about him not coming. It was only when he said goodbye, and me and the band proceeded without him, that I finally realised Joe wasn't with us any more.

We were met in New York by our promoter, Ruth Polsky. Ruth was smart and a very talkative champion of the UK music scene, and she'd had enough experience of young British bands to know that we would be impressed to arrive in America riding in a stretch limousine. Spirits were high as the four of us stared out at the city, as so many other British groups had done before. Driving over the Queensboro Bridge at dusk to see the Manhattan skyline for the first time was captivating, but it made me miss Angie and Joe all the more, and I wished they were both there with me to experience it.

We'd been booked to play the Danceteria club the following night, and on the bill with us was the hip hop artist Lovebug Starski, who I knew from hearing his track 'You've Gotta Believe' at the Haçienda. It was 2 a.m. when we went on, and no one had any idea who we were. A combination of heavy jet lag and bad eyesight caused Morrissey to fall off the stage, but he gamely dusted himself off and carried on with the set until we finished with somewhat of a whimper. Afterwards, because it was New Year's Eve and because I was in New York, I stuck around to catch up on some of the new electro records that had come out, and I hung out with Lovebug Starski.

The other reason why we were in New York was because

we were signing an American record deal with Sire Records. Morrissey and I had wanted to go with Sire because of the legacy of the bands that had been on the label, such as Patti Smith, The Ramones and Talking Heads, but what was just as important for me was that Sire Records was run by Seymour Stein. I had known about Seymour Stein not only through the new wave bands but because he was involved with Red Bird Records and the girl groups in the sixties. He had worked with so many great artists who I loved, and his story was fascinating.

When we first met in London, Seymour had told me about how he had taken Brian Jones to get a guitar on 48th Street. I already knew that I would be going to Sire, but I made a deal with Seymour that I would sign to his label on the condition that he took me to 48th Street to get a guitar too. He liked the idea and he loved The Smiths and he agreed to my terms. We signed with Sire on 2 January 1984, and Seymour, true to his word, walked over with me to 48th Street and told me to pick out whichever guitar I wanted. I looked in the window of a couple of shops and couldn't find anything, and then in a shop called We Buy Guitars I saw a red 1959 Gibson 355 hanging on the wall. We went inside, and I knew the guitar was special before I even touched it. Seymour bought the guitar for me, and I carried it back to the Iroquois Hotel on West 44th Street. When I got to my room, I took my new 355 out of its old, beat-up case, and with the very first thing I played I wrote our next single, 'Heaven Knows I'm Miserable Now', then the B-side, 'Girl Afraid'. That's what happens with some instruments. They already have music inside them.

It was really good fun buzzing around New York for the first time. Though it all looked so familiar, I felt a thrill of the unknown. The towering buildings and the winter sun were an impressive backdrop as I negotiated my way around the city through the constant rush of traffic and people on the sidewalk. Morrissey and I went over to Bleecker Street to buy some records, and I bought some clothes from the second-hand stores, and got to CBGB's one night with Grant Showbiz to see a gig by our Rough Trade label mates The Go-Betweens.

The Smiths had another American show to do, this time in New Jersey, and after that we were scheduled to travel to Boston. The tour was meant to be a short trip to introduce the band to the States, and then we'd get back to Britain, where the first album would be coming out. First, though, there was the matter of Mike. He had woken up the morning after Danceteria covered in spots on his face, his scalp and even his tongue. A doctor diagnosed chickenpox, and Mike couldn't do anything except lie in a dingy, dark hotel room with cockroaches scurrying around, so we cancelled the remaining shows and hung around in New York. After a torturous couple of days, Mike was just about able to travel and we could return to England.

The attention we were getting back at home continued as we got ready to undertake our first major headline tour of the UK. Over the previous months I had become aware that Andy was still using heroin, and he'd continued to live at home, where the scene was becoming increasingly worse. The only person I could think of who might know what to do was Joe, so I went to see him and he suggested that Andy could temporarily move into his basement to get away from the scene he was in. It seemed a good solution, and I was pleased for Andy to be freeing himself of his situation. I moved out of Janet's cottage in Marple Bridge and returned to my room at Joe's house while Andy moved into the flat in the basement for a couple of weeks to get himself straight. He and I were together all day, every day. We would hover around town during the day and visit Andrew and Angie in Vidal Sassoon, and at night we'd paint the ceilings and walls of my room with Si Wolstencroft while we drank endless amounts of vodka and listened to John Peel. Andy did what he needed to do, and by the end of it we were ready to start up again with a clean slate.

When we got back from New York, I was asked by Mike Pickering to play on a session with his group Quando Quango for Factory Records. It was an intriguing prospect to be playing on someone else's record, and I was curious to see how other people worked in the studio, especially a dance group. The record was being produced by Bernard Sumner of New Order, who I hadn't met, but I'd been told that we would get along, and when I got to the studio Bernard was working on the track using a sequencer and a drum machine. I was impressed by how well he manipulated the sounds in a way that was part producer and part scientist, and he struck me as someone with a very specific musical agenda. I was a fan of his guitar playing in Joy Division and had liked the recent New Order releases. We stayed up all night, and when we'd finished recording he played me a new track he was working on for the group Section 25, called 'Looking from a Hilltop'. It was brilliant and sounded like a New York electro acid trip exported to the Haçienda: psychedelic, but ultramodern, with hypnotic beats, abstract noises and pulsing synths. As we left the studio in the morning, we said we should work together again. I didn't envisage a time when the guitarist from The Smiths and the singer from New Order might come to work together again, but it was an interesting idea.

Earls Court

I left for the UK tour without needing to look at the itin-
erary. I dived into the prospect of playing thirty-two
shows, and was excited to be playing to audiences for whom
The Smiths were now their favourite band. Our crew were a
tight unit, mostly made up of Mancunians with an alternative
sensibility, and we'd acquired a talented young lighting engineer called John Featherstone, who became like family to us
and who would be with us for every show from then on.
Shortly into the tour, Ollie resigned as our roadie. I was sorry
to see him go, but he'd become disillusioned with the job after
Joe left and it was a sign that the times had changed. I drafted
in an old school friend of mine called Phil Powell as a replace-
ment for Ollie, and Phil became my full-time man and the
band's main roadie.

Joe's absence was obvious as the tour proceeded: there was

a strong feeling of disorganisation that occasionally fell into chaos, which was made all the worse by a manic tour manager who didn't appear to like anyone in the band or the crew. The tour manager's role is crucial, as they're responsible for running the whole operation on the road. They plan all the travel and make sure that all the technical requirements for the concert and the needs of the band are taken care of. They get the money after the show and pay everyone's wages, and they carry all the cash to keep the whole thing going. The tour manager receives their instructions about all this from someone in authority, usually the band's manager, but, seeing as The Smiths didn't have a manager, ours had to deal with someone else, and that someone else was starting to be me. Luckily I didn't care about things like food or rest; everything was hearing aids and flowers as far as I was concerned. As long as we played well every night and everyone was happy, then I was happy.

The shows were rowdy events, and I valued the relationship we were building with our audience. I could relate to the people who came to see us and who waited around to get autographs. We were the same age, and we were looking for similar things from life. Punk was long over and post-punk wasn't really ours either. Smiths fans were looking for something that expressed their times and culture, and we wanted to find it for them and find it for ourselves. Being together all day, every day, meant the band were close and had become quite an insular gang. We had our own code, and our conversation consisted of all-knowing remarks and witticisms. The roles in the band had got stronger and more defined, and we were unified onstage and off. I felt a duty and responsibility to protect everyone, especially Morrissey. My attitude towards my new-found status was fairly casual, but Morrissey's ascent to national fame and notoriety had been extreme, and he was suddenly known as the voice of his generation and public enemy number one in some areas of the press. What was required of him took a lot of physical sustenance. There was no one looking after us and making sure we ate or got enough rest, and even though I was younger I looked out for him and I could tell when he was about to get ill.

When we went back into the BBC studios to do 'What Difference Does It Make?' on *Top of the Pops*, Morrissey lay in a sick room all day and we had to use a stand-in for the rehearsals. When it came time for the cameras to start rolling, I thought he wouldn't make it through the performance, and a few dates into the tour we had to re-schedule some of the shows. There was a lot expected of him from the record company, the media and the fans. The rest of the band didn't expect anything other than whatever he had to give, and he knew we would circle the wagons and take on whatever pressure he was feeling in any way we could.

All of the activity in the pop world meant that the band now needed to move to London, and I was suddenly meeting with accountants, lawyers and PR people. The business of running everything was escalating, and I was spending more and more of my time in the back of a car on the way to appointments and photo shoots. The first thing I did when I started dealing with lawyers was to get my name changed legally so that I was finally and officially Johnny Marr.

I moved into a second-floor flat in Earls Court with Angie. She got a job as a receptionist in Vidal Sassoon's office in Mayfair, and her dad drove all her stuff down from Manchester. Angie's moving to London at nineteen was a concern for her family, but they knew that she and I had to be together, wherever that might be. Our flat quickly became the full-time hang-out and HQ for the band, and for me it was a sanctuary where I could write songs, listen to music, and hide away from the day-to-day business that I wanted to get away from. At Earls Court I learned a lot about the effects of cocaine, which makes you think you're really having fun while it sucks all of the love out of the room. It's a great drug for wasting lots of time, words and money, especially if you're a twenty-year-old pop star with a penchant for staying up all night and wearing sunglasses indoors. I liked living in Earls Court. It was good being able to walk around the streets at all hours, and it was good that I liked being around Australians and gay guys too, as Earls Court in 1984 was swarming with backpacks and leather vests.

Getting into the charts and making some money meant the band could all indulge ourselves a bit, and I discovered the guitar shops in west London. I had dragged the rest of the band into my beat group period by continuously viewing a Beatles documentary that had become available on VHS and obsessing over a Hollies *Greatest Hits* album, and it inspired me to buy an old Gibson J-160 acoustic like the ones used by both bands. Morrissey, meanwhile, had been devouring Herman's Hermits songs, which also featured the Gibson J-160, so I took that as an omen and it made the guitar an absolute must-have. I also bought a 1964 Epiphone Casino, the same guitar that Keith Richards used on the classic Stones singles, and with these new treasures I was ready to get on a roll.

The Smiths had recently had a hit with 'Heaven Knows I'm Miserable Now', which I'd written in New York, and before that we'd had success with a version of 'Hand in Glove' that we recorded with the sixties legend and Morrissey's favourite Sandie Shaw. Working with Sandie was a good experience. She brought a positive spirit to the band and educated me about Buddhism, which she was very involved in at the time. It was surreal to play behind a voice that I'd heard so much from another time, and it was unquestionably surreal that I had made a wild prediction to Morrissey that we would write a song for Sandie when we were in my attic room at Shelley's.

Our singles all had great picture sleeves, and from 'This Charming Man' onwards we always put three songs on the 12-inch vinyl. We tried to make the B-sides and the extra tracks special, and with every release I had the reaction of friends, fans and other musicians in mind. The day a new Smiths record came out was an event for fans, as kids around the country made their way into record shops. I knew that those fans would be examining the sleeves and the label on the bus ride home, just as I had done myself, and I was proud that we were continuing a tradition of pop culture that I always thought was so important.

The British music press engaged with The Smiths pretty much on a weekly basis. Morrissey was giving the papers plenty to write about, and delivered a manifesto to our audience expressing his singular passions – usually with some controversy and which I often found funny, especially if it involved the royal family or the prime minister. I was more than happy to let our frontman take care of business and he did it extremely well, although we were sometimes starting to notice just how infrequently the rest of the band were referred to in interviews.

The Smiths aesthetic drew heavily on the imagery of the early 1960s in a way that I thought was truly innovative. I became well versed in the films *Saturday Night and Sunday Morning*, *A Taste of Honey* and a lot more from the period. There was plenty to like in those films, but I didn't view them as portraying a great lost era or some romantic ideal. Life in a two-up two-down with no hot water was something that my family had managed to work our way out of, so I never mistook hardship for virtue or associated poverty with romance, nor did I want to go back there.

I had my own, quite ambivalent relationship with the media. They would rarely mention the music in interviews or want to know why I played the guitar the way I did. The press's interest in me was mostly about how different I was from Morrissey, as if we were two characters from the *Beano* comic, with me as Dennis the Menace to his Walter Softy, and the articles that did involve me would usually include the term 'gregarious'. Some journalists would interpret my geniality as unsophistication, especially in contrast to Morrissey's erudition and verbosity. I wasn't expected to have an opinion on Oscar Wilde, which was just as well as I thought his

SET THE BOY FREE

talent was spoiled by his smug self-regard and pomposity. At that point in my life I thought Sterling Morrison was cooler. Being famous and young and coming from Manchester, I learned that when someone thinks you're a thick northerner they're showing you all their cards and ultimately giving you the upper hand, and once I was able to get over the impulse to punch their face in I would go along with it and sometimes play up to it just to take the piss. My role in the band as hyper-motormouth was of my own doing though, and that was fine. My heroes had attitude, and I figured that as long as you could back it up you could wear your hyperactivity and attitude as a badge of honour. In interviews that Morrissey and I did together, I would sometimes chime in with cocky pronouncements and he would burst out laughing. I loved it when that happened, the audacity of it, and we encouraged each other because we were friends.

The Smiths had become known for many things: quiffs, jangly guitars, National Health specs and flowers. We were associated with disaffection, discontent, and how grim it was up north too. All of it was accurate, but one thing we had become synonymous with more than anything else was a thing called miserablism. If you'd have asked anyone in the street about The Smiths, they'd have invariably said the word *miserable*, and regardless of the fact that much of the band's output was laced with a lot of humour, the tag spread through the media and would stay with us for ever. Like all media tags it was reductive, but then again, if you keep putting out songs with the word *miserable* in them then you haven't really got much cause for complaint.

The Smiths' success meant that we were busy doing things for pop magazines and television shows at home and sometimes in Europe. It was at this point that I succeeded in cultivating one of the most radical hairstyles that I or any man has probably every worn. I grew my hair into a sixties-style woman's beehive after becoming obsessed with Estelle Bennett from The Ronettes. I watched a video of the three girls performing 'Be My Baby' on *The Big TNT Show* so much, it inspired me to take my hair literally to a whole new level. I'd comb the fringe down to my eyes and send the top up and over in what's known as a point parting. The make-up and wardrobe people at the TV shows would be amazed when I walked in with a perfect girl group bouffant, and it was adopted by some of the braver and more committed male fans in the audience. There would be the quiffs at the front and the beehives over my side. I started wearing a lot of blue eyeshadow around the same time too, to make the whole thing complete.

While this new pop-star life was happening, the band was always playing shows and travelling, but the best thing for me was writing new songs. One day, I was playing my Gibson acoustic on the mattress in the back of the van, on our way up to a gig, when a riff appeared, inspired by the speed and momentum of the journey. I played it over the next few days and it developed into a song that I thought would be good for the next single. Angie had gone back to Manchester for the weekend and the band had a rare couple of days off, so I found myself alone in the flat. I'd upgraded my early Teac cassette recorder for a four-track Tascam Portastudio and a Roland Dramatix drum machine. I decided that after I'd demoed the next A-side I would try to come up with the B-side and then the extra track for the 12-inch while I had the opportunity.

The A-side was fun to put down. It was a fast rush of a tune done on the acoustic, and after working on it for a while it felt complete. The Smiths hadn't had such a short song before, around two minutes. I liked the fact that Buzzcocks singles were short, so two minutes ten seconds it would stay. I approached the B-side completely differently. I'd been living in London for six months and I was missing Manchester and I hadn't seen my family for a while. Thinking about my family made me remember a song that my mother liked, and I strummed around the chords and tapped into a feeling of melancholy until I had channelled the right spirit and came up with a very pretty tune and the B-side was done. After completing the two songs by Saturday, I hung around the flat on the Sunday, listening to what I'd done and thinking about writing the third track for the 12-inch. I thought that because the A-side was short and fast and the B-side was short and waltzy, I should try to write something long with some kind of a groove. I rolled a joint, plugged in my new Epiphone Casino and started playing a rhythm. I'd been a long-time fan of The Gun Club and I liked their style of swampy blues, and with that in my mind I kicked around a trancey kind of riff that after a while morphed into a slowed-down Bohannon. As I went around and around, the tune started to get psychedelic in my headphones and I knew I was on to something. I programmed a simple beat on the drum machine and recorded the hypnotic rhythm guitar, and then came up with a two-note phrase that I put on top. What I'd done was nothing like the other two songs, and nothing like anything the band had done before either. When Angie got back I played her the demo and she thought it was great. Then I took the cassette of the three songs round to Morrissey's, having written 'Fast', 'Irish Waltz' and 'Swampy' on it. He worked on it for a few days, and when he'd finished the lyrics the songs became 'William, It Was Really Nothing', 'Please, Please, Please, Let Me Get What I Want' and 'How Soon Is Now?'.

In the meantime, Scott Piering, our radio and TV plugger, had stepped in temporarily as a surrogate manager. He didn't have the authority to sanction transactions on the band's behalf, particularly if it involved finances, and that meant I was responsible for things like approving the budget for studio equipment and vehicle hire. I found the constant calls from the record company annoying, especially on the days I was going into the studio, and Scott repeatedly tried to impress on me how crucial it was that the band appointed either him or someone else as a manager to look after our affairs. I agreed with what Scott was saying, it made complete sense, and he was a good guy and had our best interests at heart. He was worried about our situation with the record companies, lawyers and accountants, but unfortunately he didn't realise that his anxious calls and crisis meetings at my flat were becoming too much for me to deal with.

Ruth Polsky flew into London from New York uninvited and appeared to appoint herself as our manager, which I found out one day on the stage at the Lyceum. I was struggling with my guitar sound at the soundcheck, when all of a sudden she appeared on the stage beside me and declared, 'Hi Johnny!

I'm your manager!' She beamed a big smile and hugged me tightly, crushing me and my guitar. I didn't even know she was in the country, and hadn't spoken to her since the Danceteria.

'What?' I said.

'Yeah, me and Morrissey had a meeting this afternoon and I'm going to take over for you. Isn't it great?!'

I didn't know which I was more angry about, being informed by someone that they were now my manager or being informed onstage while I was trying to get my sound. I attempted to remain calm, but the look on my face screamed, *No, it's not great, it's not fucking great at all*, and her expression changed to that of a child who's been told that Father Christmas is an axe murderer.

The situation was farcical, and I wasn't going to get into it at the soundcheck. As the band all took refuge in the dressing room, Morrissey explained how Ruth had turned up at his place unannounced and insisted that she should represent us and now she was announcing it to everyone. There was a confrontation backstage between Ruth and Scott over who was going to be the band's manager, and Scott made it clear to Ruth that the band had no intention of her representing us. Meanwhile we went onstage and played the show, which went surprisingly well and was a testament to the band's resolve. Maybe we were all getting a bit too good at dealing with absurdity.

The studio was always a creative haven for me. I loved every session, and they would always go all night until the next morning. Every Smiths record was done on a budget, which meant that we had to maximise what time we had. In July 1984, we went into Jam Studios in Finsbury Park with John Porter to do the three new songs for the next single. 'William, It Was Really Nothing' came together quickly. I used a trick that John showed me called Nashville tuning, where you replace the bottom four strings on a regular guitar with the strings from a twelve-string to get a more ringing sound. 'Please, Please, Please, Let Me Get What I Want' was a matter of capturing the poignancy of the song without adding too much. I played the melody on the instrumental section on a mandolin, which was tricky to get right but was worth the effort.

Having done the A-side and the B-side of the single, the pressure was off and we started on 'How Soon Is Now?'. We recorded the backing track as a three-piece, and we spent a couple of hours playing alongside a LinnDrum drum machine in the background to get the feel right. My basic guitar track was done on the Epiphone Casino without any effects. The rhythm was steady and catchy, but I was worried that the song might not turn out as I hoped, as I thought that we'd lost the hypnotic quality and psychedelic atmosphere that I'd liked on the demo. It was a long instrumental track when Morrissey came in to do his vocal. John got a balance for him in his headphones, and I sat behind the mixing desk and waited for him to sing as the tape started rolling. After eight bars Morrissey started the vocal, and I loved it. I turned to Mike and Andy, who were sitting at the back of the studio, and we all knew we had a great track in the making. A couple of takes later and the vocal was finished.

It was already late when I started doing my guitar overdubs, and as I listened I was still bothered that something was missing. Since I was very young I'd loved the sound of tremolo, or vibrato as it's sometimes known; it was mostly associated with the great Bo Diddley. It hadn't been used on a pop record for a long time, and for years I'd been looking for an opportunity to feature it somehow. I knew immediately that the effect would work, and we decided to take what I'd already played from the tape, and send it out through the tremolo on my amp. It sounded like a good idea, and then John suggested that instead of using one amp we could use two amps for stereo, one left and one right – better still, as there happened to be four Fender Twin Reverb amps in the studio, why not send the sound through all of them? John and I went out into the live room to manually control the speed of the tremolos for them to stay in perfect time with the track. We crouched in front of the two Fenders, John on the right side and me on the left. The engineer fed the straight guitar track through all four amps, and we turned them up, really, really loud. It was a mighty sound, and the song was becoming everything it should be. It took us a long time to get the whole thing done, as every time one of the amps went out of sync we'd have to go back a few seconds and drop in. It was around three in the morning and the rest of the band had gone, leaving me and John to the Guitarchestra. The second guitar figure that went on top of the tremolo riff was good on the demo, but I wanted to make it darker so I decided to play it with a metal slide to give it more of a howling effect. I recorded it with a lot of echo and then added a harmony to make it sound more intense and paranoid. Occasionally, if you're lucky, your work takes on a life of its own and pulls you along with it. You follow the momentum and forget about time and food and sleep. You're in the flow; it's inspiration, and as Picasso once said, 'Inspiration does exist, but it has to find you working.'

'How Soon Is Now?' took on a life of its own at around five in the morning. The whole building was pulsing, and it sounded so good that I plugged in a white Stratocaster and improvised a wild lead solo to finish it off, just because I felt like it. As I sat in the back of a taxi heading home, I stared straight ahead for the whole journey, completely dazed and numb but with a strong sense that I'd really been through something. It was dark when I woke up the next evening, and I peered over at the bedside cabinet to see the cassette that I'd taken back from the studio with 'How Soon Is Now?' written on it. I wondered what everyone would make of it.

Glastonbury

The Smiths were a political band. As Margaret Thatcher carried out her systematic and ruthless dismantling of the country's industries and communities, it gave the new generation of artists a common enemy to unite against. Such was the discontent among the young, it was a given that you were in opposition to the government, and as the music press were in opposition too they gave the bands a national platform and we were literally all on the same page.

The month before we recorded 'William, It Was Really Nothing', we'd been asked to play a free outdoor concert billed as 'Jobs for Change', in support of the Greater London Council led by Ken Livingstone, and were more than willing to show our solidarity alongside Billy Bragg, who was also appearing. Billy had been playing shows himself in support of the miners' strike, and was becoming known as a champion of the people. I had a great deal of respect for Billy, not only as a songwriter but for his commitment to his beliefs. He liked guitars and loved Motown too, and we became good friends, with common foes and heroes.

The turnout for the GLC concert was huge, by far the biggest audience The Smiths had played to. I was so nervous I threw up before going on. We went out to 10,000 people, some of whom were hanging off balconies and screaming out of windows around the square behind the GLC building, and during the set I could see people climbing on the outside of the buildings and dangling from the roof.

After the show, Mike and Andy threw some flowers from a window in the GLC to fans, who then clambered on top of a vehicle belonging to the caterers, causing damage to it. There was a huge fracas as the backstage staff came gunning for us and we were threatened with all manner of retribution. The band had to be escorted out of the place to avoid a showdown, but before we made our escape I was introduced to Ken Livingstone. It was the first time I'd met a politician, and I was astounded by the self-assurance of the man. It was a surprise to find that someone who was seemingly one of the good guys could also be in the fame game. I naively assumed that if you claimed to be on the side of minority groups and represented equality for the less fortunate, you might show some signs of humility.

Nearly a fortnight later we found ourselves on our way to play the Glastonbury Festival. We'd been reluctant to participate, because to us festivals were a relic from the hippy era and were usually very low-key affairs in out-of-the-way places, with old people dancing around to forgotten bands in the cold. It was Geoff Travis who insisted The Smiths play Glastonbury. He informed us about its musical legacy and impressed on me the importance of its political agenda and allegiance to the CND anti-nuclear campaign. At the time, Glastonbury pretty much consisted of 'the big field', where the main bands played; 'the muddy field', where everyone stayed and which was actually bigger than the big field; and 'the shit field', where no one went to. The ticket price was £13.

We arrived on the site in a run-down 1970s white Mercedes limousine that someone at the record company had rented for us, probably for a laugh. It was entirely inappropriate for anyone other than a 1970s TV star, but after being in it for a few miles all the band came to like it. We were shown to the nearest empty Portakabin, and I saw for the first time an actual tour bus. It was a huge shiny thing and belonged to Elvis Costello. I thought it looked like a mansion.

The four of us and Angie stuck close together and dared not stray more than ten feet from our bleak cabin for fear of contamination by the rural festival vibes. We had a few photos taken and then climbed the high stairs to the stage. The dreary damp morning had turned into a beautiful Saturday afternoon, with everyone in high spirits as the rain finally abated and blue skies appeared overhead.

We started our set to a half-empty field, but it soon started to fill up. After playing a few songs to a crowd seeing us for the first time, it occurred to me again just how different we were from most of the music that was around. In those surroundings we suddenly seemed very fast and very intense, and a lot of our songs were quite short. Glastonbury was our first experience of playing across a huge divide between the band and the audience, but it didn't deter one young fan, who took it upon himself to scale the steep iron barrier and invade the stage. It was a daring move, and as he climbed up, a security guard rushed towards him to throw him down. Admiring his guile, I moved in to help him up, which pissed off the security guard, and we got into a stand-off while the band carried on playing.

When the rest of the crowd saw all of this, it inspired more of them to clamber on to the stage, and before anyone could do anything about it there was a whole mob dancing with us. We finished playing and left the stage having showed Glastonbury what we were about. As I was making my exit with my guitar, one of the stage crew grabbed me around the neck and tried to pull me down the stairs. Scott Piering rescued me and then hurried me into our cabin as more stage crew and security came after us. There was a lot of tension backstage, and when we came to leave we found that the tyres of the Merc had been slashed, not as retaliation for the stage invasion, but as the caterers' revenge for the damage to their car at the GLC show twelve days earlier, as it turned out they were also at Glastonbury. We decided to get out of there before we caused any more drama, and we got a ride back with the crew. Much later the consensus in the media was that The Smiths' set at Glastonbury was a turning point in the history of the festival and helped usher in a new era. If that is the case, then it was totally accidental, and you're welcome, I'm glad to have been of service.

Meat Is Murder

We continued to play shows around the UK and Europe, and I'd come back to my flat for a few days here and there before setting off on more dates and promotional duties. I'd started writing songs for the second album, and even though we'd had a great run of hit singles, the music industry and the media were taking up more of our time and all these distractions had made me disenchanted with life in London.

I was working one evening on a demo with Andy when there was a lot of banging and shouting outside. We stopped to look out of the window and saw the band's ex-tour manager from the previous UK tour standing on the street below and holding up an infant while shouting about being fired. Andy and I laughed it off for a minute, but involving his child really bothered me and creeped me out. The guy hadn't worked out for the whole band, but again it was me that everyone came to when there was a problem. It was a sign of how untenable things were becoming.

I wanted to be back in the creative atmosphere of Manchester. It had an attitude that suited the band, and as soon as we got back, I felt we were where we should be. I liked being in a community who would measure our worth against the Velvets and Iggy, rather than who we were up against in the charts and magazines that week. Angie and I had moved into the Portland Hotel until we could find a place of our own. We were both happy to be back, and ran around town as we had before, seeing our friends and going to gigs. Andrew had continued to DJ at the Haçienda and had also opened a hairdressing salon in the dressing room backstage, which served as the new daytime hangout. Everyone was getting their hair cut there, and any time I went in I would end up in a conversation with Bernard Sumner and Rob Gretton or someone from Factory Records. Sometimes bands would arrive from out of town, excited to be playing at the famous Haçienda, and they'd find their dressing room full of Mancunian stoners with no intention of clearing out. Andrew was so charming that later on the band would appear onstage with brand-new Smiths and New Order haircuts, inspired and extremely high.

We decided to record our album in Liverpool, and we'd pile into the old, rusty, white Mercedes limo and drive the twenty-odd miles to an industrial estate somewhere on the outskirts of Merseyside. The band had elected me to produce the album instead of John Porter. It was unexpected and surprising to me, as we were coming off a run of hit singles, but if the band trusted me enough to do it then I'd take it on. I'd liked working with John and he'd brought us success, but it was a musical decision, as my sensibilities were more alternative, which was what we wanted. There was no animosity, and we would employ John to work with us again in the future. Also working on the album with us was a young engineer called Stephen Street, who we'd met at an earlier session and who would play an important part in our recording career. Stephen was around the same age as us, and like me wanted to make great records. We got totally focused on the job at hand, and the album was sounding good from the start. The only problem for Stephen Street was that because none of the band could drive he had to get behind the wheel of the white limo and chauffeur us through the streets of Liverpool every night.

I took my role as the band's producer seriously, though I always credited the job to me and Morrissey, or me and Stephen Street. Working without an established producer meant I had to follow my own instincts, and there were never any arguments or disagreements in the studio between the band members about the direction of the record or the way anything was going. I was inspired by the songs we were writing, and the return to the north was definitely the right move as it influenced me to follow a sound with a northern spirit. 'The Headmaster Ritual', which opened the record, was a breakthrough for the band. Andy's bass playing was his best so far, and it demonstrated his innovation. There were so many inspired moments from everyone. Morrissey's singing had taken on an even more supple quality, especially on 'That Joke Isn't Funny Anymore' and 'Well I Wonder', and Mike's drumming on 'What She Said' and 'That Joke Isn't Funny Anymore' was exceptional. We were firing on all cylinders and doing it ourselves.

Towards the end of the sessions, Morrissey and I were sitting in the control room when he asked me what I thought about calling the album *Meat Is Murder*. I thought it was a great title: it was strong and made a statement. It fitted us perfectly. Then we decided we should do a title track. Vegetarianism was by no means an odd concept to me. Angie was vegetarian when I met her, and when I first met Morrissey and discovered he was vegetarian I never had a second thought about it. I'd always been amazed when people thought it was a radical lifestyle choice. Before we made the *Meat Is Murder* LP I ate meat because I'd been brought up eating it, but the moment my band had a song called 'Meat Is Murder' I stopped and never ate meat again.

My decision to become vegetarian was a natural commitment to the principles of the band, and a mark of solidarity with my songwriting partner and my girlfriend. I didn't know why it hadn't occurred to me before. It wasn't like I was making any huge sacrifice anyway, as my diet then consisted of chocolate, Coca-Cola, coffee and nicotine, and the times that I did sit down to eat I'd have scrambled eggs and chips for five minutes and then start running around again. There was no ideological motive for me becoming vegetarian at the time. I never thought about animals as a child, and my only experience of them growing up in Ardwick and Wythenshawe was 'I hope that dog doesn't bite' or 'Your cat hates me.' What I thought was interesting about becoming vegetarian was when I stopped eating animals I really started to appreciate them much more. I discovered an empathy with animals and started noticing the serenity of cows in fields, and the beauty of horses, which brought a new and very welcome dimension to my world. It happened quickly and I was surprised. Fundamentally I realised that animals are innocent.

My approach to writing the music for the song 'Meat Is Murder' was to make something as dramatic and doomed-sounding as I could while still allowing it to be a song to sing over. Experimenting with guitar tunings that steered me into a heavy mood, I eventually came up with some chord sequences. I thought about how horror films sometimes use a plaintive nursery-rhyme motif to convey a sense of dread, or threat to innocence, and I found a few notes on the piano that suited it perfectly. I was essentially composing a soundtrack for the horror that an innocent animal experienced. Morrissey had the music for a day, then came in with the finished words and recorded the lead vocal in one take.

The *Meat Is Murder* album was released on 11 February 1985 and went straight into the charts at number one, knocking Bruce Springsteen's *Born in the USA* off the top position. Aside from it being an achievement in itself, the album was a success to me because we still sounded like ourselves and if anything were more uncompromising than ever. The album came out in America with 'How Soon Is Now?' added at the start, which really annoyed me because we'd made a brand-new piece of work with a coherence and a unified sound, and as important as 'How Soon Is Now?' was, it came from a different artistic intention. The American record company exercised their right to disagree with me and Morrissey though, and as a result 'How Soon Is Now?' became a big alternative song and introduced a whole generation of American music fans to our new album and to the rest of The Smiths' music after that.

America

I n the mid-eighties, America was going through a healthy
resurgence in alternative music, known for obvious reasons
as college rock. The Smiths, New Order, The Cure and
Depeche Mode were all finding an appreciative audience, who
were seeking out an alternative not only to the music scene at
the time, but to the obvious jock culture that championed all
things mainstream and macho and marginalised minority
groups. This polarisation of the conventional versus the
unconventional, or 'winners and losers', was very prevalent
when The Smiths went to America on the *Meat Is Murder* tour,
and I got the message from the audience that they felt we
understood them and that we represented some kind of
liberation.

The shows were just as impassioned as back at home and
maybe even more so. There was a whole generation of

American boys who were dissatisfied with the model of masculinity they had been expected to conform to and that was irrelevant and totally out of date. They saw in the British bands a way of being that was anti-macho and pro-androgyny, where the question of whether you were gay or straight didn't matter at all. I loved the shows on The Smiths' first American tour. We were into another new phase of the band, and I felt genuine appreciation for what we were about. When we played to American kids we arrived fully formed, and they loved the fact that we were so different from all the other bands. Morrissey would whip up the crowd from the first word, and I would back him up while keeping up the intensity with Mike and Andy. Our audience understood that we were a new kind of guitar band with new values, and that we were more than ready to actually rock out.

Angie was with us on the tour, and that made me happy and everyone else happy. She and Morrissey had their own friendship and would go out on expeditions together during the day. As well as being a naturally positive person, she cared about everyone and put the needs of the band before her own. I thought I was the luckiest person alive. I had as intimate a relationship as you could have without it actually being physical with my songwriting partner, who I loved and who I thought was a great frontman; I had a girlfriend who was the love of my life; and I thought my band was the best in the world.

We played two nights in New York. There was a lot of talk going around about the place being overrun by the Mafia, and as we were walking onstage I was very pointedly introduced to an imposing-looking man dressed all in white and wearing a white fedora who definitely didn't look like a Smiths fan. Both shows were manic and highly charged as usual, and at the close of the first night I got into an altercation with a brawny security man who was being unnecessarily forceful with a fan. I kicked him from the stage, and when that didn't stop him I took off my guitar and clubbed him with it. He went down, and then I noticed that his colleagues had seen the incident. It was the last song of the show, and as soon as I hit the final note I sped out of a side door and hoped that I wouldn't encounter the man in the white hat. At the next night's show I played without looking up from my guitar the whole time, diligently concentrating on my fingers and avoiding the deadly glares from the security men seeking revenge for the previous night's slaying.

We went back to the hotel after the show and avoided the bar as usual. The band and crew would always hang out together in a couple of the rooms, smoking and drinking and listening to music. We had the next two days off, as we were travelling to San Francisco, and Angie and I were excited as it was the city we'd always wanted to go to. When we got back to our room, Angie was still buzzing about San Francisco and said, 'We could go to Haight Ashbury, or we could go to Golden Gate Bridge,' to which I replied, 'Or we could get married.' We stopped for a few seconds and looked at each other and then started laughing. 'What do you think?' I said seriously.

'Yeah,' she said, 'let's do it.'

We were both excited and kind of amused to be getting

married. Not only was it the right thing, but it seemed like a fun thing to do. The next morning I frantically started making arrangements with Stuart James, who was our new tour manager, for me and Angie to get married in San Francisco.

Our promoter was the legendary Bill Graham, who had put on all the shows at the Fillmore in the sixties. When he discovered that Angie and I were getting married, he offered his assistance in any way he could, which was very kind of him and also very helpful as I didn't know the first thing about getting married. I knew I had to find a church of some sort that wasn't actually religious. It being San Francisco, there was everything from the Church of the Living Desert to the Church of the Not Too Bothered, and we found a nice Unitarian in a circular modernist building that was perfect.

On the day before the wedding we had to get blood tests and Bill found us a doctor on Haight and rushed the legal process through. Angie was impressed that we'd got the blood tests for our wedding on Haight Street, and it had to be worth several thousand rock 'n' roll points having Bill Graham arranging your wedding, even if it was just making a few calls. We got brought back down to earth though when, coming out of the doctor's, we were stopped by three dudes wanting to inspect the contents of our tour manager's conspicuous-looking briefcase.

'What you got there, man?' one of the dudes said. 'A cool few thousand?'

'Just some papers,' said Stuart, sounding extremely weedy and very English. The novelty of his accent distracted them for a second.

'Hey, where you guys from, England?'

'Yeah,' I said amiably.

'Whereabouts? London?'

'Yeah, London,' I replied, not wanting to disappoint them or get into any further geographical details. I would've answered yes if he'd said Shropshire.

Angie and I started to walk away and Stuart followed, and as we made our way down the street a voice behind us shouted, 'Watch out with all that money!' We left our new friends laughing and moved on quickly down Haight. When we got into the taxi to take us back to the hotel, Stuart looked at me and then opened the case. Inside was $8,000 of the band's money that he had yet to put in the bank.

My and Angie's wedding was very sweet. The rest of the band and the road crew jumped in a few taxis to the church and trundled inside, where the groovy female minister was waiting to marry us. It was a gorgeous Sunday morning, and I was touched that the roadies turned up, having made the effort to shave, and obviously having rummaged through their cases to find an appropriate shirt or the nearest thing to it midway through a tour. We all stood in a semicircle and the minister said some nice words about love and commitment. I looked around and saw a genuine emotion in everyone as they watched Angie and me officially declare our devotion to each other. It was one of those times when I was suddenly aware that we were both so young. It was a timeless moment, and one that I felt was serious and significant in my life. It didn't matter to us that our families weren't there. Angie and I had been living an unconventional life for a few years now, and our families were used to our lifestyle. It was a really nice ceremony, and it was perfect that the band and crew were with us as at the time that was our world.

The two of us went to the Golden Gate Bridge to have some wedding photos taken by a photographer who'd been found for us at the last minute by Rough Trade. After we'd commemorated our special day, the photographer refused to be paid and offered his services free of charge because he liked the band. It was a nice gesture, and I promised him guest passes for the show the next night. We played at the Henry Kaiser Auditorium in Oakland, and as I was being escorted out of the building and into a waiting car I saw the photographer and heard him screaming, 'You fucker, I've been out here all night! There were no tickets! You're not getting those photos, man.'

I turned to the tour manager in shock and asked him if he'd remembered to put the photographer on the guest list. He looked at me sheepishly and said, 'Er, yeah . . . I think so . . .' A few weeks later, *Rolling Stone* magazine contacted Rough Trade to say that they had been offered my wedding photos for $5,000. They asked me what I wanted to do, and I told them to stuff it. I wasn't about to pay someone who would go to a national magazine with my wedding photos. Angie and I ended up with one photo of us coming out of the church that was taken by a fan who happened to have her camera with her. It seemed to bother everyone else more than it did us, but it would have been nice to have had some.

Having finished the American tour, Angie and I moved into our first house, a three-storey Victorian in Cheshire, about five minutes away from where I'd lived at Shelley Rohde's. Getting our own house was a big step. We got a £70,000 mortgage, and after putting down a third of the price as a deposit we had £1,000 left over for furniture, which we spent on two paintings we liked. Angie's parents bought us a washing machine and dryer for our wedding present, and we scrounged a bed off one of our friends. We kept the curtains from the previous owners and we inherited an old upright piano in the kitchen. The people we bought the house from were an Irish family with five children. They opened their cellar every Friday for the local kids to use as a disco, and there was a little stage down there with some lights, and the names of some rock bands sprayed on the walls and ceiling.

From the minute we moved in, my house became the new improved Smiths HQ, with my roadie Phil living in a room on the top floor, and Andrew making a return, along with our lighting man John Featherstone, who would stay with us whenever he was nearby. The band were around all the time, and the crew and tour buses would meet up at mine whenever we were going anywhere. I liked having my own domain, and I liked having a lot of activity around me. I was becoming ever more nocturnal, and I would often stay up with Phil or Andrew listening to music, and then I'd make demos when everyone had gone to bed. I'd wake up in the afternoon the next day and the house would be busy with people running around and the phone ringing. Morrissey once remarked that 'every room in your house is like a soundcheck', which was completely accurate and which I took to be a compliment. The other band members bought houses at the same time.

Morrissey got a place in Hale Barns, ten minutes away, and Mike got his house ten minutes away in another direction, just around the corner from Andy, who rented a flat. It was a good period for all of us. We'd made some money and were the most popular guitar band in the country, we'd come out the other side of our time living in London, and we knew what it took to have our kind of hits.

The only thing about the band's destiny that I didn't feel was in our own hands was the ongoing matter of management and how we were going to deal with the outside world. It was a problem for me that would just not go away. We'd found an equilibrium of sorts, having recently taken on a manager called Matthew Sztumpf on a trial basis. Morrissey had presented Matthew to me as a potential candidate, and after the trial period was over Matthew had done a good job and there was really no reason to look for anyone else. He was a decent guy and trustworthy, and had done very well with Madness, who Morrissey liked. It was a relief when Matthew came on board, and he and I became friendly and I thought our management issues might be over. But then on the day when we were leaving America to come back to England, I had the same kind of visit to my hotel room as I'd had from Scott Piering and a few other people: Matthew wanted to know where he stood and why he was getting strange vibes from the band that he wasn't really going to be our manager. I assured him that everything was fine and that we wanted him permanently, which I believed was right, and the right thing for the band. It was embarrassing for both of us, and I felt bad about it. I didn't see why there would be a problem. He sat with Morrissey and me on the plane home and everything seemed positive, so I assumed that all was well.

A few weeks later, the band was scheduled to appear on a live chat show. It had been arranged by Matthew and the record company to promote our new single, but Morrissey didn't want to do it and he pulled out of it on the band's behalf at the last minute. It didn't bother me, but there was a big drama at the BBC and Matthew was very angry about not being told. He confronted me, saying that his position was untenable and the incident signalled the end of our relationship with him. I didn't care if we were on the show or not, I just wanted someone else to step in and deal with it so I didn't have to.

The Queen Is Dead

I t occurred to me one afternoon that the next Smiths album had to be a serious piece of work. I was walking through my kitchen when it hit me that, amazingly, the band were now being talked about in England in the same exalted terms as bands like The Who and The Kinks, and that we had come to mean a lot to a generation of music fans. It was at this moment that the pressure of it really hit me. Our previous album had been number one, and we'd had a run of hits. As great as the situation was, it felt to me that if I was to accept that kind of praise and be compared to those kinds of artists, then I would be similarly judged, and this revelation, far from being a cosy ego trip, was suddenly overwhelming and froze me in my tracks. I knew that the next album had to be the best I could possibly do. The stakes had got higher, and greatness was a possibility for the band if we were prepared to go for it. I stood and thought about it, and then I said to myself, 'You're going to have to dig deep, whatever it takes.'

Morrissey came over to my house one night. There were some other friends knocking around, and after socialising for a while we decamped to a room on our own and I picked up my Martin acoustic. I was ready to play him the songs I'd been working on, and as usual we sat just a couple of feet away from each other, with me on a chair and him on the edge of the coffee table. There was the customary sense of anticipation as I hit the 'record' button on the cassette machine on my knees and started strumming a tune. It was a waltzy ballad that was tentative in the verse and then kicked into a dramatic chorus, building in intensity as it went along. There was a lot of promise in the tune, and we knew it would be good for the new album. I'd been playing the next one for just a few days: it had a breezy minor chord pattern that went to an uplifting chorus, and I'd inserted a rhythmic skip from The Velvet Underground for some mischief, as they'd copied it from the Stones. At first I thought the song might be a B-side because it came to me so easily, but as I played it there was something certain about it, an indefinable quality that comes out of nowhere. We were getting the feeling that we had something good. Then I threw down a third tune, just because we were on a roll. It was in total contrast to the others and sounded like Sandie Shaw or an eccentric vaudevillian romp. I drove Morrissey back to his place with the cassette of the three songs that would become 'I Know It's Over', 'There Is a Light That Never Goes Out' and 'Frankly, Mr Shankly'.

We didn't waste any time waiting to record new songs, and

the first sessions for *The Queen Is Dead* album were booked for Studio Three at RAK studios in St John's Wood.

The first song we recorded was 'Bigmouth Strikes Again', which we'd been playing in soundchecks and which sounded to me like a single. It was good to kick the sessions off with a banger, and it was good too because we'd invited Kirsty MacColl to come down and sing backing vocals. It was the first time we'd met Kirsty. She was immediately great to have around, outgoing, smart and funny, and she knew a lot about making records. She and I stayed in the studio playing songs and singing until early the next morning, and from that night my relationship with Kirsty would become one of the great friendships of my life.

The band completed a couple more songs over the following few days, and then one morning we came together to record the new one we'd just written, 'There Is a Light That Never Goes Out'. I decided to record it using the Martin acoustic I'd written it on, so as to capture the breezy quality, and I ran through the chords with Andy and Mike, who were hearing it for the first time, while Stephen Street made some adjustments to the sound. The music came together quickly, which is usually the sign of a good song. It was always an important moment for me when we were putting down something new, but with 'There Is a Light' it was obvious that we might have some magic, and it felt like the music was playing itself. All my expectations were surpassed though when Morrissey got behind the microphone and we played the song as a band for the first time. Every line was perfect as the words and the music carried us along on our own new anthem. We were high with it, and after just a few takes we had one of our best ever songs, and something that felt at the time like pop music and beyond.

I always loved working, but I also had an objective because it felt like there was a lot at stake. I took my place behind the mixing desk and smoked spliffs and drank a lot of coffee and I attended to every detail of the record. Smoking pot in the studio never hindered me. It helped me shut out the outside world just enough to do the job. I regarded smoking a joint as the same as smoking a cigarette with two sugars. Sessions would start at eleven in the morning and we would work all day until eleven or midnight, when we couldn't hear anything any more, then we'd come back and do the same the next day. I didn't need anything else in my life. My world was the studio, and I tried to ignore everything that might distract me.

I made a new discovery during the making of *The Queen Is Dead* that would be a benefit to the band and a significant step towards the future. I'd heard about a new keyboard called the Emulator, which was a digital synthesiser that could call up orchestral sounds or sound effects. It opened up a whole world for me as an arranger. The first thing I did on the Emulator was the strings on 'There Is a Light That Never Goes Out', and I would use it a lot more to make what I saw as a progression from the previous records. Using the Emulator, I could orchestrate what I was doing in addition to using guitars, and I started thinking about possibilities and a different kind of sound.

We made a good start to the record, and then came a serious

disturbance in the form of the band's recently acquired lawyer. I don't know how he came to be appointed by us, but he wore an earring and would put his feet up on the desk to show off the sneakers he wore with his suit while he tried to impress us with his rock 'n' roll credentials. The first time I met him he said there was an important issue he needed to discuss with me and Morrissey. Apparently the contract we'd signed in Joe's office between us and Rough Trade was about to expire with the completion of the new album.

The rest of the meeting was equally illuminating. The lawyer had already been in negotiations with EMI on our behalf, and he was keen to assure us that they would be delighted to give us a home, it was all just a matter of informing Rough Trade. I'd never really had a problem with Rough Trade. I liked the people and respected Geoff Travis and Scott Piering, and even though the label could sometimes be a bit makeshift, I thought things had gone very well for all of us, so leaving them sounded a bit drastic. But re-signing with the same label apparently wasn't an option; it now appeared that we needed to make the next big step in our career, which sounded logical. I had absolutely no expertise in these matters, and even though we were a very successful band it didn't occur to me that we could've signed with anyone we wanted. If it was necessary to leave Rough Trade, then EMI sounded like they were promising a regal future for The Smiths to enjoy happily ever after, and I was fine with the band getting bigger. That EMI had refused our demo of 'What Difference Does It Make?' in 1982 was an irony that hadn't escaped me, although I wasn't sure Rough Trade would see it that way when they got the news. It was a big situation and a lot to take in. I wondered what Joe would've had to say about it.

The band took a break from making the album to appear on *Top of the Pops* that autumn with our latest single, 'The Boy with the Thorn in His Side'. It was our eighth appearance on the show, and we'd become old hands at turning up to mime for the nation. It was a nice occasion for me, because Billy Duffy was also on the show with his band, The Cult, who'd been enjoying considerable success themselves. Billy and I met at the BBC, and although we didn't mention it we were both aware of the novelty of the situation. We'd started off on the Wythenshawe estate with dreams of being in bands, and here we were together on *Top of the Pops*. I watched him when it was his turn to go on, and it was the same as when I'd watched him from the stairs at Rob's house. He was a mate I could relate to, and although seeing each other didn't exactly put our feet back on the ground, it made us realise just how far we had come.

The Smiths needed to get back into the studio. We did a small run of shows in Scotland, which was good, but I was becoming disenchanted with touring. The lifestyle on the road was running me down, and it had taken me away from making the album, which had become an obsession. We decided that the best thing to do would be to go into a residential studio where we could get away from everything and work on the songs until the album was done. We settled on a big old farmhouse in Surrey called Jacobs Studios. We got to the studio the night before we started, and chose our rooms. There was a small cottage at the end of the grounds away from the main house, and I moved in there. I set up my four-track and a couple of amps so I could work on the songs and keep myself to myself if I wanted.

Earlier in the year, a new Velvet Underground album of lost tracks had come out, called *VU*. Everyone I knew in Manchester had devoured every single note of the Velvets that was available up to then, so the discovery of unheard material was like the discovery of ten new Commandments. I became infatuated with the song 'I Can't Stand It'. I loved Lou Reed's vocal and was particularly taken with a few seconds of Sterling Morrison's scratchy rhythm guitar that comes in just before the singing. Sterling Morrison had been a big inspiration for me in the early days, and I loved the way he played. I fixated on 'I Can't Stand It'; its simplicity and the way the rhythm hooked me was just the same as when I'd heard Bohannon and Bo Diddley. People are often very impressed by guitar playing that shows off technical prowess, but I've always fallen for a guitar that goes '*da-da-da-da-da*'. It's primal and human, and it avoids the ego trap that gets in the way of making a simple statement. I assimilated Sterling Morrison's scratchy style into a chord change I was working on, and from that inspiration I ended up with a six-and-a-half-minute howling wipeout track called 'The Queen Is Dead' which would be the title track of our new album. When we cut the song, I'd been playing through a wah-wah pedal, and when I put my guitar back on the stand it made a feedback noise that was in exactly the same key as the track. I asked Stephen to put the tape machine into record, and I kept the guitar feeding back on the stand and rocked the wah pedal back and forth to make a ghostly kind of howl. All I kept thinking as I was going through the track was, 'Don't die on me, feedback. Don't die,' and it kept on going. It was a glorious bit of luck. When I got to the end I walked back into the control room and the band all applauded. A couple of days later Morrissey recorded the vocal and it was one of our best performances. It was a brilliant lyric and a great composition, with space for the band members to show exactly what we could do. The Smiths had been dismissed in some quarters as a kind of whimsical indie pop. The title track of our new album would prove how wrong that assessment was.

The sessions continued and were inspired and industrious, but it came at a price for me personally. I pushed myself and didn't dare let the intensity stop for a minute. I'd always been small and ran on nervous energy, but the incessant full tilt of my lifestyle was starting to show and I dropped down to around seven stone. After working all day, I'd go back to the cottage and stay up all night, working out what I was going to do the next day. I rarely drank when we were working, but I was downing brandy at night and balanced it out with coke to keep going, then after a few hours with the headphones on I'd crash out. I'd get into the control room to start work the next day, by which time Morrissey had worked out what he was going to do on the track and was ready to record his vocal. I rarely thought about food unless it was absolutely necessary. I'd just get on with recording and sometimes someone might make me a sandwich.

It was winter now, and being holed up in the countryside on dark nights brought a mood that was good for the music. It reminded me of being in my bedroom as a teenager when the future was uncertain and the street light outside my window shone through the gloom. Once I identified it, I tried to capture the feeling on the new recordings, and when we did 'I Know It's Over' and 'Never Had No One Ever' I thought we'd created something utterly beautiful. I was hugely proud of the band and of my songwriting partnership with Morrissey.

Our lawyer turned up one afternoon when we were recording. I'd not been warned that he was coming and I resented having to stop working. Everyone vacated the room and left me and Morrissey to it. The lawyer informed us that Rough Trade had officially received notice that *The Queen Is Dead* would be our last album for them and that we would be going to EMI. It sounded exciting, but to me it felt reckless. We were alienating the people we were working with, and it seemed weird to me that we were going to EMI without having met them. We then discovered that even though they'd been given notice, Rough Trade did in fact have more records due to them, and the conversation got worse when we heard that they were threatening to put an injunction on the album and were within their rights to stop *The Queen Is Dead* from coming out. That information was devastating. All I cared about at that moment was finishing the record. Every day was dedicated to it, and now it might be shelved indefinitely. Our lawyer left, and we were supposed to continue working on the record, a record I'd just been told was probably not going to come out without a legal battle. I messed around with my guitars for a while and tried to ignore it. I'd have to put it out of my mind and just say, 'Fuck it, I'll deal with it tomorrow.'

When tomorrow came, I got a call from Geoff Travis telling

me how disappointed he was in us and that he was going to injunct the album if we tried to break our contract with Rough Trade. He talked about everything we'd been through and I felt lousy. I got back to working. Andy was putting down a bass part in the live room and I was behind the mixing desk. We were back to making music, and then I was called to the phone. Someone from Rough Trade needed to speak to me urgently. I took the call and was told that Salford Van Hire were threatening to take action against the band because the roadie had returned the van a few days late from a previous session and the invoices hadn't been paid. The record company felt the band needed to deal with it. I looked out at Andy waiting with his bass in the studio, and I screamed, 'Get someone else to fucking deal with it.' It might have been a simple thing, but after the phone call I'd had with Geoff it made me feel like I was in a situation that had become completely anti-music.

The album got made and I was satisfied with it. I always liked it when a record was finished and I could listen to it at home, before the outside world knew it. It feels like a secret that represents your world, and you're excited about it coming out because it could be good news for everyone. With the record finished, the band went back to Manchester and hung out together, because that's what we did. It was a nice time for us all. *The Queen Is Dead* was good.

Morrissey and I were supposed to meet our lawyer about the Rough Trade situation at my house in Manchester. I had gone back into the studio in Surrey for a few days to mix a song and was supposed to have driven back the night before the meeting so I would be there the next morning, but I forgot about the meeting and didn't remember until the middle of the night, by which time I was a little the worse for wear. I had to make the meeting, so I took off with Phil, my roadie, around 5 a.m. and we raced the 250 miles back up the motorway through commuter traffic to pick up our lawyer at the train station. By the time we got to Manchester, and with only minutes to spare, Phil was too exhausted to drive any further and with no way of contacting our lawyer I decided that I'd have to go to pick him up myself. There were a couple of problems with this plan: one was that I was completely deranged, having been up for two days, and was well and firmly in the rock 'n' roll zone; and the other was that I couldn't drive. Undeterred by either of these factors, I got in the BMW, started it up and zoomed off in the direction of Piccadilly station.

The journey went by in a flash as I improvised my way into town, ignoring blaring horns and oblivious to the bewildered expressions of anyone who happened to cross my path. When I got to the station, I could see our lawyer waiting with the other passengers on the pavement. I came hurtling towards them at top speed and then continued right on past as I tried to work out how to stop. About fifty feet down the road, I took my foot off the pedal and the car came to an abrupt and jerky halt. Nice job. I jumped out and walked jauntily up to my lawyer, who offered me a weak handshake and an even weaker smile. I acted as if everything was completely normal, and reasoned, 'Well, if I get into any trouble on the way back it's cool, I have my lawyer with me.' He got in the car, and as I barged into the traffic and zigzagged down the road I kept looking at him and was chatting away like we were ambling through the countryside.

I screeched around corners without slowing down and sped up at every traffic light, and his eyes went from me to the road and back again in rapid movements. We came to a roundabout and I lurched into it enthusiastically, letting out an involuntary 'Wo-agh!' and then went around again as I'd missed the turn-off. All the while he was clutching on to the door handle, the look on his face turning to dread with the realisation that dying at the hands of a deranged rock star might be his karma for wearing those sneakers with that suit. We eventually got back to mine, and I fell asleep in the chair as soon as we started the meeting. When I woke up I found out that he'd insisted that I stay asleep and really didn't mind taking a taxi back to the station.

With the album finished, I looked for something to do. The record was in limbo because of the dispute with Rough Trade, and there was no imminent release schedule to work towards. Morrissey and I took advantage of the time by making pilgrimages to record shops to track down rare sixties and seventies singles, and we made a pact to find any record that we either once owned or once loved. They were great days out, and we'd have an interesting time and always had a laugh. We both looked forward to these times away from the insanity; it was a relief to just be ourselves and have some fun. We went off around Brighton and took off to Morecambe one weekend. It gave us an opportunity to discuss what we were dreaming up for the band, and it kept our relationship exclusive.

The Red Wedge was a political movement launched by Billy Bragg to help bring about public awareness and support for the Labour Party, which was under the new leadership of Neil Kinnock. Britain had continued to witness the disastrous effects of Thatcherism, and it was felt by the more idealistic of us that there needed to be some solidarity in opposition to the Conservative government. I was of the opinion that if you were an alternative musician, you were by definition anti-right wing, and though it wasn't explicitly discussed between the bands at the time, there was an under-standing that the government was our common enemy. The Smiths were asked to play on the Red Wedge tour, but turned it down as it didn't seem like the right musical fit. I wanted to lend my support though, and I decided to play some of the shows by joining Billy Bragg onstage for a few songs.

The first Red Wedge show was at the Manchester Apollo, and I turned up for a press conference with the Labour leader during the day. After waiting around for a while, the big moment came and Mr Kinnock swept in with a huge fuss and fanfare. It was the third time I'd been in the presence of a politician, the first being when The Smiths met Ken Living-stone at the Greater London Council concert and the second when we played a concert in Liverpool for Derek Hatton. I was to witness the showbiz nature of politics once again when Mr Kinnock made his entrance with a smile so wide you wondered how he'd managed to squeeze his face through the door. His confidence was incredible as he sucked every bit of attention from the room. If Liberace and Diana Ross had been fighting naked and on fire in front of him, he still wouldn't have noticed. It was then that I decided that most politicians are ultimately fame hounds. They may have the rhetoric and may even stand for the right things, but they're more than a little ambitious and they're definitely more than OK with being famous. They just weren't cool enough to be musicians and not good enough to be footballers.

I played with Billy at the Red Wedge show in Manchester, and then I brought Andy along to do another one with me in Birmingham. Andy and I got treated with pretty short shrift in Birmingham by some of the other bands and their crews, and we took off straight after we'd played. The next day the rest of The Smiths were all at my house. I was talking about what had happened, and then someone suggested that we all turn up at the Red Wedge show that night and play as a band. We got in the car, and Angie drove us to Newcastle. I walked into Newcastle City Hall with my band, went up to the stage manager and said, 'We're here to play.' He looked at us and asked us where our roadies were, and where we would be setting up our equipment at such short notice. I told him that we didn't have any equipment, not even any guitars. The word went around that The Smiths were playing, and Paul Weller offered to loan us his gear. When the time came for us to go on, Billy introduced us, and when he said 'The Smiths' there were a few seconds of silence and then an almighty eruption of hysteria. The audience were still in disbelief as we grabbed the borrowed guitars and roared into 'Shakespeare's Sister'. For the next twenty-five minutes we played a blistering set and debuted 'Bigmouth Strikes Again' as our next single. I tore into the intro, knowing that it was the first time anyone had heard it, and Morrissey was as good as I'd ever seen him. When we finished it was as if the place had been hit by a tornado. We'd walked into the venue as a sign of unity. We'd had three years of success on our own terms, and with *The Queen Is Dead* not even out yet I thought no one could touch us. That moment was the peak of The Smiths' career.

Having the injunction on *The Queen Is Dead* was confusing. I didn't know what it meant, except that I had made an album and I was now just expected to sit around and wait for someone to do something. I was up one night when I decided to take matters into my own hands. I talked Phil into driving me from Manchester to Surrey to steal the master tapes. I had it in my mind that if the band weren't allowed to have the album then no one else was. I would break into the studio and liberate *The Queen Is Dead*. We left Manchester at around one thirty in the morning and it started snowing. I wasn't deterred but was buoyant with the spirit of indie justice. About fifty miles down the motorway the snow started falling more heavily and I sensed that Phil was having second thoughts. I turned up the car stereo and was determined to follow our quest as we forged ahead at a noble pace. Dawn was breaking when we finally got to the studio and by then I was tired out, but we'd made the journey and I didn't want to have gone all that way for nothing. We parked the car down the road and I gestured to Phil to wait for me as I tiptoed through the snow towards the farmhouse and up to the kitchen door, which I hoped would be unlocked. I turned the handle and the door opened. I crept in, hoping that whatever band was staying there had been long tucked up for the night. Status Quo had been there a few weeks before and I didn't fancy bumping into any of them. I made my way through the studio and into the store cupboard, where the tapes were kept, and as I found the shelf with our tapes the light went on behind me and I was confronted by Tim, who was one of the owners. He was startled to see me.

'Hello Johnny, what are you doing here?' he asked.

'Hi Tim,' I replied chirpily, like nothing out of the ordinary was happening. 'I've come for our tapes.'

'Your tapes?' he said, confused.

'Yeah . . . Rough Trade have injuncted them and I've come to get them,' I stated matter-of-factly.

Tim was even more confused and then he apologised and told me that he couldn't give me the tapes. He didn't want to get involved in a legal dispute, but the main reason I couldn't have them was that the studio bill for the album hadn't been paid. It sounded reasonable, and also typical, and neither of us even alluded to the fact that I was creeping around, trying to nick the album back. We drove back up to Manchester feeling like renegades, even if we had been thwarted by the man.

The Smiths and Rough Trade came to an agreement whereby we would deliver them one more album. It wasn't clear what would happen in the future, but for now we just got on with the release of *The Queen Is Dead*. It was totally fascinating to see the record sleeves coming together. Morrissey would show me the artwork he was working on, and I was as excited about them as the fans were. One night he called me to ask if I wanted to do a photo session the next day in Salford. It sounded like business as usual, so the next morning we gathered at my place, got in Angie's car and drove to Salford Lads Club.

It felt natural to have our photo taken on a street in Salford. The band's aesthetic had drawn a lot from the area, whether it was a quote from the playwright Shelagh Delaney, or images of Albert Finney or the television character Elsie Tanner, so standing on the corner of the real Coronation Street was us in our world, and not that far away from Ardwick. It was a windy and typically grey rainy morning in the North West. The car pulled up and we got out and tried not to look like we were wet and freezing. The photographer snapped a few quick pictures of us in front of Salford Lads Club, and some kids came over on their bikes to investigate. We then walked across to an alley behind some houses to take a few more shots and the session was done in twenty minutes. The photos came back to us and looked good. There were some that were better than others, and the ones I didn't like I marked as usual, such as one where I was cowering behind Morrissey because I was cold. When the record came out, the one I'd marked as bad was the picture that was used on the cover. I wondered why it had happened. It's not a good sign when you're not in control of your own image, especially when it's your own band.

With everything going right with the music, things were about to go wrong for Andy. He'd fallen more heavily into his drug habit, and there didn't appear to be a way he could beat it. We played a few shows in Ireland, and because he didn't want to be carrying drugs with him he'd gone to a doctor to get some medication to get through it. The pills were harder for him to deal with than the drugs, and they affected him badly. Eventually it became obvious to everyone that something had to be done. I talked to him, and he knew that the situation couldn't go on the way it was. Things came to a head when he had a nightmare at one show. Half of the reason was a technical issue, and the other was that he wasn't able to deal with it. Without knowing what else we could do, the rest of us had no choice but to tell him he had to leave the band. It was a moment I'd been dreading. It fell to me to be the one to tell him, and it was right that it came from me. Andy arrived at my house, and even though we both knew what was going on it didn't make the situation any easier. We were crying and hugging each other, and when he finally left and I watched him walk out of the door with his bass, it was the worst thing I'd ever had to go through.

We were all in a state of disbelief about Andy not being in the band, and we only had one idea for someone to replace him, which was Craig Gannon. I couldn't imagine holding auditions with a lot of outsiders. I first heard about Craig when he was playing with Roddy Frame in Aztec Camera and then later when he played with Si Wolstencroft in The Colourfield. He came over to my place and I explained to him what was needed. He was nervous, but we played some guitar together and we got along fine. Craig wasn't a bass player, but I thought he was the right person and I didn't think he'd have too much of a problem handling bass duties. He already looked like one of the band, and it didn't hurt that he was from our part of the world.

I stayed in touch with Andy. He came over to my house,

and it was surreal that he wasn't in the band. I would fear the worst when he would disappear for days, and one night his girlfriend called to say he hadn't come back. I didn't think too much of it, and then she called again, and again. Angie and I became concerned, and in the morning the doorbell rang. I opened it and it was Andy. He'd been busted for heroin. I didn't know if it was the shock, but he was strangely calm. He'd always been mentally strong, but it was as if by being out of the band and then getting busted, all of his fears had finally come true and there was nothing else that could possibly affect him. Andy needed help, and there was no one around to offer us any advice. We were four very young men in an indie band from Manchester and no one knew what to do. It was a bad situation, so we all rallied round and did the only thing we could do: we got Andy back in the band, and that felt right to us all.

With Andy back, it meant that Craig was effectively having the rug pulled out from under him. He'd just been offered a place in The Smiths and now it was being taken back. None of us had the heart to do it to him, so we turned the situation into an opportunity and got Craig to play second guitar. It was a novelty to have a new presence around, and it lightened the mood after all the recent heaviness. The insular nature of The Smiths was one of our strengths, but it did us good to have a distraction and a new dynamic. It was freeing for me musically too, as I could play different guitar parts live that I'd done on the records. Craig added a dimension to the sound. He could play well enough to fit in, and with Andy back we were sounding formidable.

We finally came to an agreement with Rough Trade, and *The Queen Is Dead* was released on 16 June 1986 to much critical and commercial success, and was heralded as something of a masterpiece. It was gratifying that it was so highly regarded, but the best thing about it was that fans would finally get to hear the new songs. 'Cemetery Gates', 'The Queen Is Dead', 'Some Girls Are Bigger Than Others' were all well liked, but 'There Is a Light That Never Goes Out' seemed to be universally loved.

The release meant that it was a busy time for all of us, and especially for Morrissey, as he had the press to engage with. He decided to move to a flat in Oscar Wilde's manor of Cadogan Square in London. It wasn't in my plans for the band to move to London; I thought it was better for us to be in Manchester. We had a central base at my place, the songs for *The Queen Is Dead* had been written there, and creatively things had never been better. I was fully aware that we were a big group and that we couldn't run things ourselves from the north, but the move meant we were going back to the situation we'd escaped in 1984, when we'd fled the interference of the London music scene to record *Meat Is Murder*. All the things we'd gained on our return to Manchester, the autonomy, identity, and the fact that we all lived within minutes of each other, were about to be sacrificed for a fragmented existence that was all about PR, where we would only see each other in TV stations and photo sessions. I thought it was a big mistake, and for the first time I was concerned about the differences in mine and my partner's visions for the band.

I moved into the Portobello Hotel in Notting Hill. Angie went back and forth between Manchester and London, and I spent any spare time I had in between promotional activities buying second-hand books in Camden and clothes from the King's Road and Kensington Market. One of the first things I noticed about having money was that I was able to buy books. I read everything I could find by the Beats and on American film, and a whole world opened up for me. Most nights I was in a tiny hotel room with my acoustic. I had a lot of time to kill, and I found living in a hotel to be an inconvenience as I liked working at night. I would go over to Kirsty's house to hang out with her and her husband, Steve Lillywhite, and it was through Kirsty that I found somewhere to live. She had a one-bedroom flat in Shepherd's Bush that was unoccupied. Moving into the flat meant I could have some space for equipment. It also meant that Kirsty was my landlady, which was fine unless I messed up or broke something. She knew exactly where I lived, and was not someone you wanted to cross – unless, that is, you didn't mind ten minutes of extremely colourful and creative expletives fired at you.

I was in the flat late one night with Phil when the phone rang. I answered it and Kirsty said, 'There's someone here who wants to talk to you.'

I waited a few seconds and then a very recognisable voice said, 'Hey Johnny . . . it's Keith.'

I tried to act like everything was completely normal. 'Oh, hi Keith . . . how are you?'

'Good, man . . . have you got a couple of acoustics over there?' asked my hero.

'Let me see,' I said, still trying to act normal. 'Yes . . . yes, I do have a couple of acoustics.'

'Great,' said Keith. 'Why don't you come over and we can play. I'll send a car.'

I put the phone down and was springing around like the carpet was on fire. A vintage Bentley turned up and took me to Kirsty's, where Keith Richards was waiting. I was pinching myself, but as extraordinary as the situation was, Keith is a very gracious man and a real musician's musician. He made it easy to relate to him and for us to play together. We kicked around rock 'n' roll songs with Kirsty like we'd been doing it for years, and then we'd talk and smoke a joint, have a laugh and put on an old soul record.

High on Intensity, 1986

T he legal hassles and dramas during the making of *The Queen Is Dead* had started to test my resolve, and for the first time I would have rather done anything than go on tour. Most musicians live for being on the stage, but I was more interested in the studio and I wasn't looking forward to going back on the road at all.

I'd recently been in the studio with Billy Bragg to work on his album *Talking with the Taxman about Poetry*. It was interesting playing with another songwriter, and really good fun just being a guitarist and not having to take care of anything. I enjoyed sessions, they were all about music and invention, and I was lucky in that I was invited to make records with people I liked. I got an invitation to record from Bryan Ferry, who had been one of my favourite artists ever since I'd bought Roxy records in the glam days. He'd heard an instrumental

Smiths B-side and wanted to write with me. I was honoured to be asked, and I went over to AIR Studios on Oxford Street. When I got there, I walked straight into the wrong session where George Martin was working on a Beatles track. I made my apologies and he was very friendly and let me listen to the multi-track of 'Strawberry Fields Forever'. I stood at the mixing desk and tried to act composed and not say anything stupid.

Working with Bryan Ferry was a great experience. There was a sense of discovery in his sessions, and at the age of twenty-two I was writing with one of my favourite ever singers. We hit it off and became friends, and I invited him to drop in on a Smiths session and meet the band. The rest of The Smiths were very excited about my working with Bryan and when Bryan came down to one of our sessions to say hello, it was a big moment.

The legal moves to get us away from Rough Trade and on to EMI continued. The issue seemed to just keep gathering momentum once the lawyers got to work and I was handed a shiny new contract. The whole thing was a done deal – or was about to be a done deal, as soon as we signed it. It was rushed to us at the airport, just as we were getting on the plane to go on a six-week American tour, with no manager present, just a phone call from our lawyer that morning which I failed to properly take in. It's hard to believe it, but we just signed the contract, put it back in the envelope, and Grant, our soundman, stuck it in a postbox to send it back to the lawyer. I really was that stupid.

Andy was given a break by the courts for his bust, and we

got to America for the tour. There were a couple of weeks before we left when we thought he wouldn't be able to make it, and Andy went through the set with Guy Pratt from Bryan Ferry's band on bass, which I thought was extremely professional and also very noble.

At the hotel in America on the first day, before we'd even played a note, there was a delegation from the road crew in my room, threatening to cancel the shows because no one had been paid and part of the stage set hadn't turned up. It was a situation that neither me nor Morrissey needed, and I ended up making a frantic call to the record company to ask them to loan us the money upfront so we could at least get the tour started and keep everyone happy.

The shows were always good and high on intensity. We were scheduled to play two nights at the Universal Amphitheatre in LA, and were warned beforehand by the promoter that any riots or stage invasions, which we'd had in Toronto, would mean police intervention and a ban for The Smiths in California. The first night in LA was attended by some celebrities, and Joe Dallesandro, the cover star on our first album, came to meet us backstage. The Smiths' shows in LA were always an event, and the amphitheatre was keyed up before we even started to play. Getting ready backstage was a ritual. It had been since we'd started out in Manchester three years earlier, except now we were in lavish dressing rooms with thousands of cheering people outside. I hovered around with my $10 in my pocket, my mind half focused and half distracted so as not to psyche myself out, strumming riffs on my Les Paul, usually from *Raw Power* – while Andy made amusing observations, calmly appearing not to even notice what was about to happen. Morrissey was self-contained and busy, attending to clothes, flowers, placards, and looking like he was getting ready for something pressing, while Mike tapped his sticks on chairs and Craig conscientiously played runs on the Rickenbacker to warm up. The roadies flitted in and out to consult with us about any last-minute changes and wished us luck, and the band stuck closely together while we made our way down the tunnel towards the stage. The shouts turned into a roar as the house lights went down, and Prokofiev's 'Montagues and Capulets' boomed through the arena.

The amphitheatre was totally charged when we started the set. We stormed the audience, and Morrissey took things to a new level by holding up a giant sign that read, *The Queen Is Dead*. Having Craig with us as a five-piece made a difference: we were a new incarnation of the band, with a more expansive sound and a more powerful presence. I felt more pressure to project as I looked out from bigger stages into vast venues where the crowds expected a bigger show, and it would take me a couple of songs to calibrate. Morrissey invited the audience to come closer, ramping up the energy and increasing the tension for the security, who were becoming decidedly uneasy. We introduced a brand-new song called 'Panic', and by the time we got to the encore all kinds of hysteria was about to break out. It was at this point that our singer delivered the following instruction to the audience: 'If a security guard tries to stop you, kiss them on the lips.' And with that, every member of the security staff stood back and the fans charged the stage.

We came off the stage in LA and were told that 'someone from Warner Brothers' was demanding to see us. We knew it was Steven Baker, the vice president of the label which owned Sire, and I had the feeling that he'd probably found out about us signing the contract with EMI, which meant we would be leaving Warners. Steven was one of the few people in the music industry that The Smiths related to. He'd looked after us and we were friends, so signing to another label wasn't good news and I knew it. I told the security to show him in while I went to change out of my stage shirt, and when I came back Steven was there but the rest of the band had vanished. The record company was pissed off, and Steven wanted to know why we were leaving the label. I was embarrassed, and felt my duties had gone way beyond my role as a guitar player and song-writer. All the unrealistic demands that were being made of me had become too much to ignore.

It was on this tour that I got into drinking onstage, for no other reason than I wanted to let loose and thought it would be a good thing to do. We'd get through three-quarters of the set and I'd have a big tumbler of brandy and Coke on the drum riser. The night would be really kicking off, and I'd take the party to the limit during the last few songs, with thousands of people going wild and fans diving on to the stage. It was a heady experience, and I'd try to keep it going as long as I could after the show, until eventually the adrenaline would abandon my body and I'd drop wherever I stood. I relished the opportunity to dive into the rock 'n' roll lifestyle and everything that came with it. Doing that every night started to take its toll, especially as I was so small, but it was a fun thing to do and no one could say I wasn't living the dream.

Getting to new cities and states was always good, and despite all the craziness, I'd call my family to tell them I was in New Orleans or Texas or wherever. The scheduling of the tour meant that we usually just saw the hotels, but I was always happy to be in places I'd heard about in songs and books, or because they were the home towns of bands and performers, which in America means most places if you're a music fan. There wasn't much sightseeing or shopping going on. On days off we'd all usually just stay in the hotel.

We continued to play great shows around America, but the tour was becoming more and more unsteady. The expectations on us to perform to huge crowds and keep to a hectic schedule were taking their toll on everyone. The drinking and partying after shows didn't help, but the band would walk onstage more than ready and were never less than totally professional. Things were particularly chaotic around us: the people who were paid to look after us were very loose, and with no one accountable. Young men aren't exactly known for looking after themselves, and they are definitely not known for looking after each other, so we just kept on going, and when our latest tour manager was fired for making us miss a sound-check one too many times, it fell to Angie to get us on a plane. By the time we got to the final week, we were ready to go back to the UK, and then when Andy got stung by a stingray in Florida and ended up in the hospital, we quit while we were relatively ahead and cancelled the last few shows.

We returned to England, and three weeks later were back

on a UK tour. There was some edginess and aggression at a couple of the shows, and I went straight from the stage to the hospital with Morrissey one night after he'd been hit in the head by a coin thrown from the crowd during the first song. I was tired of touring, and things weren't working out between the band and Craig. He'd always been quiet, but he became more remote from the rest of us and had even taken to travelling on his own to shows. I thought he should be more enthusiastic about the band, and the more he retreated the more I took it as a sign of uninterest. He trashed some hotel rooms, which was his way of letting off steam, but it was extreme and was an anathema to the rest of us. In the end Craig, like all of us, was a youngster trying to deal with pressure in a crazy situation. It was a challenge for him when he joined The Smiths. On the face of it he'd landed a dream job, but he'd walked into an intense situation with a tightly knit group of people who had an unconventional way of going about things. We tried to make him feel like he belonged, and it worked well for a while, but he had to either fit in with our craziness or remain on the outside. That won't work in a band for very long, and The Smiths and Craig parted company, leaving us to go back to our original four-piece.

Crash

A ngie and I went out for dinner one Sunday night with
Mike and his girlfriend after the tour finished. We were
at my house afterwards, and when it came for Mike and Tina
to go home I offered to drive them back. I still hadn't bothered
to get a licence, and had been content to take on the roads
with my own unique driving style. Angie protested about me
getting in the car because I'd had a bottle of wine and half a
bottle of tequila, but we got to Mike's without any problems
and I turned around and headed back to my place through the
rain. About two minutes from home, I stopped at a red light
and waited. Suddenly a deafening blast of music came through
the speakers as the cassette of the song I was working on
flipped around in the machine. The light changed to green,
the song kicked in, and I put my foot down and accelerated
as fast as I could go.

Within seconds I hit a bend and steered violently. I was going way too fast. The car skidded and I lost control and it smashed with an explosive boom into the wall on one side of the road before bouncing back into the air across the road and into the wall on the other side. The front of the car crumpled, the dashboard caved in and the steering wheel shot up into the roof. The car kept bouncing on the road with steam hissing out of the front until it came to a stop and there was total silence. I heard myself breathing. I was suddenly sober. I stared out of the windscreen and saw that the front of the car was completely crushed and steaming. A chunk of the dashboard was centimetres from my face. I got out of the car and looked down at my body: I had to check that I was still alive. The car was stuck diagonally across the middle of the road, and I frantically tried pushing it in case any other cars were coming. I was in total shock, but what was happening was dawning on me and I started to run as fast as I could to my house to get someone or to hide. In my confusion I was hoping that no one had heard or seen anything and that by some miracle I'd be able to make the situation disappear. I was in a mad delusion as I ran over to my house, and I fell a couple of times. Some of the neighbours came out. They'd heard the crash and had seen a demented young pop star fleeing from a smashed-up BMW, running and falling in a torn-up Yohji Yamamoto suit. When I got to the door, Angie and Phil were already on their way to get me. They'd heard the crash and knew it was me. They led me back to the car and three police vans pulled up with their lights flashing. By now there were people everywhere. 'Are you a charming man?' asked one of the cops, who happened to be a fan. I had a severe pain down my side and my wrist had started aching. The adrenaline and the booze were wearing off and grim reality was kicking in as I sat on a wall and surveyed the scene in the middle of the night. The front of the car was completely crushed like a tin can.

When the band came round the next day and saw the wreckage, it came home to me how fortunate I was to have survived. I was bashed up a bit and had to wear a brace for my neck and my back and a temporary splint on my arm. The next week the band went into the studio and I produced our new single, 'Shoplifters of the World Unite'. Two weeks later, on 12 December, The Smiths walked on to the stage at Brixton Academy. We were back to our original line-up and played a great show. It was the last one we ever did.

The crash was a huge wake-up call. I'd been living close to the line and I knew it. It was time to curb the excesses, and I had a new positivity and sense of purpose. I didn't want to do the same as I had been doing, onstage or off, and I didn't think the band should be repeating itself either. With the next album I wanted to move away from some of the things that were considered 'hallmark Smiths'. It seemed that no one could ever talk about us without using the words *miserable* and *jangle*, even though we'd proved we were much more than that, and I was eager to see where we could take things musically. In the UK there had been a movement of bands that had a specific indie sound, but I felt it had nothing to do with us, other than National Health spectacles and throwing some sixties influences around. The indie scene in England had become

After the confrontation with the Warners executive backstage in LA.

'I was becoming disenchanted with touring.'

Above: Setting up my sound with Phil my roadie and our soundman Grant Showbiz. New York, 1986.

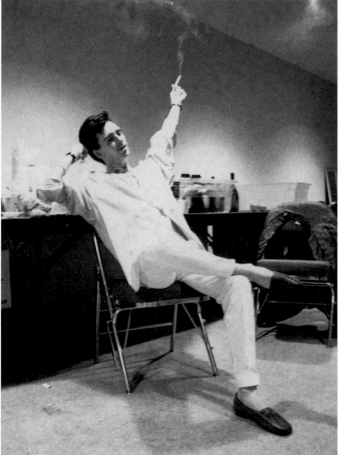

Left: Backstage. US tour, 1986.

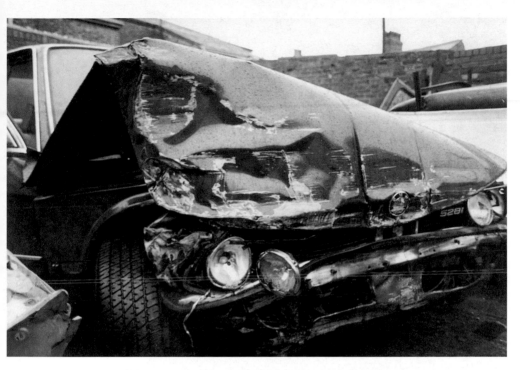

The wake-up call. 'I had to check that I was still alive.'

Kirsty MacColl. 'One of the great friendships of my life.'

The Wool Hall. 'Making *Strangeways* was a brighter time. I was in my element and then something suddenly changed.'

Opposite, top: The The, left to right: me, James Eller, David Palmer, Matt Johnson.

Opposite, below: My guitar style worked in The Pretenders and Chrissie gave me a lot to think about.

Above: With Matt Johnson on top of the World Trade Center. 'Matt and I fulfilled our pact.'

Below: Nile and Sonny, 1996.

Left: Me and Billy Duffy reunite at Electronic's Dodger Stadium debut.

Below: Electronic. 'Everyone was going through a time of liberation.'

dominated by such wimpy music that if it had been any more fey, butterflies and petals would've come out of the speakers. I was also sick of the way the band were being perceived. We were starting to be defined by all the things we supposedly hated, as if all we were about was negativity, which I didn't feel. On the rare occasions I did interviews, they were always about what The Smiths hated. I wondered if that was always going to be my lot.

I was looking and listening out for new things. There was one record which was fantastic and stood out from everything else. Matt Johnson had brought out his new album, *Infected*, and everyone took notice. It was innovative, with great guitars and strong songwriting, and it managed to be a new kind of pop while still being socio-political. I was impressed by Matt's use of new technology and his increasing skills as a producer. He was breaking new ground and I was pleased for him.

I went into the making of the *Strangeways, Here We Come* album with an agenda to use fewer overdubs and not fill up all the space in the sound. It came from a new confidence and a desire to shake things up, and was something I'd noticed in The Beatles' *White* album, which seemed to have a feeling of suspension and an atmosphere of something unresolved. I was keen to use more keyboards, and I hired an Emulator for myself at home which we'd dubbed the 'Orchestrazia Ardwick'. The first thing I came up with for the album was the synth intro for 'Last Night I Dreamt That Somebody Loved Me', after getting back into David Bowie's *Low*. Writing on the synth gave me new possibilities, and I made the decision that the first track on the new album would be all keyboards and no guitars. Even if no one else cared, it was important for me to do something different, to feel like we were going forward. I didn't know it at the time, but my experiments with new technology were going to be one of the keys to the future.

Things started looking up business-wise as The Smiths finally got a manager we all liked. Ken Friedman was an enterprising Californian who'd worked with Bill Graham, promoting shows in San Francisco. He was introduced to me by Morrissey, and as soon as he came on board things started to get sorted out. Ken was amazed that we'd spent so much on lawyers, and he couldn't believe that a band as big as The Smiths were running everything ourselves and didn't even have someone to answer phone calls. The first thing our new manager did was fire the lawyer, and find us an accountant. He then got Rough Trade and the American label behind us for the new album, and had them agree to funding for proper advertising and tour support, which was something the band had never had before. It was a relief that business was finally being taken care of, and a good sign that the manager wasn't a yes man and in awe of us, as everyone around us had now started to be as far as I was concerned.

The band went into a residential studio called the Wool Hall in Bath to make *Strangeways, Here We Come*, and I was in my element. I didn't need to know what was going on in the outside world or see anyone other than the band and Angie, and I had everything I needed. I loved the new songs. 'Unhappy Birthday', 'Stop Me If You Think You've Heard This One Before' and 'Death of a Disco Dancer' were great performances by the band and had a carefree spirit that reminded me of our first album, with Troy Tate; and with 'A Rush and a Push and the Land Is Ours' I got my track that was all done on keyboards, to start the album. The best moment on *Strangeways* was 'Last Night I Dreamt That Somebody Loved Me'. It was built around a riff that I came up with at the back of a tour bus one day when I was feeling lonely, and when it was done I thought we'd reached a level of emotion that was as good as we ever needed to be. The song epitomised everything that was unique about the band. It sounded like the drama of our lives.

Making *Strangeways* was a brighter time for me. The crash had given me a sense of clarity, and I didn't feel weighed down by label hassles or worried about the future. Every so often we'd have a meeting to make some business decisions and then go back to working on the album, which was turning out to be my favourite yet. Things were going smoothly.

In the middle of making the album, though, something suddenly changed. New allegiances were formed between band members, and I was having to defend the merits of our new manager. I didn't understand why there was a problem. The band's business was finally being looked after for the first time since Joe, we were making plans and things were going well, but the rest of the band made a sudden U-turn and it was three against one. Everything I saw as good management they saw as interference and giving up control, and I thought it was really weird that a band as big as The Smiths were trying to avoid having someone taking care of business. This new feeling of opposition seemed like it was turning into a kind of domination, with our friendships now appearing to be a secondary consideration, and I could feel all the positivity I had for the future slipping away.

We were booked to do the video for 'Shoplifters of the World Unite' with the American director Tamra Davis. Andy, Mike and I got to Battersea early in the morning for the shoot, but Morrissey didn't show up. It was costing the band a fortune with every passing minute, so I headed over to Morrissey's with Ken and Tamra to see what I could do. In a complete reversal of the day I formed the band, I banged on my partner's door but this time he wouldn't let me in. I was shouting, 'Don't do this,' but it appeared that we were no longer on the same side and it didn't even seem like we were still friends. There was no way we could continue like this. Tamra was crying, and Ken was trying to calm everyone down. I didn't know what else I could do, so I walked away.

We spoke a couple of times over the next few days, but we didn't get anywhere. I couldn't stop thinking about the future of the band. I had a sinking feeling. The Smiths were my life and I had protected the band and looked after everybody since I was eighteen, but now every day brought one new problem after another. I hadn't totally given up, and I hoped that there might be a way for us to keep going, but I didn't know what it could be.

I headed back to Morrissey's again and we started to talk. Morrissey told me that he wouldn't work with Ken. He said that he was unhappy and wanted things to go back to the way they were. I told him I couldn't do it. I was no longer prepared to deal with all the things that came up. I'd had enough of running the band without a manager, and I'd had enough of meetings with the lawyers about contracts, and meetings with accountants about tax issues I didn't understand. I was still only twenty-three, and I just wanted to be the guitar player in the best band in the world. Another manager was going to be fired, and once again someone's head was on the chopping block, but this time I refused to be the executioner. We had reached an impasse; a chasm had opened up between us and there was no way to bridge it. I knew it would mean the end of the band, but I wasn't able to face it. Our conversation moved on to something else and it was very awkward, so I left and called a meeting with the band the next day.

I needed to discuss things and tell everyone what was on my mind before Angie and I went to Los Angeles on holiday for two weeks. The two of us had never had a holiday and we hadn't had a honeymoon, so with the new album finished it was the perfect time to go away. I'd put the management situation aside for the moment, and thought that clearing the air would be a good thing for us all. The band met in an upmarket fish-and-chip restaurant in Kensington. Andy and I sat on one side, and Morrissey and Mike sat on the other. I told the band that we needed to have a rethink and get some perspective. I was trying to shake off the malaise that was taking over us, and I talked vaguely about reinventing the music, although I wasn't sure what that meant. I knew that the others no longer considered Ken Friedman to be the manager and I didn't have a solution to that. I expressed my frustrations as well as I could without trying to sound too negative, but inside I felt like I was drowning.

The band's response was unenthusiastic and unfriendly, and again it looked as though I was in a minority of one. They'd already been discussing what they wanted to do, and now Mike appeared to be the new spokesman. He informed me that the band intended to go back into the studio to record new songs, which I thought was a bizarre suggestion. We'd only just completed a new album that wasn't due out for months. I was about to go on holiday, and now I was being told to go back into the studio, and with no songs. It was like a weird test, and I was guilty of some kind of violation. The mood stayed frozen. They obviously had a problem but I didn't know what it was. I loved the others and I wanted everything to be all right, but I was aware of a new dynamic that had developed in the band, and I felt like I was being made to submit.

I agreed to go back into the studio to please everyone, and we chose the home studio of our friend James Hood in Streatham, as it was informal and wouldn't cost very much. I had no idea what we were going to do, but I set up the studio with Grant, who would be with me behind the mixing desk, and waited for the band. There was an uneasy atmosphere from the moment we got together, and then Mike came up to me and said, 'We're doing a cover version. It's a Cilla Black song.' I thought he was joking, but I looked at the others and realised he was serious. I didn't want to do a cover of a Cilla Black song, and I didn't want to be told I was doing one by Mike either. That was not going to be the new way. I was becoming angry. My dedication to the band was being tested, which was hard to take as I'd formed the band in the first place. I relented and listened to the Cilla Black song. It was a silly bit of Merseybeat called 'Work Is a Four-Letter Word', with lyrics that said, *you were born lazy* and *change your life*. We recorded it, and when it was finished I thought it wasn't even worthy of being associated with The Smiths.

The oppressive feeling affected the sessions every day. We all needed to take a break from one another, and the stress was being expressed in desperation and mistrust. The more weird everything got, the more I wanted to get out, and the more I wanted to get out, the more tense the feeling became between everyone.

In spite of all the weirdness, Morrissey and I managed to write a new song called 'I Keep Mine Hidden', and then we attempted another cover version, an Elvis Presley song called 'A Fool Such As I'. It sounded as desperate as it felt, and we abandoned it after a couple of takes. I was determined to finish the two songs we'd recorded, and I spent the next two nights sleeping under the mixing desk so I could go away knowing that everything was done. The day after the sessions ended I went to the airport in a daze after working all through the night. Angie and I got on the plane, and as we took off I felt an incredible sense of relief.

Getting out into the sunshine was exactly what I needed. I hung around for a couple of days doing very little; it was nice not having to be anywhere for a while. I was still shell-shocked from the events of the previous few weeks. Things had reached breaking point and I thought a lot about the new divisions in the band. I waited for one of the others to call but there was nothing, and the more days that went by without hearing anything, the more it pissed me off and the more I started to think that The Smiths might actually be over.

Angie and I returned home and settled back into life in Manchester. I was making instrumental tracks on my new recording set-up, and I started thinking about a different kind of music. Everyone was back in Manchester and it was odd to be only minutes away from the other Smiths and not hear anything from them. But at the same time it was a respite from what had become the band's day-to-day reality, and I felt the freedom to just be a musician again. I held out for a sign that someone might do something to salvage the situation, and then out of the blue I got a call from The Smiths' publicity agent Pat Bellis. She told me that the press had somehow got hold of a rumour that I had left the band, and she wanted to know what I intended to do about it. It didn't sound right, and I wasn't about to be forced into saying anything to her, the band or anyone else about any split by making a public statement. Two days later, a story appeared that I was leaving The Smiths. The article included a new photo of us that had been taken by the press officer and just happened to catch me scowling while the other three Smiths were all smiling away. Having the story out there I had no choice but to make a statement. I still hadn't heard from the others, and with everything that had happened I just thought, 'Fuck you.' I faced up to the inevitable and announced that I was leaving The Smiths. The other band members issued a statement on the same day. It said they wished me luck and that 'other guitarists are being considered to replace him'. I thought that it might be some kind of hoax, but then one of our friends called me to say that it was true, and that they'd gone into a studio with another guitarist. It was a difficult thing to hear that the band had been so quick to replace me within only a week of the story coming out. It was the final nail in the coffin. I couldn't go back even if I'd wanted.

All hell broke loose when I left The Smiths, and the soap opera commenced. It didn't work out for the band with the new guitarist, and everywhere I looked people were discussing the split and had an opinion about it. I kept out of the media and refused the deluge of interviews because I knew everyone wanted a sensational story and expected me to discredit the others to get my side across. The split wasn't just the end of a band; it was a break-up of very close friendships, mine and Morrissey's in particular. I didn't want to slug it out in the media. It was hard enough to deal with as it was, and too painful for me to put a spin on in public. I had to stand back and let people say whatever they wanted, whether it was true or not. The more bitter the split became, the better off I felt out of it, and soon I was just happy to be out of it altogether. Angie had to handle it too. She'd been there from the beginning, when it was just me and her, then Joe and Morrissey, and she had to deal with the disappointment of it all when it finished just as much as anyone.

As stressful as The Smiths' split was, it also brought with it a huge sense of relief when it finally ended. The fallout would continue for a long time, but as difficult as it might have been I always knew that the band would have a finite amount of time, and now events had conspired to bring it to an end. I was in charge of my own life again.

I was still only twenty-three and Angie was twenty-two when The Smiths broke up, and it was back to just the two of us. I had no idea what I was going to do. I just knew I wanted to play the guitar and do something different from what I'd been doing for the previous five years. It was a time of rejuvenation, pro-future, pro-music.

Talking Heads: 88

Talking Heads invited me to record with them for their new album in Paris. They had a few songs already down for me to play on, and they also wanted to do something with me from scratch. They'd been such an important band to my generation, and had managed to pull off the rare feat of being one of the biggest bands in the world while still maintaining their artistic integrity. I knew their stuff inside out, and I was flattered and excited to be asked to make a contribution to one of their records.

I flew over to the studio in Paris to meet David Byrne on the first day. He kindly vacated the apartment he'd been staying in to let me and Angie have it while he moved to a hotel. When I got in there, I noticed he'd left us some earplugs on the kitchen table. I didn't think anything of it until the nightclub kicked in below us at midnight and blared full-on disco music until dawn. Steve Lillywhite, who was producing the album, was in the control room when I arrived to start recording, and it was good to have someone there who I knew. I wanted to get straight into playing and I got my sound going quickly, using a Fender Strat for a suitably funky Talking Heads approach, and told him to roll the tape. Steve started the first song and said, 'This is a bit of a blank canvas.'

I listened to the sparse percussion and drum groove for a while, then Tina Weymouth's bass line came and a couple of guitar chords, then ... round and round it went. I was expecting a song that sounded like Talking Heads, and this was just a groove, albeit a pretty cool one. 'OK,' I thought, 'relax.' 'Give it to me again, Steve,' I said. I scoured my brain to try to conceptualise an approach to the track that might travel from my fingers. 'OK now ... here we go,' I thought. Then ... nothing. 'What the ...? Huh?' I couldn't think of anything. Usually I can hear, if not exactly the right thing to play, then at least something, but not this time. I was stumped. I really didn't want to freak out. There was only one thing to do: get out of the studio and get my head together. I walked out on to the Parisian street. 'What are you doing?' I said to myself. 'You've lost it.' I walked around the block and then around again, and something occurred to me: put a riff on it, and make it a big one. I was being too precious. I needed to throw on my own sound – that was, after all, why they wanted me in the first place.

I walked back into the studio, plugged in my Gibson 335 twelve-string electric and told Steve to roll the tape again. The intro started, and without thinking I played the very first thing that came to me. Steve gave me a smile and a thumbs-up, and when it came to the next section I dived straight into a riff off the top of my head. It was exactly the right thing. The song came to life and everyone was grooving. After that it was plain sailing. David added his brilliant lyrics and vocals and the song became '(Nothing But) Flowers'. It was the first single off the album that was to be called *Naked*, which I suggested they call *Talking Heads: 88*. I cut three more songs with Talking Heads. 'Ruby Dear' was recorded live, with the original four members and me on guitar. I hadn't recorded live with anyone other than The Smiths before. It was a learning curve, and as a learning curve goes, Talking Heads was a good way to start.

Angie and I got to Charles de Gaulle airport to fly home. I was asleep on one of the circular benches, and the next thing I know I'm being woken up with a rifle to my head by a French military policeman shouting, 'Move, move – *allez-vous-en*! Evacuate!' Angie hauled me up as the gendarme grabbed us and marched us away fast, shouting, 'Hurry, hurry!' Suddenly there was an explosion, with glass flying everywhere and sirens going off at a deafening volume, and the cop pulled me down on to the ground. People were rushing all over the place and as I looked around at the commotion I saw that the area where I'd been sleeping had been blown up by a bomb that was under it. Time stopped, and then all I could think off was to thank the gendarme: '*Merci! Merci!*' I expected to be taken out of the airport, but we were made to wait until we got put on a plane to Heathrow. We landed a couple of hours later, where my guitar tech was waiting for me. I got in the car.

'How was Paris?' he said.

'Good, good,' I replied. 'Talking Heads are cool.'

Back in the UK, everyone was having a field day ramping up the drama of The Smiths' split and I felt like Public Enemy No. 1. It had already turned into a saga, and everyone seemed to want it to run and run. Every day brought new carnage raining down and I didn't know what to expect next. The story was being milked for all it was worth by the media. My every move was portrayed as proof that I was the ambitious heel who hated The Smiths and was desecrating the grave of the golden goose by playing with Talking Heads and Bryan Ferry, when really I was just accepting amazing invitations from great people and really wanted to play.

The other Smiths got together as a band under Morrissey's name. I thought it made perfect sense, but the media depicted it as a symbolic statement against me by the others and used it to further dramatise the saga. I retreated into music. I wrote some new songs for Kirsty, and I snuck out onstage unannounced in Brixton one night with A Certain Ratio to play the Haçienda classic 'Shack Up'. I was at Kirsty's one afternoon when I got a phone call. It was Paul McCartney's manager asking me if I wanted to get together with Paul to play. I didn't have to think twice, and within a few minutes a fax was sent to me with a list of old rock 'n' roll songs that Paul wanted me to learn.

I knew Eddie Cochran's 'Twenty Flight Rock', and 'Long Tall Sally' by Little Richard, and there were a few Buddy Holly songs and Elvis Presley songs too. The following week I went to the rehearsal space out of town, where a couple of musicians whose names I recognised from rock albums were already there: Henry Spinetti on drums, and Charlie Whitney from Family on guitar. I was much younger than everyone and nervous as hell. I knew the songs from Joe playing them in Crazy Face, but I'd never actually played them myself before. I was just going to have to wing it. Paul and Linda came in, and it was a moment for me and probably an occupational hazard for them. Like everyone else on the planet I was thrilled to meet a Beatle, but I was also a fan of Linda. She was someone I'd liked since I was a kid. I admired her commitment to vegetarianism, and because we thought of her as a role model The Smiths had asked her to do something with us on *The Queen Is Dead*. Now here I was with her and Paul and we were about to play. They were both friendly and easy to be around, and Paul asked me about working with Talking Heads while he got his sound together. Being in the presence of a Beatle, as anyone who has ever done it will tell you, can make you feel a curious mixture of wild anticipation and mild anxiety. Add to that the fact that I was playing with one of the Beatles at twenty-four years old, and you're halfway to recognising the situation I found myself in.

The first thing that I noticed about Paul McCartney was how much attitude he has as soon as he picks up his bass. You can see his total command of the instrument. I heard it too, and at deafening volume, as he stood looking at his amp and went *BWOOOMFV!* with one note. It was the best bass sound I'd ever heard, and the loudest. We kicked into 'Twenty Flight Rock', which I'd managed to work out the night before, and it took every bit of resolve I had not to shout, 'Holy fuck! That's Paul McCartney, singing right there in front of my face! Does everybody else realise that that is Paul

McCartney . . . standing right there in front of my face?' Luckily I held it together enough not to do that, and just tried to make my playing sound as authentic and fifties rock 'n' roll as possible. At one point Paul asked me if I knew 'I Saw Her Standing There', and I tried to keep a straight face as I said, 'Yeah, I think so.' Then he asked me matter-of-factly if I fancied singing the harmony. A voice in my head started screaming, 'You mean John Lennon's part? I'M . . . GOING . . . TO BE SINGING . . . JOHN LENNON'S PART?' But I just nodded and said, 'OK . . . I'll give it a go.' The next thing I know, me and Paul McCartney are facing each other, singing, '*I saw her standing there.*' I couldn't really believe it was happening, but I made the most of it. I got brave and suggested 'Things We Said Today'. He counted it off and away we went. I thought it sounded very good.

My experience of playing with legendary musicians is that without exception playing is really what it's all about. There's not much sitting around talking and doing nothing. I played with Paul McCartney all day. When we eventually took a break, we sat together and Paul and Linda asked me about what was going on with me. Linda was a nice person, funny and engaging, and genuinely interested in what I was doing. She asked about The Smiths splitting up, and I was honest and told her that it was hard as everywhere I went people didn't seem to want to let me get away from it. She listened intently and Paul was nodding. The subject changed to general musician's talk, and sometimes Paul would interject with a 'yeah, The Beatles had that in Japan' or 'that happened to us once', as if it was the most natural thing in the world, which to him it was, as he was just talking with another musician. It was nice hanging out with them, and then it struck me that I had a once-in-a-lifetime opportunity to get perspective and insight from a man who actually knew my situation. A man who had been defined by his relationship with his songwriting partner and whose band's break-up had hung over his every move, regardless of his immense personal and professional journey. If anyone could hip me up to some wisdom and insight, it would be this man in front of me. So after recounting the basic details of recent events, I held my breath and waited for Paul McCartney to enlighten me. He paused, I waited, and then he paused again and said, 'That's bands for ya.' That was it, the sum total of his evaluation: 'That's bands for ya.' Over the years I've found myself in a similar situation when a fellow musician is recounting his tale of woe and the predicament with his band. I've thought of different things to say, but in the end the best thing to say really is: 'That's bands for ya.' I got that from Paul McCartney, and he knows a thing or two about bands.

Talk of the Town

Like everyone I'd been a fan of The Pretenders for years. When their debut album came out in 1980, James Honeyman-Scott instantly became one of my favourite guitar players. They had a style that was modern and it genuinely rocked, and with her words and vocals Chrissie Hynde had the sound and attitude of a truly great singer fronting a great band. One day Ken Friedman called me. I hadn't seen him since before the end of The Smiths – he wasn't around when the band broke up, having taken time out to get over his experience by trekking up the Himalayas. I guess managing The Smiths can do that to a man. I was glad to hear from him, and he was calling to say that Robbie McIntosh had left The Pretenders before the end of their tour and Chrissie wanted to know if I'd like to join them for some shows. It was a big ask to learn their set at short notice, but it was an exciting prospect and also a chance for me to escape all the drama that was surrounding the break-up of The Smiths and the claustrophobia I was feeling in England. I told them I'd do it, and I went over to meet Chrissie at her house in Maida Vale.

She opened the door, looking exactly how I expected and wearing a T-shirt that said, 'I Learned the Guitar in Three Minutes'. We talked for a while about Iggy Pop and Mitch Ryder, and she suggested we go out to the Marquee to see a band that was playing. When we got to the club and walked in, I instinctively felt that Chrissie was someone I could be friends with. We only stayed for a few minutes and then left to walk around the streets of Soho and talk. Chrissie was someone I could understand. Her attitude towards being in a band was positive and poetic. She'd had huge success, but she viewed fame and her career as almost a side issue compared to the real business of plugging in and playing. She was funny and had interesting opinions about a lot of things, and from the first night we met she gave me plenty to think about.

The tour was starting on the West Coast of America, and the first show was in a week. We were opening for U2 on their now famous *Joshua Tree* tour, which was being documented for the film *Rattle and Hum*. I had four days to learn The Pretenders' set, and their office sent me over VHS tapes of two concerts to study. I spent the next two days and nights learning the songs, and then went into a rehearsal to meet the rest of the band and the crew. Everyone was friendly, but I knew they were wondering if we would be able to pull off the task at hand and be good enough to walk out in front of 70,000 people. I put on my guitar and looked down at the set list. Chrissie asked me what I wanted to play, and I chose the song 'Kid' as I'd known it from my teens and had always played it in guitar shops. We started playing and it sounded good straight away. We knew it was going to work. My role in the band was not only as lead guitarist, though. There are a lot of backing vocals on Pretenders songs, which I had to sing with the bass player, Malcolm Foster. We ran through all the parts meticulously and played some more, and from then on I was singing back-up with Chrissie Hynde. Significant turns can happen in life within minutes, and that was one of mine. Chrissie said it sounded good and I could do it, which was good enough for me and would be good enough for anybody, and that was the start of me singing again.

We flew out to join U2 on the tour. My first show was at the Oakland Coliseum in California. I'd never seen that many people before, let alone played in front of them, and the gap for the cameras at the front of the stage was as big as some of the venues I'd played in with The Smiths. I walked out with bits of sticky tape stuck to the back of my guitar with the chords to the songs written on them, and I thought I'd better up the money in my back pocket to a $20 bill. We played great songs, it was a blast, and I was sky high and miles away from the past.

Being on tour with U2 was eye-opening. I'd never been exposed to ambition on that scale before, and it was interesting to watch a band connect with such vast crowds every night. I'd always respected the Edge and regarded him as a great guitar player and someone you recognised the first second you heard him. He made a point of coming into my dressing room to say hello every night, and it was nice to have someone around to talk guitars with. A totally new thing for me was having children around on a tour, and it made a big difference. Usually bands and touring are very male-oriented affairs, and you definitely don't see much of children. Chrissie had her two daughters, Natalie and Yasmin, on the dates, and as well as having adorable little people around it brought a sense of perspective and normality to everything, which I wasn't used to on the road. I'd be playing with two little kids at the side of the stage one minute, and then walk out to an ocean of people the next. It was a lovely thing and it kept the enormity of it all from getting too much.

The Pretenders were liked by everyone who was into rock music. Customs officials would ask me what I did for a living and what band I was in, and when I said 'The Pretenders' I'd be welcomed with a smile. A lot of very famous people also loved the band, and I was introduced to some interesting fans. Jack Nicholson hung out with us on both nights of our LA shows and Chrissie introduced me to Bob Dylan. One night she told me she'd invited a friend to come out with us to dinner, and I was sitting around when the doorbell rang. I went to see who it was, and Bruce Springsteen was standing outside. Me, Angie and Chrissie squeezed into his Volkswagen Beetle and he drove us to dinner, where he and I spent most of the night talking about sixties garage bands. He was great company and he shared with me his philosophy that every concert ticket sold is an individual contract with a fan, which was a real privilege to hear and a philosophy that I've never forgotten. I played some more shows with The Pretenders, going to South America for the first time and playing stadium concerts that were even bigger than the ones with U2. Chrissie and I then went to Jamaica for a Bob Marley tribute concert. I liked Jamaica and took to the local customs with aplomb, operating on the 'when in Rome' principle and 'it would be rude not to', partaking with Grace Jones and the rest of the Wailers until I was so laid-back I wondered how Bob Marley even managed to write the words 'Get Up, Stand Up', let alone do either of those things.

Back in London, Chrissie got involved in working with the animal rights organisation PETA. It was an education to see the reality and the scale of animal cruelty happening in the world. Being introduced to people so committed to a cause and witnessing their selfless dedication strengthened my own commitment to vegetarianism and taught me the value of taking action and standing up for your beliefs, no matter what. It was good for me to be confronted by issues more serious than what was going on in my own life. I'd been emotionally bruised by what had happened with The Smiths, and teaming up with Chrissie helped me enormously. She'd experienced the very real challenges of dealing with the death of two of her bandmates, Jimmy Scott and Pete Farndon, and her attitude helped me put my situation into better perspective. It also made me think that there might be some truth in the idea that the right people can show up in your life at the right time.

I stayed in London for a while, and The Pretenders went into the studio with Nick Lowe to record two songs for a film. We cut the Burt Bacharach song 'The Windows of the World' and The Stooges' song '1969' for a single. It turned out to be a perfect document of how The Pretenders sounded with me in the band. After we'd got the touring done, the question of whether I was going to stay in the band permanently came up. We'd hoped to make a record at some point, and worked on a song in the studio, but The Pretenders were in need of a break from it all. The band had been touring and recording for a few years when Robbie left, and I had come into a situation that felt like the end of a chapter, when my life was all about starting a new one.

The New Thing

B ack in Manchester, things were starting to get wild. Everyone was having a different experience when they went out to the Haçienda. The place was still half-empty, even on the weekends, but one or two of my friends were telling me about the amazing times they'd had as Mike Pickering was playing a new kind of music from Chicago and they'd been going all night on a new drug called 'E'. Something significant was definitely happening: a new attitude swept through the city and everyone was in it together.

Togetherness wasn't an entirely unknown concept in town, because, after all, we'd all been going to gigs and clubs together for years. It was just that now everybody was aware of the togetherness, and appreciated it. Dancing together, in a club together, in new fashions together, in the city together. An awful lot of people were getting into it, which was amazing and no bad thing – Manchester needed it, musically, culturally and sociologically. There were obvious parallels with the peace and love movement of the hippies in the sixties, and not only because of the presence of a love drug and people dancing with their hands in the air. Joe had always said that if the hippy movement hadn't happened in Britain, the culture of booze and aggression that was taking over at the time would've made it impossible to go out at night in Manchester, such was the amount of violence you would encounter on the streets and in clubs, where people were starting to carry chains and knives.

At the start of the new scene in Manchester, no one knew it was a 'movement'. It wasn't called 'rave' or 'acid house' yet. It was just a brand-new thing to get into, and it meant a radical change was going to happen because anything that didn't fit in suddenly seemed irrelevant and past its sell-by date, which meant a lot of the rock music that was around and the fashions too. It permeated everything, from the clubs to the streets, creating a full-blown culture that you either embraced and explored, or had to try very hard to imagine wasn't happening. People changed their clothes, bands changed their sound, graphic designers changed their direction, and druggies and boozers changed their poison. Dance music culture and E was the new thing, and there is no denying that it made a lot of people who weren't very happy much happier and some people who weren't very nice suddenly much nicer.

Angie and I were spending most of our time on the motorway, driving with the roadies back and forth from

Manchester to London, where I was recording a lot with Kirsty. I'd be in the studio for a few days, and then we'd jump in the car when the session was done at whatever time of night to make it back to the Haçienda, which was suddenly starting to get busier and more loved up until it began to feel like the centre of the new musical universe. The Haçienda had always been identified with the digital world in my mind because of the sound of the electro records that echoed around it when it first opened and because of Peter Saville's visual aesthetic that accompanied it. I liked technology, especially when it was used to create pop music, back from Roxy Music's synths and Sylvester's 'You Make Me Feel (Mighty Real)' to The Smiths' 'How Soon Is Now?'. I'd been into new music machines ever since the Emulator had shown me a way to get to the future.

I met up with Bernard Sumner after a New Order and Echo and the Bunnymen show in San Francisco – I'd gone to California to meet with the producers of a Dennis Hopper film called *Colors*, who'd asked me to play on the soundtrack. I'd last seen Bernard when The Smiths and New Order played the Festival of the Tenth Summer in Manchester, and we took off after the San Francisco show to catch up. Like me, Bernard knew all about the ups and downs of being in a successful band from Manchester, and he'd had more than a little dramatic history of his own. New Order had been recording and touring for a long time without taking a break, even after Joy Division. They'd gone through the death of Ian Curtis, and succeeded in resurrecting themselves as a new entity before going on to build the Haçienda. Bernard had come to a point in his life when he wanted to do something different, outside of the group format, and in me he saw someone who was a free agent.

We picked up where we'd left off, and Bernard asked me if I'd be interested in writing some songs, which sounded like a good idea. We'd worked together once before when we'd done Mike Pickering's record for Factory, and although The Smiths and New Order had different approaches to making music, we shared a similar sensibility, having come from the same place. New Order had more touring to do, so we arranged to get together when we were back in Manchester.

I went on to New York to work on the Dennis Hopper movie. I was stood playing the guitar, with Herbie Hancock producing me, when I sensed a very intense presence breathing on my neck. I was playing to a scene of a police car driven by Robert Duvall, and as I did so Dennis Hopper put his face right next to mine and hissed, 'Make it sound like the cops, man . . . make it sound like the cops.' I carried on playing as he prowled around the room, scrutinising the action on the screen, then what I was doing, and then the screen again. I summoned up howls and siren sounds in a way I'd never done before, and when the scene was finished he stood two feet away and stared at me, completely deadpan. I stared back at him and didn't say anything, then he broke into the most dazzling, enigmatic grin and said, 'I like you, Johnny.'

I had no idea what was going to happen when I left The Smiths. For all I knew I might have had to go back to square one and start all over again. I didn't know I was going to get a call from Paul McCartney or Dennis Hopper or Talking

Heads; I just knew that I wanted to play guitar, the same as I had since I was a kid. I did sessions simply because I got interesting invitations and because it was great; I liked making records with great people, so playing sessions seemed the perfect thing to do. I didn't want to be in a band, or at least I thought I didn't, until Matt Johnson came back into my life and invited me to join The The.

I heard from Matt completely out of the blue. He was about to enter into a new phase after *Infected*, and now that The Smiths had ended he followed up on the pact we'd made in 1981, before our paths took off in different and extraordinary directions. We arranged to meet at an Iggy Pop show at Brixton Academy, and it was great to see him again. Back-stage in Iggy's dressing room after the show, Matt was telling me about his plans to put together a new version of The The, and Iggy, who doesn't miss a trick, said, 'Are you guys working together? You should do something together.' It was the perfect initiation, an auspicious beginning sanctioned by the great man himself.

In the intervening years since I'd slept on his couch to get The Smiths a record deal, I'd followed Matt and what he was doing, and with *Soul Mining* and *Infected* he'd made a couple of albums that I really loved. The The had not been a group in the conventional sense but was more of a title or moniker for whatever project Matt was working on, having collabo-rated with different musicians and pursuing his interest in video and film. The plan was to put together a band to make a record and go on the road for the first time, and as well as being an opportunity for Matt and I to work together, it was good timing. I'd taken on a manager in London called Marcus Russell on the recommendation of Ken Friedman, and my office then became the management for The The. I was already living between Manchester and London, so I would work with The The and then go back up north to record with Bernard when he wasn't working with New Order. The only remaining thing that Bernard and I needed to sort out was a name for what we were doing. We were in a meeting with Peter Saville and he was pressing us about it. Bernard looked around the room and saw that the name on the air-conditioning unit was 'Electronic'. He pointed to it and said, 'We're called Electronic.'

The mood around The The and Electronic was really positive and forward-thinking. Bernard and his girlfriend Sarah moved in with me and Angie while they were looking for their own place. I'd known Sarah for a long time, and the four of us became very close. In 1988 everyone in Manchester seemed to be going through a time of liberation, and it was no different for me. I was young and I felt free for the first time in ages.

Matt Johnson is one of the few partners I've had who is the same age as me. We're both self-taught working-class boys who grew up in the seventies Britain of Harold Wilson and Edward Heath and came of age as the Thatcher regime took its toll on our generation. While I had been busy in The Smiths, Matt had been on an intrepid journey of his own, and had been putting himself in some extreme situations physically and psychologically during the making of his most recent work. He immersed himself in world events and turned me on to a lot of things, most notably Noam Chomsky and the essays of Gore Vidal. HQ for The The was in an old building in

Shoreditch that had once been a gentleman's outfitter's. It stood on the corner of two streets, with Matt occupying the one big space of the store's second floor, so that we spent most of our time in an intense orange glow from the street lights that flooded through the windows around us. In the daytime the place felt like a Hitchcock flick or a detective movie from the fifties film noir, and filled with suspense. At night the ambience was nocturnal and more like New Orleans at 3 a.m. or Alan Parker's *Angel Heart*, and Matt and I would stay up drinking vodka and listening to Ennio Morricone, Tim Buckley and Howlin' Wolf.

Shoreditch in those days was really run-down and edgy. Sometimes we'd go out in the small hours to a dive in King's Cross and come back at dawn, the London traffic and commuters blighting our reality. Being in The The also opened my eyes to the psychogeography of London, as the two of us would wander around the parts of the city that Matt had written about in songs like 'Perfect' and 'Heartland':

Beneath the old iron bridges, across the Victorian parks
And all the frightened people running home before dark
Past the Saturday morning cinema that lies crumbling to the ground
And the piss stinking shopping centre in the new side of town
I've come to smell the seasons change and watch the city
As the sun goes down again.

Matt often looked out at the world for his inspiration rather than just talking about himself. His words evoked his environment, and I could personally relate to the songs I was playing.

The other two members of the new The The were musicians I already knew. David Palmer had played on *Infected* and was in demand by everybody. I first became aware of him when he was in ABC; he was the drummer all the drummers I knew wanted to be. The bass player was James Eller, who had been in Julian Cope's band. I'd heard a lot about him from my friends, and he would've been the first person I'd have called if I was forming a band myself. All four of us wanted to play together, and when we were eventually joined by an ace keyboard player called D. C. Collard, The The became very tight as friends as well as a very good band.

When it was announced that I had joined Matt Johnson in The The, it was rather predictably met with negativity from some areas of the British music press. Matt was called on to defend our collaboration and was denounced for having the audacity to harbour a fugitive from The Smiths. That we both maintained a belief in the mission of The The made the indie militia all the more suspicious, but the pettiness galvanised us. We were committed to what we were doing, and we thought that people who actually bought records and paid to go into concerts might like what we were doing. They did, and the album we made, called *Mind Bomb*, went into the Top 5 and the shows sold out everywhere.

The first thing we recorded was a song called 'The Beat(en) Generation', which became Matt's first Top 20 hit. When we recorded the album's opening track, 'Good Morning, Beautiful', a story of a satellite addressing our planet and an exposition on humanity's self-destruction, we did it in the middle of the night, having been ingesting psychedelics for several days. When I plugged in my guitar, Matt approached me conspiratorially with saucer eyes and said, 'Can you make it sound like Jesus meeting the devil?' His request made total sense to me and I summoned up the appropriate response, which he followed by hollering demonically into an old blues mic, '*Who is it? Whose words have been twisted beyond recognition in order to build your planet Earth's religions? Who is it? Who could make your little armies of the left and your little armies of the right, light up your skies tonight?*' It was stunning.

Playing in The The, I was given the freedom to try anything and encouraged to do things I'd not done before; fuzz sounds, industrial noises and radical echoes were all employed in the spirit of experimentation.

In contrast to The The's intensity, we were seriously into having fun, and the more puerile the activity the better. AIR Studios was several floors up on Oxford Street, the busiest street in London and always teeming with shoppers and tourists. Every morning Matt would buy fifteen pounds of overripe tomatoes and we'd have a contest to see how many of the public we could target. We didn't hold back and we didn't discriminate. We splattered women, businessmen, children and pensioners. We did it a lot, and the more out of hand it got the funnier it became. I'd be laughing until my face hurt. It was the best recreational pastime anyone's ever devised in a recording studio.

Because Matt had made a lot of abstract and what's known as 'textural' sounds on his previous records – playing keyboards through old effects pedals that radically alter the natural sound of things, together with some studio techniques – I had to devise ways to reproduce them on the guitar when we eventually went on tour. It was a challenge trying to make such diverse sounds. I'd remembered seeing a quote from an older guitar player that said all musicians reach a creative plateau where they've learned all they are going to learn and they stop developing, something that struck me as a really depressing notion. I've always intended to keep improving and learning my craft, even if I have to lock myself away to do so. When I joined The The, my guitar technique improved considerably. I learned everything I could about the new guitar technology: programming devices, filters, modulation, backwards effects, and any way of changing the sound with pedals, something that I came to think of as 'producing with your feet' and which would become invaluable in the future.

The The went around the world, and I finally got to go to Japan and Australia. I was twenty-five years old and miles away from where I'd been as a member of The Smiths. I felt like I was back to the person I'd been before then, and in a new place, having new experiences, in a new situation. In Greece we played at the Acropolis in Athens. I'd been out doing interviews in the sun all day and got sunstroke. I had no idea how incredibly unpleasant sunstroke can be. I was sick and hallucinating when I walked onstage, and after standing completely still and holding on through the first song, Matt came over to me and asked if I was all right.

'Are we on the Acropolis, Matt?' I enquired.

'Yeah,' he said, laughing.

'Oh, good,' I said. 'That's OK then.' And I carried on with the show.

The The had been out on the road on and off for almost a year when a terrible tragedy struck. Matt's younger brother Eugene lay down on the bed one day, complaining of a headache, and died suddenly aged twenty-four. It was devastating. The band all tried to rally round for Matt and his family, but we felt useless and it was heartbreaking to see my friend having to deal with such a catastrophe. We broke from the tour for a short while and then took up again. I don't know how Matt did it, but he got through it and at the end of it we made a live concert film from the Royal Albert Hall called *The The Versus the World*, which captured the band as it really was during that period.

Get the Message

It was just me and Bernard Sumner in the studio when Electronic first started working together; no producers, no engineers and no other musicians. We moved around, plugging things into other things, and did everything ourselves. We had no strategy other than to try something new, and for me that meant a wide-open set of possibilities. I saw working with Bernard as an opportunity to experiment with electronic music and to learn as much about working with machines as I could. I wanted to program drumbeats and write the most out-and-out synth pop I could muster, regardless of what anyone might think. Bernard thought I was mad to be going so against my own grain, and our conversations were often on a similar theme:

Him: 'Put some guitar on it.'
Me: 'No.'

Him: 'Put some guitar on it, Johnny.'
Me: 'It doesn't need it.'
Him: 'But everyone's going to blame me and say it's my fault.'

We worked on and off for a while in between The The's and New Order's schedules, recording a lot of ideas until we had our method of writing. I would start off a song with an idea for a verse or something on a synth, and Bernard would make suggestions, then he would take over for the next bit and vice versa. Other times one of us would have an idea for the whole song and the other one would help him realise it. In spite of my urge to do otherwise, I would still always play guitar on the songs, but usually after I had tried to make it sound like a synthesiser. It was important and necessary for me at the time to do different things from what I was known for. It's the prerogative of any artist not to want to repeat themselves over and over again. Unlike in the visual arts, it's one of the stranger aspects of pop culture that musicians are often expected to try to repeat things that have brought success, which to me is as absurd as expecting David Hockney to continue making splash paintings for the rest of his life.

Bernard and I genuinely hadn't anticipated how incessantly we would be asked by the press, 'Are The Smiths going to reform?' and 'Are New Order splitting up?'

My new partner liked plenty of The Smiths' songs and respected what we'd done, but he really didn't give a fuck about dealing with the gossip or the media in general, and he wasn't into maintaining an aloof persona, even though he'd been a successful frontman for years. His philosophy was to get the music out there and to enjoy what you work hard for, and to try not to let the destructive aspects of fame affect your sensibilities or your inner world. Amen, brother.

Building my own studio was an inevitable next step for me, and I was really excited about it. I could do whatever I liked and go in there whenever I wanted, which meant I was in there all the time. When Bernard went away for a week, I found myself messing around one sunny afternoon with a bass sound I'd sampled off an old soul record. I was playing around with it and came up with something that sounded really good. I programmed a drumbeat, and with the rhythm track happening it sounded perfect already and I knew exactly what the guitar should be. I played some chords on a twelve-string acoustic and added a string arrangement, and before I knew it I had an instrumental track that was unlike anything I'd done or heard before. On the Saturday night, when Bernard got back from his week away, there were a lot of people round at my house before everyone went out to the Haçienda. I snuck on the new song in between the other records and said to Bernard, 'What do you think of the new demo?'

He looked at me curiously and said, 'Is this us? What?!' It was a great moment. We played the track a few times and everyone was loving it. Bernard said, 'Call it "Get the Message".'

Having a lot of people on the scene permeated a lot of what we did. There was so much partying going on it's amazing anything got done, but it absolutely reflected the times and it all fed into the direction of our record. There would usually be a gathering like that somewhere before everyone went to the Haçienda. We would go into town and surrender to the revelry and hear the great new music that was becoming more and more influential by the week. 808 State, The Stone Roses and Happy Mondays were all on our home turf, and Manchester was the centre of everything.

Some nights I'd stay working in my studio when the city was buzzing. Around five in the morning, my brother Ian would phone to warn me that a gang of loved-up crazies was heading my way from a house party in Moss Side. Ian was the Vibe Protector, heading off the wrong kind of people with me on their radar, and making sure I wasn't harassed. He was only sixteen, but he was street-wise and very protective of his big brother.

Shortly after Electronic formed, we got a message through a friend that Neil Tennant would be interested in working with us and that maybe we could record something with Pet Shop Boys. We loved the Pet Shop Boys' records, and on the day that Neil and Chris Lowe were due to come to my studio I started work on an idea that sounded like a chorus for a song. When Neil and Chris arrived, we all worked on the idea until eventually we had a backing track for Neil to take away; he wrote the lyrics and it became 'Getting Away with It'. We went to the Haçienda that night and all reconvened the next day to write another song, called 'The Patience of a Saint'. It was an interesting and successful collaboration that was exactly what Bernard and I had envisioned for Electronic when we'd first talked about a new way of doing things, and it was the start of a creative relationship between me and Pet Shop Boys that would last a long time.

The impact of the Manchester scene could be seen all over the country as more and more people flocked to the city to join in the 'Madchester' experience. Suddenly it was the hippest thing in the world to pretend that you'd come from the most socially deprived areas of the city and speak as if you were a barely educated urchin from a young offenders' institution. Unfortunately a lot of people started to act that way too, which was a side effect of the scene that I found disappointing. Having come from the inner city, I'd seen the aspirations of working-class people and suddenly there were these characters walking around wearing their lack of opportunity as a badge of honour, which was confounding to me and a regression for ordinary people. It may have been part of putting Mancunians in the spotlight for a while, but it also devalued what some people had been working for all their lives, namely pride and the victory of elevating themselves through betterment and discipline. What had started out as authentic was turning into a depressing stereotype of the northerner, which set back the image of the northern working class forty years, and created the dreaded cultural phenomenon that is the 'Manc Man', or professional Mancunian. There were even people around who were pretending to be from Manchester, which I doubt had ever happened before.

A new, much more serious aspect of the culture also took hold. The economic opportunities of the new drug trade created heavy violence, and the togetherness that had been there at the beginning turned to edginess. Gangs started to take over, and became self-appointed kings of the nightlife, especially in the Haçienda, which was by now the most notorious nightclub in the world. Manchester had become Gunchester. It was a dilemma for Bernard, one of the owners of the club, and I found myself in a couple of encounters with some dubious people who were part of a world I had no interest in.

One night, I pulled up outside the Haçienda and two characters who I knew were in one of the gangs approached me and offered to park my car. Valet parking was not a service you expected at the Haçienda, but I knew better than to refuse and played along. Later, when I was leaving, one of them approached me and said, 'Wait here, I'll get your car for you.' I waited on the street, and then my car appeared, which was a convertible, with the roof down and the two gangsters in it. They stopped and got out, and as I got in my car they sat on the bonnet and one said, 'All right, John? Just like to have a chat.'

'Uh-oh,' I thought.

'How's it going, man?' he said, smiling while still sitting on the car.

'Yeah, great,' I replied, trying to sound not unfriendly yet as remote as I could be under the circumstances. 'What are we doing?' I asked.

'We just wanted to have a word,' he countered, 'about the gig at the G-Mex.' I had no idea what he was talking about. 'We're putting on a night at the G-Mex . . . you and the Mondays.'

'I don't know anything about it,' I offered, not knowing where the conversation was going and trying to get a game plan in my mind as quickly as possible.

'Yeah, we're putting you on, you'll be headlining, don't worry about that,' he continued. 'We've got the merch all sorted and we've got some DJs.'

By now I'd got the gist of what was going on and I jumped in: 'Oh . . . right. The thing is, I'd be up for it, course . . . but it's Bernard, you see. He doesn't like playing live . . . hates it.'

'Well done, Johnny boy,' I said to myself, 'problem solved.'

Unfortunately, my new friend on the car was well used to blag and he was already way ahead of me. 'No, we've sorted it with Barney, he's well up for it. He said to talk to you about it.'

I knew that was bullshit and my instinct kicked in and told me to just start babbling. 'Well, the thing is, right . . . we've only got a few songs . . . and they're very complicated to do with just the two of us, you see.' As soon as I started talking like this, his manner changed from conceit to contempt. I saw my chance. 'We'd need a lot of samplers, yeah? Samplers, for the sound, and the er . . . the EQs, y'know? Graphic equalisers . . . with midi and hard drives, a lot of hard drives.'

Mr Gangland looked totally baffled, as if he'd just realised that I was a poncey artist and not one of the lads after all. I could tell that he was suddenly disappointed in me and was thinking, 'That Johnny Marr's a bit fuckin' weird.'

I started my car and tried to maintain a look of disappointment about all that midi and hard-drive business, and with a 'Shucks, maybe next time, fellas' resignation I pulled away as fast as I could and put my foot down. Back at my place I told Angie, Bernard and Sarah about it and how brilliantly I'd saved us from a very tricky predicament with one of the gangs. Bernard listened for a bit and then said seriously, 'I think it sounds all right, maybe we should do it.'

'Getting Away with It' was Electronic's first single and featured Neil Tennant on backing vocals. It was released in December 1989 in advance of our first album, which was on Factory Records, a gesture of respect from me to Tony Wilson and something which Bernard did out of loyalty to the label. In America we were contracted to Warners because of The Smiths and New Order. One night I got a call from one of the heads of the record company on the East Coast to say that he was meeting with Morrissey and that I should consider getting back together with my old partner. When I politely declined, he said, 'It would be better for Electronic if you reconsidered.' I never knew what prompted the call but I thought it was inappropriate when I was working on some-thing potentially lucrative for the label.

The popularity of 'Getting Away with It' took me by surprise and it became the most successful song I'd had in America. With it came Electronic's reputation as a 'super-group', a press angle we understood – after all, we were, or had been, members of The Smiths, New Order and Pet Shop Boys. But we were uneasy about it too, as the supergroup tag usually conjured up an image of bored, self-indulgent rock stars who only got together when the limo came to pick them up. Electronic was far from that. We worked in the studio every day and considered ourselves more akin to the club musicians putting out 12-inch records on independent white labels, or the new kind of group that was emerging, like Mark Moore's S'Express, which I really liked. I was also inspired by Brian Eno, who didn't appear to impose any limitations on what he did or how he did things, and his method of using the studio as an instrument was an idea I was interested in taking as far as I could.

In August 1990, Electronic played our first shows with Depeche Mode at Dodger Stadium in LA to 80,000 people each night. When we got to the airport to fly out, we were met by a reception committee of Mancunian gentlemen who I'd known from round the clubs. They'd taken it on themselves to embark on a field trip and form our entourage for the duration, only letting us out of their sight to go to 'check out that Compton an' all that', which they'd seen in rap videos and decided was the place of most cultural interest in the Golden State. When we arrived in LA it just so happened that Happy Mondays were also in town, recording their album *Pills 'n' Thrills and Bellyaches*, and Sunset Boulevard was suddenly infiltrated with unusual-looking girls and boys, all loved up in Travel Fox trainers and 22-inch flares.

For our first shows we assembled a collection of our friends to play with us, and I brought Ian out to work as an all-round Mr Fix-It. Having my brother with me was great; he had just left school and we had always been really close. Ian could play drums, guitar and bass but never actually wanted to be in a band. He's extremely conscientious, and us working together meant that my family were more directly involved in my world again.

The two nights at Dodger Stadium were a brilliant debut,

and Pet Shop Boys did a couple of songs with us. On the second night, Bernard, who had been out celebrating the night before, having forgotten he had to do it again the next night, was extremely hungover. He walked up to me during one of the songs and said gravely, 'This is the worst fucking moment of my life.' All right, Bernard . . . yeah! Woohoo! He survived, and did a remarkably good job considering. Those first two shows were my favourite shows Electronic ever did.

Anyone who knows Bernard Sumner or knows much about him will know that he's very into sailing boats – big boats, yachts. I had never been in a band with anyone who could sail before, and as time went on it became clear that I would prob-ably end up joining him – either that or Bernard would continue to refer to me as 'Mr Studio' and 'Mr Chronically Unsociable'. I was intrigued by the idea of sailing. Me, Angie, Bernard and Sarah, on a yacht on our own, in the middle of the sea – what could go wrong? I guessed that Bernard was probably pretty good at it, seeing that he spent so much time doing it, and thinking about it, and reading about it, even in the recording studio.

I first went sailing with him in the Lake District in England. It was pouring down with rain and very windy and everyone thought I'd hate it, but as we cast off and I stood at the front of the boat with the rain lashing down I loved it. The four of us sailed a lot, around the Mediterranean and the Caribbean and California. Having to deal with the ocean, I learned that aside from negotiating a sixty-foot vessel through open waters it's also a great lesson in acceptance and mindfulness. You have to accept that nature is in charge and is a much bigger force than yourself. You can't outsmart it or overpower it; if you don't comply you are in serious trouble, and even if you do comply you still have to be pretty vigilant and pay attention.

In Hamburg, Bernard and I decided to conduct our interviews for the day while sailing around the lake in a little dinghy with one sail. The journalists turned up, expecting an intense, in-depth discussion about The Smiths and New Order, but instead they had to try to act cool while rocking around on the water and ducking their heads to avoid getting hit every time we decided to turn, which was every time they asked a question about The Smiths or New Order. That is how to do interviews.

As Electronic was just the two of us, it meant that Bernard and I ended up doing a lot of travelling together, and if you travel a lot with someone who is afraid of flying you will catch it off them. I caught my fear of flying off Morrissey. He and I always sat together on planes and he hated flying. In my attempts to calm him I became hyper-aware of every whiff of turbulence, as he would clutch the seat or me, until eventually I was worse than he was. Billy Bragg hated flying too, and he didn't help matters. One day, on a flight to San Francisco when I made the mistake of asking him about tranquillisers for Morrissey, he said, 'Tranquillisers won't save him as we're hurtling towards our doom, John. Do you know that when a plane hits the sea, it has the same impact as when it hits concrete?'

'Er, no, Bill, I didn't know that,' I said, suddenly more nervous.

'I'm just saying,' added Billy, 'and don't forget we're in a pressurised metal tube hanging 30,000 feet in the air – it's unnatural. Peanut?'

What was wrong with these guys, these bards of England? It was one of the downsides of my empathy with lead singers that I assimilated some of their idiosyncrasies, and my experiences as an international traveller were ruined by hideous terror until I got myself over it, but not before I managed to pass it on to Bernard Sumner.

In spite of many years of blissful air travel with New Order, Bernard was now in a band with me, and Electronic did a lot of flying. We hit the mother lode when we went to the Philippines to make a video and had to fly in a helicopter several times over a volcano to get a dramatic aerial shot. We discovered that we were going in a military helicopter, which meant it didn't have any doors, and being something of a trooper, and eager to prove that unlike me he wasn't a total wuss, Bernard heroically let me sit in the middle of the plank of wood that was our seat, with him on the outside and the cameraman on the other. As the chopper rose and hovered unsteadily above the ground, I saw something in his face I hadn't ever seen before: I saw dread. For some reason I found Bernard's unease really, really amusing and it set me off on a fit of uncontrollable laughter, and the more acute his discomfort the funnier it became as we zoomed across treetops and over the jungle where *Apocalypse Now* was made. I was having the time of my life, howling and whooping and absolutely loving the experience. I realised that Billy Bragg had a point about a pressurised metal tube in the air being unnatural. But this was fine: I was totally OK with no doors and the open air and the propellers whirring above us – in fact it was great. Bernard, however, had very different feelings about it, and he was praying for it to stop with an expression of both utter terror and wild anger at my hysterics. 'Fuckin' hell! Fuckin' hell!' he screamed. I thought I was going to die from laughing. From that moment I never had a problem on a plane ever again. No matter how bad the situation, I'm cool with flying. Thank you, Bernard, you're a mate.

'Get the Message' was a record I was really proud of. I first heard the finished version on the bullet train from Tokyo to Osaka one night after I had played a show with The The. Angie had arrived with a tape of the mix with Bernard's new vocals on it, and she was excited for me to hear it because she knew I would love it. I sat in the low-lit coach on the train in Tokyo station, and as it pulled away to Nagoya I put the song on. As I heard it start up, and then the half-spoken vocal began – '*I always thought of you as my brick wall, built like an angel, six feet tall*' – I was blown away. I didn't know what it was, but I knew we had done something totally unique. It wasn't The Smiths, it wasn't New Order, it was our own – and it was cool.

Because we weren't a band in a traditional sense with a permanent line-up of musicians, Electronic didn't tour, which was mostly my decision. We promoted our records by doing interviews and lots of them. We'd fly into a city in Europe or

America and spend the whole day talking to the press, and then fly to the next city and then the next, and so on. It was intensive and we were always asked the same questions, but we managed not to send ourselves and each other insane. Our decision not to tour was partly because we'd both done a lot of it recently with The The and New Order, but mostly because I enjoyed making records so much, and if you gave someone like me the opportunity to spend as much of my life in the studio as I could, then that's what I would do. I'd been doing sessions since the start of my career, and I'd played on other people's records all through my Smiths days. I considered it to be one of the privileges of my life to be able to collaborate with someone I respected and to contribute my sound and ideas to their record.

I had been visiting Billy Bragg in the studio when I heard him kicking around an idea that was half reggae and half 'Louie Louie', with some interesting phrases about sexuality. I heard something good in what he was doing, so I took a tape of it home. I worked it up into what I thought was going to be a demo, but it was sounding so good I decided to make it into a record and hoped that Billy would like it. He came to my studio and liked the track, and over the next few days we made the single 'Sexuality', with me producing. It was a great pop song with brilliant lyrics. 'Sexuality' became a chart hit in the summer of 1991, and I produced and played on some more things with Billy.

One morning, in the middle of the Madchester scene, I answered the door with no idea that I was supposed to be doing anything. I was greeted by an extremely awake and lively Billy and band, bright-eyed and chipper, having arrived from London to make a record as we'd planned. I immediately saw that to Billy I probably looked like I thought I was a rave messiah, dressed all in white with bare feet and a bright orange David Bowie *Low* haircut. Throughout the session, Billy kept complaining that he didn't like his producer not wearing socks. I protested that it was a seventies new wave thing rather than any Mediterranean beach situation; but I was also living a life at that point where I couldn't fathom socks, or anything else for that matter that didn't make sense on hallucinogens. It was remarkably fortuitous that the song we were recording happened to be a very psychedelic track, called 'Cindy of a Thousand Lives', which I thought was totally brilliant. Luckily for me too, Billy is someone who understood my genuine attempts to balance unpretentiousness with an occasional hedonistic eccentricity befitting a rock star, and he was amused by my quirks.

When we did 'Sexuality' and 'Cindy of a Thousand Lives', it was obvious that we should get Kirsty MacColl to sing on them as we'd all worked together before and were a bit of a gang. I'd recently written an instrumental track and sent it to Kirsty to get her opinion on it. She called me back the next day and said, 'I've written a vocal on it and it's a single.' We did the song, which was called 'Walking Down Madison', and it became a hit. When she was finishing the album, she needed a title for it. Kirsty was very witty, and her working title for the album was *Al Green Was My Valet*. I thought she needed something else, and because I used to live in her flat I suggested *Electric Landlady*, as a pun on the Jimi Hendrix album. I was joking when I said it, but she ended up using it for her album.

The other sessions I did at that time were with Pet Shop Boys. I always looked forward to them, and I never knew what I'd be called on to play. Sometimes the records would be symphonic and orchestral, and sometimes they would be hi-tech crafted pop. Although the image of the Pet Shop Boys is of two stylish men in well-appointed rooms letting the machines do all the work, this is not entirely true – except for the stylish and well-appointed bit, which is completely true. My sessions with the Pet Shop Boys have been concentrated affairs and have always been inspiring. Neil and Chris are never short of ideas, and I've ended up employing a lot of different guitar styles. I've played on more Pet Shop Boys songs than any other musician, my favourite song being 'This Must Be the Place', from the album *Behaviour*, but there have been so many good ones, and when I've worked with them I've always felt a sense of occasion.

Nile

I got off a plane in 1991 after being on a promotional trip with Electronic, and Angie was at the airport to meet me. It was a hot day in England, and she arrived in my old Mercedes convertible. I was driving home on a country road when she said, 'I have something to tell you, we're going to have a baby.' I was delighted, and pulled the car over to the side of the road to process the news. Finding out you're going to be a parent means fifteen minutes of total elation followed by a brand-new parental concern – concern that it's going to be all right, concern that you can handle it, and so on. There's a lot of excitement and joy, but being a parent for the first time you worry about most things until the baby is born. The news was great for all of us, and starting a new generation brought both our families closer together.

My son was born on a Friday night in Manchester, and

Angie and I named him Nile, after Nile Rodgers. We loved the music and respected the man, and we liked the idea that our child had the same name as a river. When he was born I already knew my son, which is something often said by people about seeing their kids for the first time, but it was true. I got an impression of what his nature was, and it's never changed since the moment I first saw him. After staying in the hospital for a few hours, it was late and time for me to go. I drove back with all the windows down and went through every red light on the way. I reasoned that if the police were to stop me, they wouldn't be so heartless as to bust a guy who's just become a father, and even if they did I really didn't care.

Dusk

In early 1993, The The went back into the studio to do the follow-up album. It was to be called *Dusk*, and I knew it was going to be special. We moved into the basement of the building in Shoreditch and immersed ourselves throughout the whole process in atmospheric darkness lit sparingly by psychedelic oil lamps projected on the walls. I was staying in South Kensington, and I'd drive by the river and along the Embankment on the hazy summer mornings with the roof down on my way to the studio, accompanied by our keyboard player, D. C. Collard, who was staying with me. The journey to the sessions in the morning was the only daylight I'd see, as once I'd descended into the studio I was fully engaged in the world we were creating and I rarely came out less than fourteen hours later.

By the time we made *Dusk*, The The had been together as

a band for almost five years, and we'd played all over the world and knew each other very well. It was always creatively intense in The The, but the atmosphere in the studio when we made this album was especially poignant and affecting, and I sometimes found myself having to leave the studio for a while because I was overwhelmed. The song that was the most powerful and emotive of all, and which I think is one of the greatest songs of all time, is 'Love Is Stronger Than Death', with its opening line *Me and my friend were walking in the cold light of mourning*, which described Matt and I walking through London after Eugene died. As the track went along and I listened to Matt singing, I played the harmonica with tears streaming down my face. There were other moments on *Dusk* that were totally The The, and which only that band could do. 'Dogs of Lust', 'Helpline Operator' and 'This Is the Night' all conjured up the restless nocturnal life I'd known with Matt in London and New York, and 'Slow Emotion Replay' was so pretty that on the take I sang an impromptu harmony down my harmonica mic just because I was so happy when we were doing it. I love the record. It captured a spirit that I share with Matt, and 'Slow Emotion Replay' has some of my favourite The The lyrics:

> *The more I see*
> *The less I know*
> *About all the things I thought were wrong or right*
> *And carved in stone.*
>
> *So, don't ask me about*
> *War, Religion or God*

Love, Sex or Death
Because . . .
Everybody knows what's going wrong with the world
But I don't even know what's going on in myself.

When I was in The The, Matt was criticised for addressing such issues as the war in the Middle East and religious fundamentalism by some people who said that he was taking things in pop music too seriously. Songs like 'Armageddon Days Are Here Again' and 'Sweet Bird of Truth' proved him to be prescient and also courageous for a modern rock musician. Spiritually and mentally, Matt is one of the bravest people I've ever known. The way he appears in the videos for 'Infected' and 'I Saw the Light' is what he's actually like, although he's also very funny. In The The we were trying to find some truth, truth about the state of world and truth about the human condition. Matt once said to me, 'True inspiration travels through the ages like an arrow.' It's a big concept to take on for a rock group, and *Dusk* is one of the best things I've ever done. Sometimes, when I'm out in the world, someone will present me with a copy of *Dusk* or *Mind Bomb* to sign and they always ask, 'When is Matt Johnson going to make another record?' The records mean a lot to people, and being in The The was a very important part of my life. It's amazing that after our first meeting in Manchester as teenagers, Matt and I fulfilled our pact and had success together.

When the time came to go on the road again with *Dusk*, though, I had to take a step back. I didn't want to leave Angie and the baby, and it was time for me to explore somewhere closer to home.

Having a baby around the house brought a lot of change to our lives, and it was great being a family. It was hardly a conventional household as the place was always busy with musicians coming and going. My studio was state of the art, and Bernard was sometimes working on things for New Order, and used it to record some of the music on their World Cup song, 'World in Motion'. As always, my life was following whatever music I was making, but I'd take time to get out to the park with Nile and watching him gaze at the birds, and chasing him around, put me into the real world, which I no longer always felt the need to escape.

Kids love music, and Nile loved Kraftwerk and also Bob Dylan, and he would amuse himself in the studio, playing with the gadgets and listening to everything while I was working. My son's first ever favourite song was 'There She Goes' by The La's. It was a big hit when he was an infant and it was on the radio all the time. Lee Mavers, who wrote and sang it, came over to my house for us to feel out the possibility of doing something together. We got along, and after a while we picked up two acoustic guitars and started playing some songs, 'I Can See for Miles' by The Who, and some Stones and Bo Diddley. We were really getting into it when my son came toddling in to hear what was going on. Lee said hello to him and asked him what his name was. Nile answered, and then I asked him, 'What's your favourite song, Nile?'

'"There She Goes",' Nile said matter-of-factly, not having any idea who the man was or why I was asking, and with that

Lee stood up and delivered the whole song like he was singing to 20,000 people. Nile stood motionless in astonishment, his mouth wide open as Lee Mavers sang to him. It was a lovely thing, and also quite full-on. Lee and I played together a couple of times, but we didn't take it any further. He had his thing to do and I had mine.

The guitar scene in England post-rave was still very vague and had yet to find its *raison d'être*. The revolution in electronic music in the previous few years meant that regular rock bands seemed strangely redundant, and although some bands were trying to assimilate the new technology while still keeping the values of rock, I wasn't much interested in that.

The time was right for a new paradigm in guitar music, but at that point I didn't know where it was going to come from. The La's were the guitar band that everybody I knew was talking about, and when I first heard them I sensed that they might signal some kind of sea change.

Electronic were planning our follow-up album, and the studio was being taken care of by Ian, with Angie overseeing everything. Ian was in and out of town quite a lot, and he was often given cassettes of bands' demos by people wanting him to 'pass this on to your kid'. He always conveniently forgot to bother passing anything on to me, having grown up with people asking him to do that kind of thing all the time. We were busy one day when he mentioned in passing that he had a friend who was putting a new band together, and then he mentioned it again a few weeks later, saying that he had bumped into this friend in town and the new band were pretty good. For Ian to say that a band was 'pretty good' meant 'very good' in any other language, and he passed me a cassette with a cover that had a picture of a Union Jack that looked like it was being flushed down a toilet. I put it on a shelf somewhere and forgot about it. A few days later, we were driving through town when we passed a hunched figure in a duffel coat walking in the pouring rain.

'That's Noel,' Ian said.

'Noel?' I asked.

'Yeah, Noel,' said Ian, 'the guy whose tape I gave you a few weeks ago.'

It was raining hard and I pulled the car over and we shouted to Noel to get in. I said hello and he seemed fairly reserved. I was playing a Bob Marley and the Wailers live CD at full volume, and we drove around for a while before going to find a guitar shop. After that, we went for a cup of tea, and the first thing he asked me was what I thought of the tape, which I hadn't heard. Realising there had to be at least one song on it, I told him, 'I really like the first one, a lot.' I took to him straight away. He was smart and had an inscrutability about him. I saw his passion for what he was doing, and he was very serious about being a songwriter. It was obvious that he had a vision that he had to follow through.

After talking about Neil Young and guitars for a while, I dropped him off at his place, and when I got back to my studio I rifled through the cassettes on my shelf and pulled out the one with the flag on it and read some of the titles: 'Columbia', 'Married with Children', 'Fade Away', 'Rock 'n' Roll Star'. I stuck it in the machine and pressed 'play'. What I heard sounded new yet immediately familiar in a good way. When music sounds familiar it can sometimes mean it's just ordinary, but it can also mean it's very right. I recognised some reference points: it was flying the flag for classic rock but had a thing of its own, and there wasn't anything else like it. It was so . . . Manchester. I listened more closely and then decided to call Noel now that I had examined his band more thoroughly. He picked up the phone and I told him that I liked his band and asked him if he had any shows coming up. He told me he was working on getting some gigs, and we arranged to meet at his place the following night to go and see The Verve, who were playing in town.

Noel, along with nearly all of Manchester's bohemian aspirants, was living in an apartment block called India House. I knocked on his door, and when he let me in I was introduced to a young kid sitting on the couch with an amazing haircut – super short at the front and long at the sides – and who was flanked by two pretty young girls so enthralled by him and his hair that they didn't seem to notice anyone entering the tiny flat. I looked around the cramped space, and Noel proudly showed me his two most valuable possessions: an Epiphone guitar and a large fish tank.

I looked into the tank, pointed to one of the fish and said, 'What's that blue thing called?'

And then from behind me came the voice of Mr Haircut, who said, 'Fuckin' fish.'

'Oh,' I thought, 'attitude – very good,' and we took off to go and see The Verve.

We stood near the back – me, Noel and Ian, and the haircut kid in his blue Adidas tracksuit top with white stripes. His look and stance echoed the Manchester casual look from the late eighties, but because he was young it now meant something different – less nightclub, more street and rock 'n' roll.

The Verve played a new kind of rock for a new time. Based on the classic touchstones, their music was a reaffirmation of the values of guitar bands that had been put aside in recent years, and it resonated with a new generation of lads, who were tired of the contrived mainstream techno pop and who couldn't relate to the negativity of the new American bands. British kids were reclaiming punchy, catchy guitar culture, with the look and message to match. It had started with The La's, and I'd heard it in Noel's tape. Something was in the air and summer was coming.

I arranged with Noel to see his band play. He'd run round the corner to the students' union in Manchester and insisted that they give him a gig or else they'd burn the place down. They were the first band on that night, and so at seven o'clock Ian and I went to the top floor of the university building and waited for the show to start with the twelve other people who were in attendance. I didn't know who the other members of the band were, besides Noel, and as they walked on the stage I noticed the drummer had short curly hair – not Syd Barrett, weird-guy curly hair with groovy ringlets, more like Dave Barrett, normal-guy-who-sits-behind-you-in-science-class curly hair . 'O . . . K,' I thought, he can always grow it. Then I saw the bass player, who Ian told me was called Guigsy. He looked very chilled out, and he was followed by a regular-looking fella carrying a hollow body guitar over to his amp. 'Is that the singer?' I thought. 'Ian, who's that?' I said.

'Him?' said Ian. 'He's Bonehead.'

'What?'

'Bonehead,' Ian confirmed.

'Bonehead?' I asked. 'The rest of the band call him Bonehead?' I wondered if it was meant to be an insult or endearing or both – either way it was funny.

At that point I noticed that Noel had sneaked on from behind his amp. He looked very serious with his Epiphone and he appeared to be scowling. He was surveying his equipment and inspecting the audience when on walks the kid who I'd met in the flat – Mr Haircut . . . Mr Fish. He sauntered over to the middle of the stage with his nose in the air and was looking around at everyone quizzically while shaking a white, star-shaped tambourine for no apparent reason. I thought he must be the dancer, like Bez from Happy Mondays, then Ian said to me, 'That's Liam, he's the singer.'

'Well', I thought, 'if he sounds half as good as he thinks he looks then this is going to be interesting.'

I didn't know he was Noel's brother, but when I saw the two of them together I suddenly saw that this band had a real front line, and within a few seconds of howling feedback they crashed into a deafening assault on a tune that I slowly came to realise was 'I Am the Walrus'.

The sound was massive and deliberate and electrifying, and thirty seconds into it I knew that a lot of people were going to like them. I had no idea how big they were going to be exactly, but I knew that they were going to connect with people and that they had something great and an authentic spirit. They played a six- or seven-song set, and when it was finished Noel came over and asked me what I thought. I told him I was blown away. I was happy for him that his band were so good, and over the following week I couldn't get that performance out of my mind. I called my manager, Marcus Russell, and told him all about this band and that he really should come to see them. I was persistent, and he agreed to check them out when they next had a show.

I called Noel again and asked him if they had any shows and he immediately replied, 'Yes, this Friday.' When I asked him where the gig was, he said it was at the university again.

I don't know if he put the phone down and ran round the corner to sort it out, but I got back on to Marcus and said, 'Oasis are playing on Friday, you have to come up,' and up he came.

When we went to the university this time, the crowd had swelled to twenty-five. On come Tony – the drummer – Bonehead and Guigsy, and on come Noel and Liam, and they go into 'I Am the Walrus' very, very loud. The set was just as good as the last time, and when they were finished Marcus turned to me and asked, 'Well, what do you reckon?'

Ian and I said, 'Yeah, they're fucking brilliant.'

Noel came over to me and I introduced him to Marcus and they talked for a while. On the way back to my place I was thinking about the show and how good it was to see something new. A few days later I got a call from an unusually excited-sounding Noel to say that he'd played a show at King Tut's club in Glasgow and run into the Creation Label boss, Alan McGee, who'd offered them a record deal on the spot. Noel wanted to sign the deal but he didn't have a manager and he asked me what I thought. I interpreted his call as a scrupulous display of protocol to see if I was cool with him approaching my management, and I said, 'You and Marcus should get together.' He asked if I was sure and I assured him he should do it.

I could already sense that some momentum was starting to build for the band. I told Noel that if I had one bit of advice I could pass on to anyone it would be to keep writing more and more songs, because when you do everything can fall into place, but without the songs no amount of business can take care of anything. It was the smartest thing I could think of, although I'm pretty certain he knew it already.

Another thing I told him was to get a back-up guitar, because he was taking so long tuning up in between songs. 'That's all right for you to say,' he said. 'I've just got my Epiphone.'

I put the phone down and thought about it for a minute, then I went into the studio and looked at my guitars. I decided it would be good if I turned up with the 1960 Les Paul that I'd used on 'Panic' and 'London' with The Smiths and which used to belong to Pete Townshend. I put it in its case, drove round to his house and said, 'Here, you can use this.' It was the only moment that I or anyone else has ever seen Noel Gallagher lost for words.

Oasis put their first record out and they immediately started to get a lot of attention and were suddenly everywhere. Noel was talking about the guitar, and he said the first thing he'd done with it was to write the song 'Live Forever'. I went to see the band, and when I saw him playing it I realised that the guitar belonged to him. The way he held it, the timing of us meeting, him starting out on his journey and the songs he was writing with it . . . it all felt right and it all made sense and I was very happy for him. I had no idea how big Oasis would be. I just liked Noel and I liked his band.

Their success was so phenomenal it meant big changes in my office. What was originally just me and my manager and an assistant on a borrowed landing space in west London turned into a big new office with lots of extremely busy assistants and was complete madness in a very short space of time. Midway through their first national tour, I got a manic phone call to tell me that the night before in Newcastle the band had got into a fight onstage with some of the audience and the Les Paul I'd given Noel had got damaged. 'So what do you want me to do about it?' I asked.

'Have you got another one we can use?' came the reply.

I looked at my guitars and reasoned, 'Well, he's accustomed to playing a 1960s Les Paul from The Smiths and The Who, so I can't send him something crappy.' I grabbed my black 1970s Les Paul that I used on *The Queen Is Dead* and stuck it in its case with a note that said, 'It's a bit heavier, in weight and sound. If you get a really good swing on it, you'll take some fucker's head off – Love from Johnny' and I sent it up to Newcastle.

One of Kraftwerk living with one of The Smiths is a mad concept, but it happened. Mark Reeder, a friend of mine and Bernard's who ran a record label in Berlin, suggested that we invite Karl Bartos to work with us on Electronic's second album. We knew all about Karl's time with Kraftwerk, and we arranged to meet him in Düsseldorf. Bernard and I had expected that because Karl was one of the pioneers of electronic music he might want to employ the latest technology when we worked together. We imagined him sending us files of programmed music for us to play on, via the wonders of the new modem line. When we got to Düsseldorf, we were met by a cool-looking guy who was very much a working musician and nothing at all like a showroom dummy or a robot. We sat outside a cafe and had ice cream, and when we asked Karl about how he would like to proceed with the recording he said, 'Easy, we get in a circle with our instruments, and we jam,' which was a surprise. Karl then showed us around his studio and demonstrated how Kraftwerk made the sounds on some of their records. Bernard Sumner was astounded as Karl casually played 'Computer Love', 'Autobahn' and 'Trans-Europe Express'.

We started working on a new Electronic album, and Karl moved into my house with us. It was a good arrangement as Karl was a friend, and by then my house was essentially a residential studio with a family in it. Working with Karl, I learned first-hand about German history: composers, philosophers, and what was really happening with the musicians in the German counterculture. We influenced each other, and we would sometimes go out to investigate the music that was happening in the clubs. Karl could memorise the records and would then write the music down on a white board when we got back to the studio. One morning after a late night, we were all in the kitchen and Karl was there wearing a black

T-shirt and shorts. Andrew Berry sidled up to me and said, 'Johnny . . . your life is mad.'

'Oh yeah?' I said. 'Why's that?'

'Well,' he said, 'there's one of Kraftwerk . . . in his underpants.'

Sonny

It was midnight on New Year's Eve 1993 when Angie told me we were having another baby. We were super-excited to be having another child, and I had a strong feeling that we'd have a girl.

The morning Angie went into labour she grabbed my arm extremely tightly without any warning and just said, 'NOW!' I jumped into the car and my wife looked at me very seriously and said, 'We need to get there FAST!' It was the height of rush hour and the traffic was bumper to bumper. I was trying to keep calm as we manoeuvred up Princess Parkway, while things in the car were developing very quickly indeed. I weaved in and out of the traffic, gesturing apologetically and saying, 'Sorry, mate . . . sorry about that,' and then, as we came to a standstill for what seemed like for ever, muttering, 'COME ON! COME ON!!' The baby was going to arrive any minute, and my blood pressure and stress levels were going through the roof with every 'argh!' and 'woagh!' that Angie yelled out. We weren't moving very far at all, and there was a real possibility that my next child was going to be born in Whalley Range. I prepared myself to pull over to the side of the road and deliver the baby myself, thinking, 'Oh God, at least wait until we get to Ardwick.' We finally crawled to within ten minutes of the hospital and I sped off through the back streets of Moss Side, screeched up to the doors of St Mary's and shouted to the hospital staff, 'No, really, she's having it NOW!' as a concerned-looking porter raced Angie to the delivery room, where the baby was born before I even had time to take my coat off.

We called her Sonny, which was a name Angie and I had thought of for a long time. I looked at her for a while, imagining all the things she was going to experience in her life. As a kid I'd grown up with my sister, and ever since I'd been with my girlfriend: I'd always had girls in my life. Now I had a girl who was closer to me than anything, and I watched her and thought, 'You and me are going to have a good time.' I raced over to get Nile from his nursery school and drove him back to the hospital with the roof down as The Kinks played on the radio. Nile was enthralled with his baby sister, and with the four of us together for the first time, me and Angie had our own tribe. That night The Pretenders played in Manchester at the Apollo and Chrissie dedicated the song 'Kid' to Sonny. My friend Greg Dulli was also playing a show that night in Manchester with his band The Afghan Whigs, and he dedicated a song to Sonny too. She was born to the sound of music and it was a good day for my girl to come into the world.

I loved being a father, and Angie was an amazing mother. Everything we did, we did it together. It was important to me and Angie that our kids were educated, especially as our own schools had been a let-down, and we wanted them to be around as much nature as possible and to pursue all their curiosities and be citizens of the world.

High Court

Electronic were going through a difficult time. Bernard was dealing with some issues with the Haçienda as the gang violence at the club was having serious legal and financial consequences, and he often had to break off from recording to attend meetings that were becoming increasingly stressful. I was being dragged into a lot of meetings at the time too about my old band, as a situation which had been brewing, and which I'd made many attempts to resolve, had now turned into a legal action; depressingly, The Smiths were going to court.

Mike Joyce had served a writ against Morrissey and me, claiming that he was a partner in The Smiths and because there was no agreement to say otherwise he was an equal partner. This was based on the Partnership Act of 1890, which says that unless there is a clear agreement all partnerships are equal;

he was therefore entitled to an equal share of the band's recording and live earnings. Andy was part of this action too, but he settled and agreed to take 10 per cent in the future. My position was that Mike had agreed to 10 per cent of the band's earnings when the band decided the splits on a very emotional day in Pluto Studios in 1983. Mike argued that he never knew what the splits were, and as it had never been written down and signed, he was entitled to 25 per cent of the profits. It turned out in the evidence at trial that, through our disorganisation, the splits had not been consistent. It seemed odd to me that you could be in a band with three other people for five years and not know what everyone's splits were; no one had disputed or rejected the finances at any time during the five years when the band was together.

The Smiths as a band were not equal. People might want to think otherwise, but anyone who was around us in any capacity would tell you that The Smiths were not a band of equals. Morrissey and I formed it, and apart from the first year when Joe was with us we managed it, and usually managers take 20 per cent of a band's income before the band members take their share. We had the legal obligations and the responsibilities, and it was our names on the contracts. We hired everyone and fired everyone, and we ran everything with the record company. Morrissey did all the artwork and I produced most of the records. It would be nice to think that we all did as much as each other, but we didn't, and in that respect it was more like The Kinks, or Kraftwerk, where the two founder members are in charge. It's that way in many other bands, and that's how it was in The Smiths. If Mike Joyce wasn't happy with a 10 per cent share, he should have walked. He should have said, 'I'm not happy about this, get another drummer.'

I was surprised by the legal action, but I wasn't hurt by it. What really baffled me was that he brought this action against me and Morrissey but had continued to play in Morrissey's band after The Smiths had split. Mike and I had been good friends, but now it was just a matter of who was going to dig the most dirt. My instincts told me to get on with playing music, which I did by making a second album with Electronic and working with Pet Shop Boys.

The Smiths met up again in the High Court. I bumped into Morrissey outside the building as we went in, and as surreal as the situation was I was pleased to see him. Then I saw Mike and Andy, which was difficult. I didn't know how to feel. Andy looked shell-shocked and Mike was very friendly. We took our places in an empty courtroom and waited for whatever was going to happen. As I tried to make sense of the situation, I thought about how I'd come to be in a courtroom in a war with three people I used to love. Since I was a kid I'd worked to be a musician. I'd been in different bands as a teenager, getting on buses with amps, and had dedicated my life to it until I was able to form The Smiths. We went on an incredible journey for five years, and made our own kind of music that a lot of people loved, and broke some rules. We'd had amazing success on our own terms, but our modus operandi was dysfunctional on a grand scale and had caused a lot of problems for the group that led to our inevitable demise. I'd travelled a long way, and this band had gone too far.

The people I was with at the court – my manager, barrister and his assistant – were standing next to me, but I thought they were all useless – not because I didn't like them but because they were all outsiders. They weren't there when The Smiths were together. They weren't there when me and Morrissey spent every day chasing up people to do our first demos. They weren't there in the dressing rooms backstage. They weren't there when we worked together on the records, and they weren't there when the band discussed money.

The Fleet Street reporters scurried in and scribbled in their notebooks before proceedings even began, checking every flickering eye movement and scrutinising body language for anything that could be interpreted as drama.

When Morrissey took the stand, it was uncomfortable from the word go. He argued with the judge, who was surly and pompous, and at one point Morrissey lost his temper and walked off the stand in frustration. Mike's barrister made sure he planted a few bombs for the court and the media by putting it to Morrissey that he regarded his bandmates as 'replaceable as parts on a lawnmower'. I watched the reporters as they devoured that phrase and scribbled it down, and a couple of them exited to phone their editor – job done, now everyone had 'the angle'. The phrase became assimilated into the newspaper reports and then the proceedings as if it had been said by Morrissey, which it hadn't: Mike's barrister had planted it. He knew exactly what he was doing and it worked. The judge fell for it, and the press fell for it, then the public fell for it.

I watched the bullshit and it was like being bound and gagged while everyone threw dirt around. For the band to be wrung out like this and put in such a lowly position was degrading, not only because we were arguing over money, but because to me The Smiths were too cool to end up like that. I'd tried to find a way to settle it without having to go to court, but I couldn't achieve a settlement on my own. With each minute I grew more and more disdainful of the whole thing. I didn't respect anyone on either side, including my own. I envisaged the barristers and lawyers sitting around together after the day's hearing, scoring points and exchanging quips about how each other had done. To them it was all in a day's work, and we were just rock stars with unlimited amounts of money that we'd acquired easily in the fame game. They couldn't imagine they were desecrating someone's dream; to them it was 'just business'. Having to listen to the story of The Smiths told in such twisted terms by cunning cronies with no understanding of what a band is about was galling and grotesque. Every bit of love the band had for what it did and for each other was extinguished and interpreted in the worst possible light until there was nothing left. A few weeks before, I'd had to call Joe to inform him that he was required by law to give evidence. He wasn't happy but he attended just the same. He was summoned to the stand, and we all watched as Mike's barrister ripped into him with accusations of deceit and duplicity, because he was known to be close to me and therefore needed to be discredited as comprehensively as possible. Nice.

All four members of the band were called to the stand. I knew there was no point in trying to be clever, and by then I was under no illusions that Morrissey and I might win. I just answered as directly as I could, without letting Mike's barrister succeed in winding me up. I'd been forced to go to court, and I decided that whatever happened I was going to speak up for myself and get the satisfaction of putting a few things straight. At least that way I'd have no regrets and I could walk out of there my own man.

When the judge ruled in Mike's favour, he made a point of sticking it to me and particularly to Morrissey, who he really didn't like, making remarks about him that were personal and fairly shocking. As well as giving Mike everything he'd asked for, he also ruled that Morrissey and I pay for Mike's legal costs, which for the previous seven years had already been paid for by legal aid.

Morrissey mounted an appeal to the Court of Appeal which was unsuccessful, and Mike revised his claim against Morrissey and secured orders on his income and assets. They continued their legal battles for a further eighteen years. I paid my share up in full and have done ever since. I wasn't going to have it in my life any more. I wanted out once and for all. A great thing did come out of that court case though: Joe Moss and I decided we should work together again.

When the hearing was over, I went straight from the court to where Electronic were rehearsing for a show the next day. In the band with me and Bernard were Jimi Goodwin from Doves and Ged Lynch from Black Grape. I was drained and emotional when I walked in, but the band were all waiting by their instruments and gave me a hug. Having just gone through the court case, it felt right to be standing with three good guys in a group. I plugged in my guitar and heard the buzz coming through my amp, the drummer counted off 'Forbidden City' and I started to play. It was the only thing to do.

It was great to be back working with Joe again, and I felt like the returning prodigal son. Although life had changed since we'd last seen each other, our relationship was much the same. He'd come over to the studio and listen to the songs I was working on with Electronic, and we made up for lost time. In the previous couple of years he'd been busy nurturing new bands and setting up a live venue in Manchester called the Night & Day Café. One of Joe's bands was called Haven, who I really liked, and I ended up producing their two albums. I'd had a lot of offers to produce different bands before and had turned them down. It's a real labour of love producing a record for someone else, and you have a responsibility to deliver a magic outcome for the artist. It was great to be back doing something with Joe though.

In LA, I did a session with Beck on his *Midnite Vultures* album. I went into the studio, and after meeting everyone I noticed that there were pictures of Prince all over the place. I took this to be ironic, especially the posters where Prince was wearing women's underwear and a sexy face, but then when I heard the music I realised the posters were for real, as the record was very, very funky. I played on a song called 'Milk and Honey' and on another one called 'The Doctor'. After one session everyone was eager to go to a local bar to see a Van Halen tribute band. It was explained to me that this band, who, except for the singer, looked nothing like Van Halen, were the crème de la crème of eighties poodle-hair tribute bands, so I was in for a treat. As my formative years had been in England in the indie eighties, I didn't quite get the cultural gravitas and importance of Van Halen, and I could only marvel at how enthralled and excited everyone else was, and the joy that these fellas in spandex brought to the faces of my American colleagues. I liked working with Beck. Aside from being supremely talented, he's also very funny, as are his band, and I stayed good friends with his producer, Mickey Petralia.

Boomslang

It's amazing who you meet in an elevator. I've met actors, musicians, footballers, fans and Mancunians on holiday. I was in an elevator in New York when a wiry and intense-looking guy said to me in an English accent, 'I like that new Electronic song.' It was obvious he was a musician from the way he looked and carried himself. I didn't know who he was at first, but something about him was familiar. As we got out of the lift he said, 'See you downstairs,' and after making a couple of calls I went down to the hotel bar, where there were a lot of rock 'n' roll people with laminates and crew T-shirts who all seemed to be involved with The Who. After saying a quick hello to John Entwistle, I sat down at a table with my vaguely familiar new acquaintance, and at that moment I realised who he was.

'Do you play the drums?' I said.

'Yeah, I'm playing with The Who tonight at Madison Square Garden.'

'Right!' I said. 'Are you Zak Starkey?'

I'd heard a lot about Zak over the years. He had a reputation for being an amazing drummer, and I knew his dad was Ringo Starr. Our mutual friend Alan Rogan had told me many times that Zak and I should get together as he thought we'd have a lot in common. My and Zak's friendship took off with supernatural velocity. It was as if we were trying to catch up on every day since we were born. The two of us were really alike. We both knew why our quirks were worth protecting, and we chased down things in life the same way. He was the only person I knew who didn't drink and was into running but was still kick-ass. As a kid he was into music with as mystic a mindset as I had been, and when I was transforming myself with glam and my guitar, he was doing the same with his drums. The only difference was that when I was watching Marc Bolan in *Born to Boogie* on the cinema screen, he was watching it happen in real life on the set. I thought that was brilliant, and he did too, and I thought it was brilliant that he did.

We got together to write some songs. It was just the two of us having a good time with a guitar and drums for a while, and then I remembered that Lee Mavers had told me about a bass player from Liverpool called Edgar 'Summertyme' Jones. I contacted Edgar, and before we knew it the three of us were playing a few times a week and I started to think about having a new group. I wrote some songs and I sang on the demos I made so that when I found a singer all they had to do was just show up and not have to worry about writing the words. I'd heard about a singer from an unsigned band in Manchester and was impressed enough by him to think I'd found the right person to stand out front. I played the guy's CD to Zak and Edgar, and after they heard it Zak said, 'I thought you were going to be the singer.'

'What?' I said.

'We don't need anyone else,' Edgar said. 'He's a bit boring . . . I think your vocals are better.'

I had to think about what they were saying. I respected Zak and Ed's judgement as they really knew what they were doing. We got back to work and all I was thinking was, 'I'm going to front it?'

Me and Angie and the kids had moved into a house in Cheshire called Forest Edge. It was run-down and funky when we got it, and the place needed fixing up and some love. The house had been built in the 1920s by the chairman of Rolls-Royce and had beautiful gardens and a courtyard, and outside the front gate was a 200-acre deer park. Forest Edge was the classic 'rock guitar player's pile in the country', or more accurately 'indie guitar player's pile in the country' – like Jimmy Page if he had signed to Rough Trade. We didn't have a moat, but we did have a big recording studio on the grounds and our own woodland. It was a wonderland for the kids. As with everywhere else Angie and I had lived, our house became the HQ for whatever I was working on, and over the years our place had been used by The The, New Order, Pet Shop Boys, The Charlatans and Oasis, as well as quite a few others who I let use the studio because I liked them. Nile and Sonny grew up around artists and musicians, and the other kids in the neighbourhood liked to come over to our place because there was always interesting things going on and a big black Newfoundland dog called Boogie. It was good for whoever I was working with too, as my musician friends had the benefit of a proper studio while being around a family atmosphere and curious children. My personal life always followed the direction of my artistic path, whatever it meant and wherever it took me, and luckily for me, my family wouldn't have it any other way. Our home was a residential studio often populated by interesting people, all of whom were great, and some of whom were sometimes a bit crazy, including me.

In 1999, Bernard and I made the final Electronic album, *Twisted Tenderness*. It was a much more guitar-orientated record, and I had a really good time making it. It had been nine years since we'd started working together as Electronic, and in that time we'd done everything we'd set out to do and more. Not touring had worked out fine for me, as I was able to be around for my kids, which is a luxury for a musician, although I did pretty much live in the studio. I was working on a lot of different things during this time with a lot of different people, and I'd taken my interests in technology to the limit and learned all the ways of making records. It was time now for me to get back out on the road with a band, and Bernard felt the same way about reconvening with New Order.

As always, I was looking to do something different. I was listening to the psychedelic bands of the sixties, and the German bands commonly referred to as 'Krautrock', especially Faust, with their combination of tranced-out slink and pastoral spaciness. I wanted to play songs that were hypnotic, and in one of our meetings Zak declared, 'We should have a two-hour set list, with just five long songs on it, and be lucky if we get through three.'

The mindset I was in was reflected in the books I was reading. Madame Blavatsky, Gurdjieff and P. D. Ouspensky opened my imagination to a lot of concepts and possibilities. I liked the imagery of esotericism. The language intrigued me, and the more material I devoured, the more it influenced my life and my thinking. I wanted to know everything about it, and when I found Aldous Huxley he became my absolute favourite writer and thinker. I collected first editions and tracked down tapes of his lectures, and the more I found out about his work, the more I had to explore. It was interesting to me that in spite of the fact that he got better as he got older, Huxley's reputation rests on the work he did in the first half of his career, and as masterful as *Brave New World* is, it's comparatively slight compared to the towering achievements of *The Perennial Philosophy* and the essays and lectures in the second half of his life for which he is far less known. The culture surrounding *The Doors of Perception* is a legacy which is much less than Huxley deserves, and it illustrates the reductive nature of fame and how you can become defined by something you did in your youth, despite doing work in later life that's equally substantial.

Through all my reading and thinking, I kept coming across a word: *healers*. I was reading Blavatsky's *The Secret Doctrine*, and the word jumped out at me as a great band name. I remembered a conversation I'd had with Keith Richards about bands with good names, and having informed him that 'The Rolling Stones' was pretty much as good as it gets, we both agreed that Little Richard's 'The Upsetters' and Bob Marley's 'The Wailers' were decent contenders. I thought the name 'The Healers' was perfect, and I decided I wanted it to be the name of my new band. I told Joe and Zak about it, and they suggested that it should have my name attached to the front to make it more commercial. I saw the logic in it and agreed, but I secretly plotted to drop my name from it once people knew who we were.

The Healers was an experiment to break out of the 'four guys with guitars' format. It was liberating to be part of a large group, and the line-up grew with the addition of Liz Bonney on percussion and Lee Spencer on synthesisers. We were all set to start playing when Edgar Jones left to join Paul Weller's band, but after a recommendation from Noel Gallagher we enlisted Alonza Bevan from the recently defunct Kula Shaker on bass, and with the addition of a second guitar player from Manchester called Adam Gray, The Healers were one big, happy, six-piece electro space-rock family ready to sneak out into the world.

Going out as the frontman with The Healers was a step into the unknown, and because we hadn't put out any songs yet, none of the fans or press knew what I would be doing. My plan was to develop the band's sound by doing it live and I adopted the philosophy 'I'll do what I feel like, even if it means the audience have no idea what's going on'. It's a noble idea, but a bit of a drawback when you're known for doing something else entirely, and people definitely wondered why

I was standing in the middle of a bunch of space-rock trippers. I was also asked a lot about how daunting it was to be the frontman, as if by migrating from lowly stage left into the glory of centre stage I would dissolve under the blaze of the spotlight. I wasn't daunted, but at the beginning I had no idea how it was going to go – I hadn't been the frontman since I was a kid. I'd heard John Lee Hooker say that when he was onstage he would get the feeling from the audience and give it back amplified, and when they gave that back again he would amplify it some more. It sounded like a good strategy. I employed it and it worked out well. I liked fronting my own band, and it helped that they were all heavyweight people. The shows were loud and loose, and the audiences were with me.

As it turned out it I made my actual debut out front with Chrissie Hynde and The Pretenders backing me, at the Linda McCartney tribute concert at the Royal Albert Hall in April 1999. After playing with The Pretenders, I then played a couple of songs with Marianne Faithfull and then played again with Paul McCartney.

Going out with The Healers was good, and felt very natural. I would always work at getting better, same as I try to do with everything, and it was the next new road to creative possibilities.

Bert Jansch had been out of the public eye for a long time when I met him. He continued to be a great musician, performing low-key shows and putting out records through the eighties and nineties, but as far as the music scene and certainly the media went, Bert conducted his career well below the radar and without the need for critical validation. He was someone who'd really inspired me in my formative years, and had done the same for Jimmy Page, Neil Young and Bernard Butler, along with a legion of other guitar players. His influence had stayed with me throughout my career, and I'd borrowed his style for 'Unhappy Birthday' and 'Back to the Old House' by The Smiths.

Bernard Butler and I had become good friends and I thought of him as a kindred spirit. Bernard told me that Bert Jansch was playing a show in a little room in the basement of a pub in Crouch End and suggested that we go along. We watched in awe and due reverence along with Bert's loyal following – who Bernard dubbed 'the Muswell Bills and Muswell Jills' – as Bert moved brilliantly through his repertoire of old classics and introduced some good new songs too.

When Bert had finished and was packing his guitar away, Bernard said to me, 'Go and say hello to him.'

'What?' I replied.

'Go . . .' he said, now enunciating very slowly, like he was taking to an old-age pensioner, 'over . . . and introduce yourself.'

'OK,' I said meekly, and I shuffled towards the man who had been an enigmatic figure in my imagination for years. 'Hi . . . Bert?' I muttered.

Bert stopped what he was doing and looked up at me. 'Yeah?' he enquired with a stern look on his face.

'I'm Johnny Marr, and I'm . . . er, a guitar player. I . . . just wanted . . . to say great show and . . . I'm a big fan . . .'

At that point Bernard came over to bail me out. He'd met

Bert before, and gamely attempted to get a bit of conversation going between his suddenly very inarticulate friend and his friend's hero. After our first awkward meeting, Bert and I became very friendly. I would visit him and his wife Loren at their house in Kilburn and we'd play guitar together. Bert's reputation for being uncommunicative and terse wasn't accurate; he just wasn't into small talk. He had a lot to say about a lot of things. He told me about hitching around France in his early years, and about tracking down guitars and guitar players as a young man in Edinburgh, and he also talked a lot about the beatnik scene he'd found himself at the centre of in London in the early sixties. One of the first questions I asked him was whether, when he was in Pentangle and they were playing their hybrid psych folk music, they thought the so-called 'heavy' bands were really lightweight posers, the way I had imagined? He smiled; he'd never been asked that before. He picked up his tea and, still grinning, he said, 'What do you think?'

Bert and I talked a lot, and about serious things. I was honoured that he thought highly of me and that he valued our friendship. He was a discerning soul with an authentic cool, and as with Joe Moss I sensed Bert saw something in me that I didn't see myself. I always felt good after I'd spent time with him. We communicated some deeper things when we played guitar together, and the playing was often really wild. One of us would pick up on the atmosphere in the room and start a riff, and the other would join in. Once we'd established what we were doing, we'd both start to take the music further out until we were on a journey together. When we got to a place that was pretty or heavy, we'd stay on it until we'd had just enough, then we'd move on somewhere else and where we'd been was gone. Sometimes these guitar excursions were long, and other times we'd just go out for a little spin. Wherever we went, though, was always good.

Once when he was on the road, he came to stay at my house. He arrived when Angie was out, and we were playing our guitars in the kitchen when she came in. Angie was a fan of Bert's, and it was the first time she'd met him. He and I were in the middle of an intense improvisation, and as I looked up from my guitar she was standing behind him, wide-eyed and mouthing the words, 'OH ... MY ... GOD! IT'S BERT ... JANSCH! OH ... MY ... GOD!!' She was dumbstruck. I had never seen her as impressed. She really knows her guitar music and hadn't heard us improvising before. She's always said that it was the best guitar she's ever heard me play.

In 2000, The Healers played at the Scala Cinema in London. I walked off the stage at the end of the show, and five minutes later my guitar tech ran into the dressing room, ashen-faced and shouting, 'Where's your guitar? I think your guitar's been stolen!' The house lights went up and everyone scurried about, looking for my Gibson SG, which I'd played throughout the whole tour. I knew it was gone. It being London there were a lot of guests filing into the dressing room, and what was supposed to be a celebration was turning into a wake as everybody came to say how sorry they were about my guitar being stolen. The police came, and on the security-camera footage we saw a guy walking out of the front doors with the rest of the audience, holding my guitar as if it were normal. It was amazing: he'd just clambered up onstage, taken it and walked out.

Even if you're very lucky and you get to own a lot of guitars, you still get very attached to an instrument. I choose the guitars I use not only for the sound or the way they make me play but also because I have an instinct about them. You get a feeling for a model you think you need to play, and when you find the one that clicks you love it. I go through things with my guitar like it's a companion. Standing backstage, waiting to go on, I'm playing it, locking in with it, and thinking about me and the guitar. When you turn up at a recording session, your guitar needs to deliver something for you. I'd been playing that SG exclusively, and when the realisation hit me that it was actually gone, I was depressed. Since I'd been a kid I always thought that anyone who could steal a musician's instrument was lower than the low. I issued a statement with the promise of a reward for any information leading to the return of my guitar but heard nothing back. It was on the national news, and I had guitar dealers all over the country calling me to say they were on the lookout.

I was in a taxi going through Hyde Park a couple of days later when I heard about the theft of my guitar on the radio. I told the driver to turn around and take me to where Bert lived in Kilburn, and when I got out of the cab I really hoped that he'd be there. He answered the door and I sat down with him and told him about my guitar being stolen. He sat quietly, and when I was finished telling him he looked at me for a few seconds and said, 'You'll find another one.' I knew he was right, he had such serenity about him. I finally felt a Zen-like acceptance of the situation, and it became a perfect lesson in detachment that the Dalai Lama himself couldn't have matched, even if he'd had his guitar stolen and he knew Bert Jansch.

I did get another guitar that I loved, and people would sometimes ask me about my stolen SG. Ten years later, I was in Toronto when I got a call from Joe. A policeman who was a fan had taken it upon himself to try to find out what had happened to it. After putting the word out for months, he eventually got a tip-off about a guy who had once claimed to have had a guitar that was mine. The policeman followed up the information and went to investigate it. He found the guy and in his apartment was my guitar. I'd finally got it back.

The lifestyle I'd fallen into had started to be not good. Over the previous few years I'd got into the habit of drinking on a night-after-night basis, and night after night turned into week after week and month after month. Staying up in the studio, getting together with friends, hanging out with whoever, or even on my own, had become habitually accompanied by booze, and even though I never drank in the day, whenever I heard myself say 'I never drink in the day', I knew I was actually saying 'I drink every night', and that became an issue for me.

I knew a couple of people who didn't drink. I noticed that they didn't look like death in the morning and never needed to apologise for saying some stupid shit the night before. I hated the idea of falling into the cliché of the middle-aged rocker, hanging out in my friends' dressing room drunk. It's messy, and it was not a vision I had for myself. I thought about it a lot and I knew I had to change, but it took me a while to get my head right. Society is set up so that everybody drinks, and it's unusual if you don't join in. I was lucky in that I've always liked to change, and once I saw that I was giving myself the gift of freedom from something that was no longer fun, and giving myself something good, as opposed to thinking that I was denying myself something nice, I kicked drinking into touch for ever and never looked back.

When I stopped drinking, I would meet people who would often assume that because I didn't drink I must have suffered a 'my drink-and-drugs hell', especially because I'm a musician. They would hear I didn't drink and imagine that I'd spent the eighties dangling my children off a roof with Ozzy Osbourne, which I didn't. I like not drinking, and I'm not one of those people who have to be cosseted from other people's partying. The other thing that happens when you quit drinking is that some of your friends start acting weird and getting paranoid about being drunk because they think you're going to judge them. I wouldn't judge anyone, and I doubt I could ever be a puritan. Other people's choices are their own business, although as a drug I don't think booze has ever managed to make anyone cooler. I've stayed up late all of my life and I still do, and if I'm having a good time with people who are drinking at 4 a.m. and it's funny or interesting, I'm right there. If, however, I'm stuck with some fucked-up person who's telling me the same thing over and over again, then I'll look at my watch and get out of there and I'm already into tomorrow.

The Healers' album was called *Boomslang*, after a dream I had about a snake, which I took as symbolic because of the idea of snakes being unpredictable and shedding their skin. I had the songs all worked out before I recorded them by playing them live, but before the record was finished I felt I needed to capture a particular feeling that was around me at the time and had become a concept in my mind for the whole of the summer. The idea was to cross the sexuality of the blues with the eroticism of electronica. I was staying with The Healers' electronics wizard Lee Spencer and percussionist Liz Bonney in London, and I came up with a song called 'You Are the Magic'. When we finished the recording, I had a seventy-minute 'aural movie' that was essentially a soundtrack for psychedelic sex. I intended to release the song in its full form and may still do it some day. The Healers' album was finished in 2003, and 'You Are the Magic', 'The Last Ride', 'Bangin' On' and 'Down on the Corner' represent what my life sounded like at that time.

I'd take time out from music by going snowboarding, and escape to Canada or France with Angie and the kids to get energised. These vacations were a lot of fun – precious time that I'd spend with my family and get away from everything. The mountains provided a different mentality and outlook from the music business. It's a good thing for the mind as well as the body to get away from the obsessive nature of being an artist, and as anyone who's ever been on a snowboard will tell you, it takes a mindful approach and plenty of physical attentiveness to go to the top of a mountain and throw yourself down on a piece of plastic, hurtling at top speed.

The End of a Perfect Day

When the phone rings at an unusual hour, you get a fleeting sense of dread. I heard about Kirsty MacColl's death from my friend Matt, who guessed that I might not know and thought I should hear it from a friend before I heard it on the news. I couldn't believe it. She'd been killed by a powerboat while she was out swimming with her sons? It couldn't be right, no, no, it wasn't right. Kirsty had been scuba diving in Mexico with her two boys when a powerboat owned by a rich business tycoon had sailed illegally at high speed into designated safe waters and killed her. The last thing she did was to push the boys out of the way and save their lives, but she couldn't save herself. I'd spoken with Kirsty not too long before. All I could think about was the upbeat conversation we'd had and how well things were going in her life. She had a partner, James, who she adored, and she'd finally got over the stage fright which had plagued her for years and was loving playing shows and singing onstage. I could tell she felt loved, not only by James but by music fans, and as her mate I was pleased for her because she really deserved it and I knew music fans did love her. Kirsty and I always talked about writing more songs together, and I was proud of the records we'd made. She had been kind to me when she let me live in her flat when I was in The Smiths, and she was a good friend who would call you out if you were being a dick. Her death hit me really hard, and was made all the worse because of how it happened. It's bad enough to lose someone through illness or even from a tragic accident, but that she was killed by an act that was suspect and should've been avoided was a tough thing to accept. She really was a magnetic person, and my eternal memory of her will be of when I was round at her house and she'd entertain us by playing her favourite records while she danced around and sang along. She would lose herself in 'Surf's Up' or 'See My Baby Jive', and it was a lovely thing to see her carried away by her passion for melody. It was a privilege to know her, and when she died I felt, like all her friends did, that me and Kirsty just weren't done.

Shortly after Kirsty's death, I went out to LA and stayed in the Hollywood Hills, where Aldous Huxley lived. I had started to feel unwell and I didn't know why. I stayed on my own in California for a couple of weeks and read and tried to get better. I would look out at the view of the city at night and think about life in the music business. I've always felt lucky to do what I love, and I have done since even before I was in The Smiths. When you follow a path that's a vocation, without ever stopping to question why, you can sometimes get caught up in other considerations and forget that what you're doing is about expressing something that's in you. Some people do it through painting and some people do it through acting, and if you have something that connects with other people then you're lucky. Through music, the people who follow you have something of you in their life, and in some ways they're like you, even if they think they're just a fan. It was a strange time, and I needed to think about what I was doing. I wasn't getting better and my symptoms were getting worse. I'd developed a constant cough, even though I no longer smoked, and I seemed to be walking around with a slightly high temperature. At first I thought I might shake it off, but then it rocketed into a full-blown fever with freezing-cold sweats. I got to a doctor who recommended that I get home as quickly as possible. On the plane back to England, I was in bad shape. As soon as I got to the doctor in England he told me that I had pleurisy, and if I could I should lie in front of a fire for a few weeks, wrapped in blankets, until I got better – that or go into hospital for a while. I did as he said and sat in front of a fire with a blanket around me every day. It was bad news. I was freezing and shivering and felt like I had a truck parked on top of me. After a couple of weeks I started to get better and then I'd have an occasional relapse for a day or two, which was worrying, but slowly I came out of it and got back to normal.

One evening I got a phone call from Neil Finn, who I'd met at the Linda McCartney concert in London. He was planning to put on a week of shows in Auckland with his friends and favourite musicians, and wanted to know if I'd fly over to play the concerts with him. I wasn't sure that I was ready to get on a plane and fly to the other side of the world after recently being sick. I was planning on lying low for a while, but after hearing Neil's new solo record *One Nil* and really liking it, I decided to go.

Angie and I flew out to New Zealand, and on the plane were Ed O'Brien and Phil Selway from Radiohead. It was good to meet them and we compared notes on the songs we needed to learn for the week of shows. It was an intriguing prospect. Neil Finn's shows have been known to be spontaneous and free-flowing, and he sometimes selects whatever song he feels like from his catalogue. It means that as a musician playing behind him you have to be on your toes and sound like you know what you're doing, but it's also stimulating and a lot of fun.

When we got to Auckland, Neil and his wife Sharon welcomed us into their world and the feeling around their family and all the musicians was positive and warm. In the band with Ed O'Brien and Phil Selway were my friend Sebastian Steinberg from Soul Coughing, a songwriter and singer who I loved called Lisa Germano, and Neil's long-time friend Eddie Vedder from Pearl Jam. The shows were sold out and due to start three days later, and Neil let it slip that we would be playing around twenty-eight songs and also filming the gigs. We rehearsed each day for around twelve hours, and I took advantage of the jet lag by waking up at around 5 a.m. to start learning some of the songs on my own. When the day of the first show came, the whole of Auckland

Joe looked after me from when I was eighteen.

With Bert Jansch, 2003. 'We communicated when we played together.'

Above: The Healers.
Ardwick Green Park.

Dr Johnny,
The Night Tripper, 2003.

Left: Modest Mouse: 'The best time of my life.' Tom Peloso, Joe Plumber, Jeremiah Green, Eric Judy, Isaac Brock.

Left: 'Hey!... Busy!'

Below: 'On our nautical balalaika carnival to who knows where'.

The Cribs. 'I had to concentrate to not get swept away by the cyclone howling around me.'

'Pop music doesn't get much more powerful than that.'

The Messenger, 2013.

With Angie. Ivor Novello Awards, 2010.

My band. Iwan Gronow, Jack Mitchell and James Doviak.

Above: 'David Cameron, stop saying that you like The Smiths, no you don't. I forbid you to like it.'

Left: There's no substitute for experience.

Playing on Noel's album *Chasing Yesterday* in 2014.
'It was obvious that he had a vision he had to follow.'

'Being the best live band seemed a good ambition.'

knew about it. People stopped me in the street and shouted from their cars as I walked to the theatre, and it occurred to me just what an amazing thing it is to have people on the other side of the planet know who you are just because of the way you play the guitar.

The musicians went under the collective name of 'The Seven Worlds Collide' and everybody involved had to be on exactly the same wavelength to make it all work. It was ambitious, but Neil's so good up front that with the right intention and some luck it promised to be a pretty special event. When I walked on for the first night, my head was swimming with titles and key changes for all the music I'd just learned. At the soundcheck, Neil asked me if I'd mind playing a Smiths song. I'd not played a Smiths song since the band split, and I hadn't intended to. The idea spun me out at first, but I had to make a quick decision and I realised that I had to be OK about the past and that The Smiths are my legacy. When we played 'There Is a Light That Never Goes Out', everyone went crazy. It was a nice thing to give that song back to the audience and to give it back to myself, and I have Neil to thank for it.

After the shows in Auckland we all felt like we'd really gone through something together, and the friendships Angie and I made with the Finn family and the other musicians have been long-lasting. In Ed O'Brien I found another kindred spirit, who as a musician has gone from strength to strength with Radiohead and who remains one of my closest friends.

I was burned out by the time Zak and I had taken The Healers back around the world again. I needed to find some new inspiration and make some new memories somewhere, and I wanted to change my story. I decided to go to Morocco and see what might happen. I'd always wanted to go to Tangier because writers and artists like Paul Bowles, William Burroughs and Christopher Gibbs had lived there, so Angie and I packed up and headed out to an ancient riad on the edge of the desert. When I was out in Morocco, I got into nutrition and started studying metabolism and practising meditation. I wanted to see if the isolation could take me to another place in myself and in my life. I would go up on the roof when the sun came up, watch the Atlas mountains in the distance and shed the effects of the touring and studios. I was determined to change my lifestyle beyond just not drinking, and find a fresh perspective to take me into the future. I'd long since grown out of any interest in drugs, and I wanted to try to rid myself of as much toxicity as possible. I made every effort to disengage with any media as much as I could, to see what effect if any it might have on my life. Everyone seemed to be hooked on the world news. I avoided all newspapers and any television, and it was interesting to discover that I didn't feel uninformed about anything that I thought was important. It was liberating, and I figured that anything I really needed to know I would get to hear about eventually.

One evening, I was sitting on the roof looking out at the dusty red road that stretched out towards the mountains and it seemed like a good place to run. I didn't think about it too much, I just went out and started running and it felt natural. I was enjoying the novelty of it, and I told myself that I could stop any time, and pretty soon I forgot it was supposed to be difficult. I kept looking ahead and soon I fell into a rhythm, just noticing my breathing and the sound of my feet hitting the floor. I've been hearing music in my head for as long as I can remember, and noticing the stillness and quiet of my surroundings with the silhouettes of the palm trees scattered around felt good with every step. When I got back I made a pact with myself to go again the next day. They say that it takes eight times for something to become a habit and eight weeks to become a lifestyle. I started running every day and it became a habit, then it became a lifestyle that, no matter how hard it might get now and then, I have never regretted.

When I got back from Morocco things had changed and my regime gave me a new kind of idea about who I could be. I liked not drinking, and not drinking made getting healthy a lot easier, if only for the fact I no longer had to deal with hangovers. People think that if you get into fitness you have to deprive yourself of all the things you like, but if you're super-fit you can eat whatever you want and drink as much as you like and stay up late. You just tend to not want to do those things because you're feeling too good to bother with them. As for any idea that getting healthy means that you automatically become conservative or 'straight', that's complete nonsense. If anything, getting super-fit gave me more attitude and sped me right up.

Portland

I n 2005, Joe came over to see me because he'd had an unexpected enquiry from the American band Modest Mouse,
who wanted to know if I'd be interested in joining them. It
was a strange thing: I'd been given a lot of music on The
Healers' tour by a friend who thought I'd like the bands on
the current American scene, and I'd been listening exclusively
to Lilys and Yeah Yeah Yeahs, and particularly Broken Social
Scene and Modest Mouse. The new American bands gave me
a renewed enthusiasm for current guitar music and provided
a perfect antidote to the UK's post-Britpop scene, which aside
from a couple of bands I considered to be something of a
dead-end, one-way street.

I was intrigued by Modest Mouse. When I hear something
for the first time, I'm usually able to identity the influences in
it, but with Modest Mouse I couldn't put my finger on what

it was they were doing, I just liked it. It seemed to oscillate between some kind of bleak poetic emotion from an American landscape one minute, to tough confrontation and then the absurdity of life the next. I loved the imagery in the words and the way it was built on guitars. It could only have come from America, which at the time sounded like a good thing to me.

I got a call from the band's leader and frontman, Isaac Brock. We had a long discussion and he invited me over to Portland, Oregon, to join the band straight away. It was an unusual conversation. Isaac was a total stranger, calling me out of the blue, but having heard his music I was curious about him as a musician. He was engaging and he had a strong vision for what he wanted to do. We agreed to talk again, and after giving it some thought I proposed that we get together for a writing period in Portland to see how it turned out.

I looked forward to visiting Portland. It was somewhere I'd liked when I'd been on tour, and I'd never had enough time to really see it. I was aware of its reputation as one of the more liberal-minded American cities, and the singer-songwriter Elliott Smith had told me a lot about it when I'd met him a few years before, as he was living there at the time. I thought playing with Modest Mouse could be good, but I purposefully avoided absorbing myself in their music from then on, as I wanted to bring my own sound and sensibility to it. It was an interesting prospect and might be an adventure, but before I could go I had something else to do.

Patti Smith had invited me to play at the Meltdown Festival she was curating in London. She'd been an inspiration since the night I stood at the front of the stage at the Apollo as a fourteen-year-old boy. I got to the Royal Festival Hall with my band and I was introduced to Roy Harper, who was also on the bill. I was a fan of Roy's music and I was pleased to meet him, then I discovered Neil Finn was in London to play, so I invited him on stage to do a couple of songs. During the soundcheck, Patti's guitar player and band leader Lenny Kaye suggested that he and Patti and Roy join me in my encore. Patti came to the stage to say hello, and I thanked her for filling up my mind with *Radio Ethiopia* in the mornings before I went to school and I told her how she'd been a connection between me and Morrissey when I formed The Smiths. She was happy to hear about it and told me she was pleased how things had turned out, and when it came to the encore I played a Strawbs song called 'Lay Down', with Patti Smith singing on my mic on one side of me and Roy Harper singing on the other, and I wondered what I'd done for things to have gone so right.

When I went out to Portland, I didn't have any idea about how things were going to go with Modest Mouse. To some people it could seem like eccentric behaviour to just up sticks and travel 4,000 miles, seemingly on a whim, to go and play with a band I'd never met before, just as I was about to record my own album, but to me I was doing what I'd done since being a kid, and following a musical instinct. In the back of my mind I was prepared for it to not work out, but something told me that if it did work then it could be really great. I knew a few people who had had some dealings with the band, and the words that kept coming up were *brilliance* and *unpredictable*, which seemed OK to me, and made the prospect all the more intriguing.

I checked into the hotel and unpacked my bags and Isaac came over to take me to his house so that we could start writing straight away. We were talking on the journey from the hotel, and it turned out that the things I'd done that he liked most were the songs with Talking Heads. It was unusual for me to be better known for something I'd done after The Smiths, and I was excited about what we might do together.

The two of us set up facing each other, and I noticed that Isaac played full volume through a Fender Super Six amp, which is three times the size of a usual amp and was pointing right at me. I knew that my regular Fender Deluxe would never compete, so I plugged into one of his spare Super Sixes so we were even. As I did, I spotted a black Fender Jaguar guitar on a stand, gathering dust. I liked the look of it and I asked Isaac if he'd mind me using it. A jug of wine then appeared next to Isaac, and the two of us switched on and started playing, full blast and full assault.

Twenty minutes later we were improvising manically and blasting riffs at each other. I was starting to feel woozy as the journey and jet lag came down on me, and things began to get surreal. Isaac put on a 1940s flying cap and goggles, and halfway through playing he stopped and came three inches up to my face and asked, 'Got any riffs?' I liked his directness, no messing about, and I did have a riff. It was something I'd been playing in Morocco that was funky and jerky, and I started to play it. Something about playing the Fender Jaguar made the riff lift off, and Isaac grabbed a mic and started singing words from straight out of the air – '*Well it should've been, could've been, worse than you would ever know, the dashboard melted but we still had the radio*' and then reeled off a stream of verses about a car tearing down a mountain with bits falling off but it was all OK because we still had the radio. Verses went by as he sang a complete song in his flying cap and his goggles. I liked it. I'd never seen anyone reel off verse after verse like this before: '*The windshield was broken but I like the fresh air you know?*' I liked playing the Fender Jag too, it felt like the guitar I had been looking for all my life, and we developed the song until the two of us were a bit crazy with volume, wine and jet lag.

'Have you got any more riffs?' asked Isaac, and as it turned out I did, and we both dived into it with heedless enthusiasm. Another lyric appeared: '*We've got everything, we've got everything, we crashed in like waves into the stars.*' It was 3 a.m. and I'd been going for about twenty-eight hours. 'We've Got Everything' sounded like another good song to me, and we were joined by a member of Modest Mouse called Tom Peloso, who started playing a trumpet and a synth.

Back at the hotel, I was awake after a couple of hours, wondering where I was. As I came round I realised that I may have written a couple of really good songs for Modest Mouse with someone who wasn't a stranger to me any more. We arranged to get together early the next day, by which time I was feeling like it was time for bed, and we listened to what we'd done the night before. It appeared that the Portland experiment might work out.

The plan for the next few days was that the other members of Modest Mouse were going to arrive one by one, and we would eventually all be playing together to work on the new songs.

Tom Peloso, who was the band's multi-instrumentalist, was already with us, and Joe Plummer was the first of the two drummers to arrive, followed by Eric Judy and Jeremiah Green, the bass player and drummer who had formed the band with Isaac in 1992. It's a slightly odd situation arriving with your guitar into an existing group of tight-knit people. The first thing you want to do is assure everyone that you're all right and don't think you're a big shot. All the guys in Modest Mouse were intuitive and smart and very welcoming, and they liked the songs that Isaac and I had already started writing. Since I was young I'd usually avoided standing in a room and hoping that songs might happen just by simply jamming. I learned that it can often lead to hours of aimless meandering, and it had actually been a motivation for me to learn how to write songs in the first place. With Modest Mouse the atmosphere around everyone was easy-going but still creative enough to be pulling music from out of the ether, which is what started to happen.

I'd work every day with the band and always go through a woozy zone of jet lag in the evening. I'd play through it and use it as a surreal and creative state of mind. It helped that the vibe around Modest Mouse was a mix of punk rock, comic, stoner, testosterone and alcohol, with some costumes thrown in, and it was all just part of being in the band. As well as riffs and some jumping-off points for songs, a contribution I made to the process was buying a big cheap cassette recorder from Radio Shack, which I carried with me at all times. The band would take a cigarette break, and if I noticed someone messing around on their instrument alone, in a way that sounded good, I'd record it and then we'd all work on it together. Throughout the days these little ideas would develop between two or three different permutations of the band, like little fires starting around the room, then the others would hover around and join in bit by bit and eventually we'd have a blazing bonfire. I would record everything and we'd pick through it, and then we'd break it down and then play it again.

A few days in, I decided I was with a really good bunch of people. We were playing one afternoon, and as I listened to what we were doing it occurred to me that I had no idea what this music actually was. One of the drummers was playing trashy, the other drummer was doing something completely different, the bass playing sounded like it was from a Celtic tune and the keyboards were a sea shanty. On top of it all, Isaac's guitar was raging mad punk rock and I was doing something punchy and melodic. I was playing in this band and I still didn't know what the music was. All I knew was that it sounded good and it felt great, and that's a rare thing, especially when you've been doing it a long time.

I'd go back to the hotel each night around 1 a.m., sleep for a few hours and then wake up. It was the start of a sleep-deprived, Mid-Atlantic state of mind that would stay with me for the next few years. I always had the tapes of the jams with me, and I'd get up in the night and listen back to what we'd done and start working out some ideas for the next day. When it got light outside, I'd put on my running gear and get out to explore Portland. I was starting to really enjoy the place: it had all the things I liked about America and a refreshing lack of the things that I didn't. There wasn't much busy traffic around, and the downtown skyline looked American enough but wasn't imposing and dominating as some American cities can be. The river that divides Portland into east and west was wide and pretty, and I'd run for miles along its broad paths, going south to north, and then cross over whichever one of the beautiful bridges took my fancy. Every day was a new experience, both with the band and with the city. I ran each morning around a place I was starting to love, knowing that I'd be making great new music with new people.

All of the guys in Modest Mouse were interesting. Joe Plummer, who played drums, showed me around and introduced me to everyone, which I appreciated as I didn't know anyone in Portland at that point. We got friendly straight away and had a lot in common, and he also introduced me to things that were going on in the American art scene. Tom Peloso, who played everything from stand-up bass to lap steel guitars and synths, showed me the town at night in his car, a beat-up Ford which he'd bought for $500 from a guy at the side of the road and that I named 'The Duchess', and every night after practice we'd cruise over bridges and through the streets downtown, listening to classical music. Tom was from Virginia, and through him I got to know about the new-time old-time Appalachian music, which I was able to relate to because of Ireland and knowing a bit about country music. Jeremiah Green was one of the most innovative musicians I'd

369

ever heard. His approach to drumming was totally unique, and he played with a creativity that he applied to pretty much everything in his life. Eric Judy was the roots of the band, and through him I got a sense of the story behind it all. Eric welcomed me into the band in a way that was really warm and genuine, and like all good musicians his personality came through in his playing. Having Isaac as the leader meant things were always going to be lively. He's extremely creative and likes it when things are on the edge; he hates it when life gets boring. Isaac and I worked out an approach to our guitar playing from the very first night where we would both be full tilt but could still complement each other. I would listen very closely as we both played off one another at high volume, and it felt like two race cars going around a track – sometimes we'd physically bump into each other. It was exciting to play and it was exciting to hear, and it gave us our own style that was as powerful as any guitar band I've heard.

After one week of me being with Modest Mouse, everybody knew it was really happening. When you all work intensely and you feel like there's a lot at stake, you go through something together and it becomes a brotherhood. The band wanted me to join and I felt I belonged. I went back to England as planned, and we arranged for me to get back to Portland as soon as possible. We were on a mission, and I was looking forward to seeing the songs through. Angie, Nile and Sonny were with me as I played the tapes at home, and the Marrs were all on board the good ship Modest Mouse.

While I'd been in Portland I'd heard from Joe that Andy Rourke was trying to contact me. It had been almost ten years since Andy and I had seen each other in court, and I got Joe to pass on my number. Andy sent me a text that said, *Hi Johnny. I hope everything's going well. I think we should be friends.* It was a nice thing. I was happy that we could be above the old Smiths dramas that had happened, and we arranged to meet in the Night & Day Café in Manchester before I went back to Portland to rejoin Modest Mouse.

It was good to see Andy again, if a little strange. So much had happened at the end of The Smiths that there was a lot to get over. I assumed that the reason Andy had decided to get back in touch was because our friendship meant something to him, and after sitting down to talk we knew each other well enough to see that we were still the same people.

He was on good form, having put his demons behind him many years before, and I appreciated that he'd taken the initiative to make a reconciliation happen. We spent the day catching up and reminiscing, and at the end we agreed to do it again and stay in touch. A few weeks later I heard from Andy again. He was putting a big concert together to raise money for the Christie cancer treatment hospital in Manchester, and he invited me to join the bill. It was an ambitious enterprise and a great cause, and I was impressed and proud of him for doing it. New Order were also playing, and I agreed to appear and asked Andy to come onstage to do a song with me. I put a version of The Healers together with a great musician I'd heard about called James Doviak on second guitar and keyboards, and we did a set of some new solo songs I'd written and also a couple of Smiths songs. When it came to 'How Soon Is Now?', I introduced Andy onstage. It was the first time we'd played together since the final Smiths show in Brixton, and everybody in the place went wild. I was playing with my friend who I'd been in bands with since we were schoolboys, and who'd been there when I'd first got together with Angie and when the police had me up against the wall. It was a good moment for us and a good moment for Smiths fans, and it put things behind us in the best way we knew how.

I went to Mississippi with Modest Mouse to record our album. A U-Haul truck arrived outside Isaac's house for us to pack up all our equipment, and I wondered aloud why American bands didn't have roadies. We loaded up our amplifiers, organs, banjos, synthesisers, guitars and two drum kits, and then our lead singer climbed into the driver's seat and he drove the 2,000-mile journey with the band's gear to meet us in Mississippi to make the new album. I was amazed to be in a band with a frontman who would drive the band's gear across America to make a record, but it was symbolic of the way that Modest Mouse had stuck to their original ethos, regardless of their success, and an example of the authenticity of the man who made records called 'Interstate 8', 'Truckers Atlas' and 'This Is a Long Drive for Someone with Nothing to Think About'.

Oxford, Mississippi, is a pretty town in the county of Lafayette, and is known mostly for being the home town of William Faulkner. We were going to stay for a couple of months, in rooms that were once barns and stables, on the grounds of an old Southern country house. The album was to be called *We Were Dead Before the Ship Even Sank* and was being produced by Dennis Herring, who'd produced Modest

Mouse's previous album, *Good News for People Who Love Bad News*, which featured the hit single 'Float On'. Our working regime was intense, with two weeks of fourteen-hour days before a day off, and then another two-week consecutive stretch, and so on. Mississippi in the summer was hot and insanely humid, so spending any time outside the studio was like being in an oven. Every day I would be lying on the floor of the parking lot on the phone to Angie, baking in the heat as she filled me in on everything that was going on back home. It was hard being away for so long. All the family were excited about the album, but it was the longest Angie and I had ever spent apart and the time difference made it even more difficult. While I was making the record we got the news that Angie's dad had been diagnosed with cancer. It was a blow to all of us and especially the kids, who were very close to their grandfather. I'd call to find out about what was happening and do whatever I could, but Angie's dad was fading and it was heartbreaking that I wasn't there with them. I'd just have to work on getting the record done and hope I could make it back sometime soon.

All the work that the band had put into the writing was paying off, and having the guitar parts already worked out meant that I could put a lot of my energy into developing sounds in the way that I had learned to do with The The, when I was 'producing with my feet'. Being in a rootsy American band was a whole new thing, and I enjoyed mixing guitar science with the vibe of the Mississippi swamp.

One very big idea I had during the making of the record was to build my own Jaguar guitar. I'd become so accustomed to playing the black one, which I'd bought from Isaac, that I couldn't imagine playing anything else. I'd been very fortunate to be able to acquire a large collection of guitars that I would employ to do very specific things over the years, and now with Modest Mouse I had found a guitar that not only suited me perfectly but did the job of several guitars, and which was also taking me into new territory, in much the same way as the Rickenbacker had done in The Smiths. I became obsessed with Jaguars and also Jazzmasters, and I used them exclusively on the album. Then, one day, my friend Clay Jones told me about a guy in Tupelo, Mississippi, who had a number of rare guitars. I didn't need much of an excuse to go to see some guitars, but when I thought about the possibility of getting one from Tupelo, the birthplace of Elvis Presley, I wasn't going to miss the opportunity. I set off to find Elvis's old house and get me a Jag.

When I got to the place where the man with the guitars was, I did what any other guitarist in my position would do, I went mad and bought a bunch. The fact that I was from England and suddenly finding myself in the birthplace of the King of Rock 'n' Roll seemed to make it absolutely crucial to take advantage of it and get myself some genuine treasures from the place where it all began. I got an old 1962 Jaguar, a '65 Jazzmaster and a seventies Guild Acoustic, before going to find 306 Elvis Presley Drive to pay my respects and cosmically seal the deal. I came to the little white house where Elvis Presley had been born, and there was not a soul around. There was a swinging chair on the porch which I couldn't resist. I sat on the porch and thought about where I was, and I had to call Angie to share the moment. I just hoped she would answer.

She picked up the phone and in my best Elvis Presley voice I started to sing, '*Are you lonesome tonight?*' She let me sing the whole song, and then Angie, who it has to be said is not an Elvis Presley fan, replied, 'You are such a dick.'

One of my favourite ever things to do in Modest Mouse was to go out shopping with Jeremiah. The whole band were the most acquisitive people I'd ever come across in my life, and each gas station we stopped at was an opportunity to stock up on hats, 3D sunglasses, and fishing nets. Being in the Walmart in Mississippi at 3 a.m. with Jeremiah was an education and a treat, as he would saunter around, picking out an array of objects from children's toys to garden tools with the casual air of a consummate expert, and I would marvel at the man's aesthetic diversity. Things to make signs, things to make things, and things to stick on top of other things: they would all be launched into the basket. When we'd get back to the studio, he'd disappear with his haul and then reappear days later, having made some amazingly crafted item. One morning I went into his room and noticed something unusual. The furniture had been sprayed gold. It was on these nocturnal raids that I first started finding things to stick on my guitars. It was something to do at three in the morning, and it looked to me like decent art.

When the record was finished, I thought we'd done something that sounded like nothing else. I liked the fact that we didn't analyse anything too much, but Isaac's description of it as 'a nautical balalaika carnival romp' seemed to fit the bill. Watching Isaac writing his lyrics was fascinating, because if you weren't looking out for it you wouldn't even notice he was doing it. We would already have what I thought was a really good song, and then he would seemingly write more, investing the words with extra nuance and meaning until they sounded like a collage of otherness, and another level would appear. In Isaac I'd found someone whose words I could read just for personal pleasure, whether I was involved or not.

While we're on the subject
Could we change the subject now?
I was knocking on your ears
Don't worry you were always out
Looking towards the future
We were begging for the past
Well, we know we had the good things
But those never seemed to last.

Everyone's unhappy
Everyone's ashamed
Well, we all just got caught looking
At somebody else's page
Well, nothing ever went
Quite exactly as we planned
Our ideas held no water
But we used them like a dam

Oh, and I know this of myself
I assume as much for other people
Oh, and I know this of myself
We've listened more to life's end-gong
Than the sound of life's sweet bells

The Good Ship Modest Mouse

Angie and the kids came to Portland and we all felt at home. Nile related to the culture in Portland and at sixteen was becoming serious about songwriting and guitar playing himself, having been influenced by Elliott Smith and Broken Social Scene. He was immersed in the music of the Pacific Northwest, and Modest Mouse had been his favourite band. I'd moved out of hotels and was renting an apartment, and the family came over as often as they could during this time, given my work schedule and the kids' school, and the rest of Modest Mouse welcomed them into the band's world just as warmly as they'd welcomed me.

With the album coming out, I was set to go out on the most extensive touring schedule I'd ever undertaken. It was a challenging prospect to be away for so long, but the anticipation that we all felt around the band and the record meant that there was also a lot of things to look forward to, and I was committed to Modest Mouse for the long haul. We were making our last-minute preparations in Portland when I got bad news from home. Angie's dad was now very ill and I needed to get back. I got home just before he died. I'd known Angie's dad since she and I had first met almost thirty years before. We'd got very close over the years, and he was a great man. My main concern was to look after my family. My wife had lost her dad, and my kids had lost their grandfather. It was something we all had to go through together.

It was a little strange being back in England and seeing first-hand how my joining Modest Mouse was being reported in the press. The band were already big in America, but only the more switched-on music fans knew about them in the UK, and the tone of the story in the British press went along the lines of 'Smiths Legend Joins Weird American Rockers with Beards'. It didn't trouble me to have the usual slant put on what I was doing, but it bothered me sometimes when my songwriting partners had to deal with the Smiths baggage, when all they wanted was to make good music with their guitarist and friend. Luckily my band mates were all grown-ups and artists in their own right, and all had had plenty of success and enough sense of themselves to handle the obvious line of questioning that would come our way ten minutes into most of our interviews. Still, I wished people would think a little higher sometimes.

I was at home, packing, when I got a call from the band's manager, Juan Carrera.

'Hi Johnny, what are you doing?'

'I'm packing for the tour . . . why?'

'I just thought you'd like to know that the album has gone into the American album charts at number one.'

It was an extraordinary moment, and one I never expected. I stood on the spot for a while and was thinking, 'No? . . . Really? . . . Really?' But it had definitely happened. The Modest Mouse album had gone straight into the American charts at number one. I called Angie and told her, and she came back from where she was to hang out and celebrate. Then Joe called. He was elated. In all the time I'd been playing with The Smiths and beyond, I'd never been one to pay too much attention to chart positions. I was proud and felt a huge sense of achievement when *Meat Is Murder* went to number one in the UK, and it meant something that Electronic had had hits, but I never remembered what number anything went to, and I genuinely didn't care if a single didn't get high in the charts. When a record was done, and if it sounded great, then I was happy about having written and recorded it. Once it was released, my focus was on the next thing. Modest Mouse getting to number one in America, though, was different. I took it not only as an achievement for the band and the work we'd put into writing the songs, but as a triumph for alternative guitar music. Music like ours didn't get to number one in America, but then we did it.

Back in Portland, I climbed on the bus and in true Modest Mouse style it felt like we were embarking on some epic voyage. Hundreds of dates spread out over the horizon as we set off to take our nautical balalaika carnival romp around the world to who knows where. I'd been in the band for a while by now, and my role as British guitar specialist seemed to fit me quite nicely. Although there was a unity in the band, it was a huge novelty for everyone to have a British guy around, and no one missed an opportunity to belittle, lampoon and ridicule all cultural differences between us. My Englishness was a great source of amusement, and I got to hear the most bizarre cockney accents and brutal mockery, until I had to loudly remind everyone that I was actually a legendary rock star and they really shouldn't take the piss. I liked everyone involved with Modest Mouse: I liked the crew, the management and the band's friends and families. I really liked the audiences. The band had a special relationship with their fans, and when I walked onstage I was aware I was playing to interesting people. The shows were unpredictable and usually very wild as the six of us clambered up between pump organs, trumpets and banjos, and assaulted the place with full-on force, setting off on roaming explorations within the music. As the mood of the night dictated the show, we'd some-times discard the set list and play whatever song we felt like, and maybe play it differently from how we'd played it in the past. Sometimes I'd treat the stage like an improvisational place. It was about playing in the moment, more than I'd done with any other band before. Isaac would go off into a spon-taneous idea, and depending on what we were all feeling we'd fall in with an entirely improvised jam that could last two minutes or ten. It was out-of-body music, and music for the head. Out-of-body head music.

We travelled and travelled, and the band's history and status in America meant that we went to a lot of places that I'd never been before. My lifestyle on the road became more ascetic. I went completely vegan, which I'd been considering for a long time, and I upped my running distance to ten miles and would time my runs so that I'd finish just before showtime and I'd be vibrating as I walked onstage. The shows were so much fun as I felt so good, and I couldn't imagine living life any other way. When we were in Canada, I ran in the snow along the road towards the traffic as the cars were making their way to the venue, and wherever we were and whatever conditions we were in, I'd get out and do my routine, even if I was completely stuck and it meant doing laps around an arena in Arizona.

The band would go back to Portland periodically after being away for a few weeks. It didn't make much sense for me to be going back and forth to England, and eventually Angie and I bought a house and the family came out to stay whenever I got back into town. One Sunday, I was in Portland and was invited to a party where I was introduced to a British guy who, it turned out, was Gary Jarman from The Cribs. Before I'd left England there were two bands that I'd really liked: one was Franz Ferdinand and the other was The Cribs, who I first heard when 'Hey Scenesters' came bursting from the car radio one night and nearly stopped me in my tracks. Gary and I saw quite a lot of each other in Portland. We were the only English musicians in town, and we'd get together when we were both back in between Modest Mouse and Cribs tours.

I started to miss England, and I was missing my family and Joe. British music culture was an undeniable part of my DNA, and being away for a few years had made me think about my influences and the sound and attitude of the bands that I'd grown up with. My and Gary Jarman's friendship was a connection to the UK and to home for us both, and it was good to find someone who had similar interests. I went back to the UK with Modest Mouse on tour, and the shows were all sold out. We played Glastonbury and the Royal Albert Hall, and it was nice to be back.

The morning of the Manchester show, I was in a hotel and was woken up by a phone call from Angie to say that Isaac was in the hospital. He'd been attacked the night before in Nottingham after the rest of us had left town, and had been hit in the face with a bottle. It was a serious situation. He'd had to have his face stitched up at three in the morning, but he was on his way with the band's legendary mascot and spiritual leader, Tim Loftus, to make the show because he didn't want me to miss playing Manchester. When he met up with the rest of us, his face was so cut up I couldn't believe he'd be able to play, but we did the show and Isaac got an excuse to legitimately wear an eyepatch onstage. Being back in Manchester for a couple of days gave me an opportunity to introduce everyone to Joe Moss and show the band around my home town. One day I was with Joe Plummer, and I pointed out Shelley Rohde's house, where I'd lived when I put The Smiths together and where Morrissey and I wrote our early songs. It was the first time that I'd remembered that the road was called Portland Drive. Later on, when we got into town and I showed Joe where The Smiths had rehearsed in Joe Moss's Crazy Face offices and where we first played 'Hand in Glove', I noticed that we were on Portland Street.

The Pacific Northwest coast of America and touring with Modest Mouse was my full-time existence for four years, and it brought a huge amount of changes in my life. My kids had grown up with me being in an American band, and in Portland we had found a new home town. I'd cultivated a completely new lifestyle while travelling and playing with Modest Mouse and it had been the best time of my life. I'd had a number one album in America, had started building my own guitar, and had even sung 'Are You Lonesome Tonight?' to my wife on Elvis's porch. It was all good, and I felt like it was time again to write some songs and make a new record.

Modest Mouse booked another round of touring in Japan and Australia, and then America again, this time with REM. I was tour-fried and I needed to go back to England, and with no recording for the band on the horizon I felt like the next tour would probably have to be my swansong with Modest Mouse, for a while at least. There was no bad feeling, everybody understood, and me and the band felt that we could easily work together again in the future. We went out on the road with REM, and at one show the stadium got struck by a bolt of lightning during our set. I saw it come from the sky and hit the venue, and the band all stopped for a few seconds as the audience started fleeing, then we continued with the song very nervously until we were called off the stage by officials.

Peter Buck from REM and I were already friendly, having hung out together in Portland. I saw him holding his set list one day, and I grabbed a pen and wrote 'Fall on Me' on it because it was my favourite REM song. The band added it to their set, and they asked me to play it with them every night in the encore. After the shows, depending on the time difference, I'd stay up and call Joe. I'd be out on my own with the trucks behind the venue, and we'd catch up with everything and talk about all sorts as always.

During the tour, the Fender guitar company, who'd heard that I was redesigning my Jaguar, approached me to make my own signature guitar. I could design a guitar to my own exact specifications, which they would then add to their range and sell in guitar stores around the world. It's a prestigious thing to have a guitar named after you, and a real honour to follow in the footsteps of people like Les Paul and Chet Atkins, who were the pioneers of the modern electric guitar. I'd been playing a Fender Jag since I'd joined Modest Mouse: it was perfect for my style and it sounded like me. But as much as I loved them, there were a number of things about the Jaguar that I knew I could improve, and I started to think about how to make it perfect. I tried out a lot of old Jags, testing them and comparing them in different environments to get the best out of them that I could. I was experimenting in rehearsals and soundchecks at first, but then I got brave and started testing them during concerts, as there's nothing quite like standing in front of several thousand people to help you make your mind up about something quick. The Modest Mouse and REM tour got to New York, and we were playing Madison Square Garden. I'd borrowed an old 1960s Jag to test it out, and I was supposed to make sure it was working before the show but I'd forgotten to do it. Midway through the set, I plugged it in and went to kick off a song, I started strumming and there was . . . nothing . . . just complete . . . silence. The band were all looking round at me, waiting to start the song, and my roadie was frantically running around the stage and cursing me for not checking the guitar before the show. I picked up my working one and I got through the rest of the gig, but it taught me to always make sure that an old guitar is actually working before playing it at Madison Square Garden. Modest Mouse had booked a second show in Brooklyn later that same night. After our set I played with REM and then jumped in a cab to catch up with Modest Mouse and get onstage in Williamsburg. We started the Modest Mouse show at around three thirty in the morning, and when the night was over I walked out on to the sidewalk at seven o'clock, dazed but feeling good, having played three times in one night in New York.

The New Fellas

B ack in London I was being given a lifetime achievement
award by *Q Magazine* at the Grosvenor Hotel when a
striking indie rock star bounded up to me and said in a York-
shire accent, 'Hey Johnny, I'm Gary's brother Ryan, from The
Cribs. We should do a single together,' before he bounded off
in another direction. I liked the idea of it – a 7-inch EP of
explosive guitar music. I got it in my mind and I thought we
should do it.

I had some ideas for songs: I was being pulled back to the
clang of two guitars and the adrenaline of punk, and I was
picking up the sense of disaffection that informs the best UK
music. I wanted to kick up some noise and I had some good
riffs, and then The Cribs asked me to join.

I first played with The Cribs in February 2008 at Glasgow
Barrowlands, and it was not unlike when The Smiths played

there in 1985. I sidestepped every pint of beer that came towards my guitar, and swerved every shoe that rocketed past my ear. Their gigs were a high-energy experience and an exuberant communal celebration. It was loud and exciting, and I had to concentrate to avoid getting swept away by the cyclone that was howling around me. To me The Cribs played street UK guitar music but with the attitude of an American band. They had grown up devouring the US alternative culture in the nineties that had been led by bands like Sonic Youth and Nirvana, which meant that The Cribs were different from their peers, who didn't have quite the same anti-corporate ideology, nor the same force.

Musically I fitted in by weaving my guitar playing with Ryan in much the same way as I did when I played with Isaac, and I tried to make it an agenda for us to have a very deliberate two-guitar assault. When I first met Ryan, he was a prominent figure in the music press, and seemed to them to epitomise the kind of unpredictable character who could throw himself off something dangerous any minute. It would have been easy for him to accept the mantle of the new Mr Notorious, but he was too serious and too multifaceted a person to go for it. The band cared too much to fall for a short-term pay-off and had no taste for the mainstream. They had their sights set on a legacy of impassioned shows and making records that meant something to fans.

When we came to write songs, I suggested that we go to a dingy practice room in a big old mill on the outskirts of Manchester, because I thought what we were doing needed to be able to work in that environment first, and then once we knew that it was working we could take it back to my more comfortable studio. It might have puzzled the band that someone with a professional studio would choose to go to a run-down room somewhere, but they understood the logic of it and trusted that I knew what I was talking about. The key moment for me and The Cribs came when we set up our gear to play. It's a simple thing, but to me that process is both ritualistic and completely natural, as if you're born to do it, and if you see that in someone else you know you're made of the same stuff. The Cribs set up their gear the same as I did, and when we were ready to go I said, 'I've got this one,' and played a stinging riff that we all fell in with immediately. It sounded good, and within forty minutes we had our first song. The next few days we all threw in ideas, and by the end of the week we had a bunch of good songs, which perhaps appropriately enough sounded just like The Cribs only with me playing. The chemistry worked, and because of that we decided to keep playing together. I'd thought that the idea of being in a gang was behind me, but there are some things that you can't change. I guess it just depends on meeting the right gang.

I was asked a lot about being in a band with three brothers, as if plates were being thrown around backstage and guitars were always being smashed over people's heads, but there was none of that. What it really means is that they have a bond onstage and off, and for them this is a strength. It was definitely unusual to be joining a band that's a family, but it turned out that being in the Jarman family was a special privilege, and my role was more like the half-brother who'd come back from the indie wars. We all stayed at my place in Manchester when we were first recording, and both our families became very close. My kids had spent their teenage years around Modest Mouse and The Cribs, and they couldn't have been happier about it. We were all in it together: the Marrs and the Jarmans, and a Rhodesian ridgeback called Riff.

The Smiths business was ticking over in the background, on and off and now and then. The band's catalogue had been signed to Warners by Morrissey and me in 1992, when we were advised to rescue it from Rough Trade, who were on the brink of bankruptcy. Rough Trade owed a lot of money, but they had managed to hang on to their business by selling Smiths records and then using the money they made to pay off debts before paying the band, so none of the band received any royalties for a long time. With very few options and no time to do anything else, Morrissey and I managed to make a hurried deal with Warners to put The Smiths' records out and to stop the catalogue falling into the hands of the receivers. It wasn't the greatest deal in the world, but at least it got the music to people we already knew.

The first thing Warners did when they acquired The Smiths' catalogue was to reissue all the albums on CD, which meant that they remastered them. Mastering is the last stage of making a record, whereby all the songs are put in the correct order with the required length of silence in between them. The volume of each song is checked and adjusted so everything is at the same level and it all hangs together and hopefully will sound perfect.

I always attended the mastering process for The Smiths' records. I regarded it as a professional obligation as a producer, and I wasn't about to let someone mess around with the sound of the records after I'd put so much work into making them. There's a lot you can do in the mastering process to make a record sound better if needs be. You can add high-end equalisation to make it sparkle more, or you can add or reduce bass levels to make it more or less weighty. Unfortunately for The Smiths, I wasn't consulted when the catalogue was remastered for the CDs in the nineties. The albums all came out after some mastering engineer had randomly made all kinds of adjustments, which meant they sounded nothing like they did to me when I made them. It was a huge source of frustration and disappointment to see the albums released when I knew that they sounded wrong, and I was determined to put it right. Warners and I spent a lot of time trying to come up with a solution, which was further complicated by the continued legal battles between Morrissey and Mike Joyce. After a lot of struggle, I reached an agreement with Morrissey and Warners. I would take The Smiths' master tapes and master all the records again with a top mastering engineer so that our catalogue would be as it should be, once and for all. It would be a long process and a massive undertaking, but I believed it was worth it.

Going through The Smiths' album catalogue and working on it song by song was a real labour of love. I started with 'Hand in Glove' and went chronologically to the end. I knew every guitar part, bass note and cymbal crash, and when I analysed the records I was struck by how good the band were as an ensemble and just how young we all were when we were together. My job was to be as technical as possible in restoring the records to exactly how they sounded in the studio, but I was able to recall the exact intention and emotion that went into every note and word when each song was originally made. Working on the records again made me proud of the band, and I texted Morrissey and Andy and said, *You can really hear the love in it*. It was good to get a nice reply from both of them.

The negotiations with Warners meant that Morrissey and I were in a rare period of communication. One day in September 2008 we contacted each other, and as we were only a couple of miles away in south Manchester we arranged to meet up in a pub nearby. I was happy to see my ex-songwriting partner. It had been ten years or more since we'd last seen each other. There was a lot to talk about. I was interested in what he was doing, and we compared our experiences of living in America. Both of us had been touring a lot over the previous few years, and we talked about playing shows and the places on our travels, things we liked and things we didn't like so much. It was good. We caught up with personal news and family and reminisced a bit, and we talked about how the list I'd made for the band on the day we first got together at Shelley's had come true.

The orange juice went down and the beer went down, and our conversation turned to deeper things. Morrissey started to talk about how, with so much water under the bridge, our relationship had become owned by the outside world, and usually in a negative way. We had been defined by each other in most areas of our professional life. I appreciated him mentioning it, as it was true. The landlord couldn't believe what he was witnessing, as the drinks kept coming and we sat talking for hours in his quiet pub. We talked, as we always did, about the records we loved, and eventually our conversation turned to 'that subject'. There had been rumours for years in the press that The Smiths were about to re-form, and they were always untrue. I had never pursued any offer for the band to re-form, and I had never wanted to. We talked about the most recent rumours and where they might have come from, and it was interesting that the subject appeared to be up for discussion. It was definitely nice to be together, and then suddenly we were talking about the possibility of the band re-forming, and in that moment it seemed that with the right intention it could actually be done and might even be great. I would still work with The Cribs on our album, and I made it clear that I'd do that first, and Morrissey also had an album due out. We hung out for a while longer, and after even more orange juice and even more beer we hugged and said our goodbyes.

Over the next few days we were in contact and planned to meet up again. I was genuinely pleased to be back in touch with Morrissey, and The Cribs and I talked about the possibility of me playing some shows at some point with The Smiths. For four days it was a very real prospect. We would have to get someone new on drums, but I thought that if The Smiths really wanted to re-form at that point it could be good and it would make a hell of a lot of people very happy, and with all our experience we might even be better than before. Morrissey and I continued our dialogue and I went to Mexico with The Cribs a few days later, and then suddenly there was radio silence. Our communication ended, and things went back to how they were and how I expect they always will be.

We Share the Same Skies

The Cribs planned to record our album in Los Angeles with the producer Nick Launay, who we knew from his work with Yeah Yeah Yeahs and Nick Cave, but first we went to a stranger's barn in Oregon City that Gary had found advertised in a local newspaper. The place had the ambience of a serial killer's hideout mixed with a touch of kidnapper's lair, and looked like the Amityville Horror had actually taken place there. Every day we'd drive down the deserted country roads into the middle of nowhere and the owner, who was an amateur guitar merchant with a slightly sinister air, would be waiting to drink some beers and have God knows what kind of fun with the fellas. There were tatty old dolls and children's toys lying around but no children, and our mulleted host was always alone. We were stoic though, and there was an album to be written, so we stayed in the dimly lit barn without ever coming out in order to complete our mission, and also because we were frightened. Being imprisoned in a barn did the trick. We wrote some good songs in record time and then got the hell out of there and didn't look back.

We made it to California to make the *Ignore the Ignorant* album. The sessions should have been plain sailing, but I was out at a friend's place one day when I got a call from Ryan to say that Ross was in hospital. He'd taken up skateboarding the day before the sessions were to start, went to the steepest hill in LA and threw himself down it. Suffice it to say he was going very fast, and when he jumped off to try to stop he fell and broke his arm. It was bad news for a drummer, and completely out of character for Ross, who is one of the smartest people I know. The day before the sessions, and he was in the hospital with a broken wrist. Somehow he found a way to play the drums, and we recorded the album in the LA sunshine. Ross suffered for his art, and there was pain in every beat.

Having a good producer and bandmates working as a team meant I could get a bit of time to myself. We were staying in the valley where the roads are straight and long, and my running regime went into overdrive. If I had the time before 11 a.m. I would run five miles in one direction and then come back. Alternatively, if I had some time in the evening, I would get more ambitious and take off towards the mountains in the distance, with the road stretching out ahead of me. I'd be thinking over things and clearing my head or listening to old northern soul or some electro. After seven miles the endorphins would kick in and I'd be running towards the hills. I'd carry on until I reached ten miles and then I'd turn around. On the journey back I'd be tranced out; the music would be going and I'd be in a meditative state, feeling amazing, the sun now low. I'd have run twenty miles when I got back to the studio, and every couple of days I'd do the same. A few weeks went by, and I was so fit I reasoned that if I just went the three extra miles on the way out, then by the time I got back I'd have run twenty-six miles, which is the marathon distance. I went for it one evening, and afterwards I was totally wrecked and spaced out. My mind wasn't functioning and I had nothing left. I walked into the kitchen in the studio and I saw a strange look on Ross's face, a look of concern that his new guitarist might expire before the record was finished.

'Are you all right?' he said.

'Yeah . . . I'm . . . er . . .' I couldn't talk and I couldn't think.

Twenty minutes later I came around, having fallen into the deepest sleep I've ever slept, even more than when I went out digging with my dad. I had to mentally reset, but aside from aching a lot I was then fine and ready to get back to recording. The day afterwards I felt great. I was on a high from the achievement of doing the marathon distance, so I did it again. This time it was mentally easier as I knew I'd done it before. I got back and reset, but I avoided Ross as I didn't want to worry him. Two marathons in two days sounded good. I felt OK the next day, so I attempted a third. There's a theory that the third time of doing something difficult is the hardest, as you're over the feeling of achievement, and the novelty has worn off, like day three of quitting smoking. My third run was really difficult for those reasons, and probably also because I was wrecked. I didn't run the next day, but I did one the day after that, and then the day after that. By the time I'd finished I'd done five marathons in a week. I surprised myself and it really felt like an achievement, even more so when I looked back on it, but I was doing so much running at the time that I didn't make a big deal of it.

From then on I kept my runs down to ten and fourteen miles, but I would do the marathon distance once every few weeks if I could. I stayed with that regime for a year or so and then fell into a pattern where some months I would do less and sometimes more. Eventually I ended up averaging around thirty-five miles a week, eight miles some days and ten miles others, and now if for some reason I go for more than two days without running at all I really don't like it.

In LA around that time I woke up to the news that Michael Jackson had died. I was staying in town, and when I tried to leave the hotel I couldn't get out of the building because there were so many people on Hollywood Boulevard. A reporter recognised me and stopped me to ask what my favourite track was from *Thriller*. I was wondering how best to answer the question, so I decided to just be honest. I told him that I didn't like *Thriller*. He looked at me like I was mad or joking, or was a very bad man, but I was just being honest. His death was tragic, but of course I didn't like *Thriller*, I was in The Smiths.

The Cribs' album *Ignore the Ignorant* was great, and went into the Top 10 in England. 'We Share the Same Skies', 'City of Bugs' and 'Cheat on Me' were all stand-out songs. We toured for eighteen months, playing frenetic shows to very raucous crowds. There were almost as many girls at Cribs shows as boys, and from the moment we took to the stage in a howl of feedback a mass of bodies swarmed in celebration and forgot about school and college for a night. I'd let the fellas go on in front, Ryan bouncing on as everyone went mental, and Ross starting the gig by standing up on his drum stool while crashing his cymbals, and I'd follow Gary, who walks onstage cooler than anyone I've ever seen. I'd plug in and go into the riff to 'We Were Aborted' and it was full-on, screeching guitar noise and the audience singing along from start to finish. The Cribs play to the max, and by the end of the set Ryan would be laid out on the stage, spinning round, while Gary rammed his bass against his amp and Ross kicked his drums off the riser. I made the loudest and weirdest noises I could to accompany the chaos and it was carnage; everyone was spent.

I finished touring with The Cribs in 2010 after doing the summer festivals. It was a good time, and the sun even came out at Glastonbury. The last show we did together was at Reading Festival, which was a fitting place to finish as it completed the circle on the stage where I'd made my first official appearance as a member of The Cribs. The thing about all the bands I've joined is that we became very close friends. I couldn't have travelled around, sleeping in bunks and waiting around airports and venues all day, if it hadn't been that way, and that's the way it was with The Cribs. It was great to have been part of the band, and it kept me connected to what being in a band is really all about. We'd toured for a couple of years and made an album, and when the band were planning to take some time off I, as usual, started to think about doing something different next.

The New York Marathon is the most prestigious one to run. Angie had entered me without telling me, and so I found myself standing on Staten Island at six in the morning in the freezing cold with 50,000 other runners, waiting to cross the starting line. When you begin a marathon, you feel like you're involved in something really momentous, and it's a strange thing and an odd proposition to have to tap into a feeling of solitary concentration while being surrounded by so many people all feeling the same way, to say nothing of the twenty-six miles that lie ahead. It was a good day to run, blue skies and bright sunshine. I was glad that I'd done the distance before, and I was thinking about all the bridges and taking in the views. Like most people I love New York, and running freely down the streets through all the boroughs is definitely the best way to see the city. The thing I had to adapt to the most was the crowds. I'd got into running by myself, and the solitary nature of it was one of the main reasons why I liked it. But having everyone cheering and seeing all the smiling faces makes you get into the festivity of it, and it feels like a celebration of the city as well as of the human spirit. The diversity of the tens of thousands of people you're running with in the New York Marathon is extraordinary. There are people there from all over the world and every kind of life, and as you all struggle through this serious test of endurance together, you realise that you really are a part of the human race. My goal was just to try to enjoy it and finish under four hours, and I did it in three hours fifty-four, which I was OK with. By the end of it I was pretty wiped out, as you might expect, and finishing in Central Park I'd forgotten just how hilly that place is, but it's these kinds of experiences that make you realise you really can get over your limitations sometimes. I felt like I'd really been through something, and I'd do it again.

Inception

Angie and I were at the movies one night in Manchester. We were watching the trailers when Angie leaned over and said, 'There's a new Christopher Nolan film coming out that looks really good.' A couple of trailers went by and then one came on for a new film called *Inception*, with Leonardo DiCaprio. 'This is it,' she said, 'check it out.' I watched it and I liked the music and noticed that it was composed by Hans Zimmer. When we got back home from the cinema, we'd only been in the house five minutes when the phone rang.

'Hello, is that Johnny Marr?' said the voice. 'This is Hans Zimmer.'

I'd never met Hans Zimmer before or spoken to him, but he'd got my number and told me that he wanted me to work on a film he was doing. Hans had written the score and had intended to get 'someone like Johnny Marr' to play on it, but then realised he should track me down and get me to do it. I asked him what the film was, and he told me it was the new Christopher Nolan film *Inception*, so I told him about the trailer and he explained that they'd used a different score as it hadn't been finished. It was a very weird coincidence, too much to get my head around, but our conversation was great and Hans was charming and the idea of doing something with him on the film was too good to miss. I'd first become aware of Hans Zimmer's work from the film *True Romance*, and then became a big fan of the soundtrack for *The Thin Red Line*. I'd just scored a movie myself called *The Big Bang* starring Antonio Banderas, which had been a good experience, but working on a film with Hans Zimmer was something else.

I went to Santa Monica to meet with Hans and Christopher Nolan and saw the film for the first time. *Inception* was a conceptual story about the potential of the human mind and the world of the subconscious, where the main character steals secrets and seeks redemption by breaking into people's dreams. I thought the film was great: it was something new and clever. It was totally original, and Hans's score was emotive and beautiful. Hollywood soundtracks don't usually feature guitar, but I could hear myself on it as soon as I watched the film. Hans and Christopher were very open to me trying out different things, and I was free to approach the movie whichever way I wanted.

Working on a film is entirely different from writing songs. A song is a subjective endeavour and you're working to meet your own criteria, whatever they might be. The music for a film has to express some aspect of the emotion that's happening on the screen, and emotion doesn't necessarily have to mean 'emotional'. A scene can have many different emotions – tension, fear, sensuality, joy – and while you're watching a film and engrossed in whatever's happening, the music can help to tap into all kinds of things. It can give the story another dimension and more complexity.

I worked long days and late nights on *Inception*, immersed in the emotion of the film as I played. It's a curious thing, but there are some artists who, when you hear their music or see their paintings, have a quality in their work that makes you connect with them and so you assume that you will get on. That happened with me and Hans Zimmer. He was the person I thought he was when I heard his music. We understand each other, and what we do together has become a very important part of my musical life.

The night of the premiere of *Inception* I played the score with Hans and the orchestra at a special concert in Hollywood. Performing such dramatic music, with some of the greatest musicians in the world in the orchestra behind me, was one of the high points of my life, and afterwards, when the film was done and *Inception* was number one at the box office, it occurred to me that I wouldn't have been able to do it when I was younger. I didn't have the technical facility or mindset to accomplish it back then. Sometimes there really isn't any substitute for experience.

Individual Citizen

Being on the move with Modest Mouse and The Cribs for five years, I was onstage more than I'd ever been before, and my world turned into the space between me and my amp. I was travelling so much that I had to get into it or I wouldn't have been able to make it work physically or mentally. When you're young and first start touring, the constant travel and lifestyle always has an impact, and health, home life and relationships between band members are affected by physical burnout, hangovers and living in a bubble. I adapted to years of touring when I got older by getting as fit as I could, and using the travel and activity to energise me, especially in cities. I got to see more of the places I went to than I had done at any other time in my life, and I had the disposition and mentality to make the most of it.

On those tours I got a lot of ideas for words and music.

Some things went into the records, and other ideas I collected in notebooks. After a while I started to imagine a record inspired by the things I saw in the cities and from observing people and the culture. Musically I was more interested in the punchy riffs that were not unlike what I was doing in the bands I was in before The Smiths, and I kept writing down words and titles with a sense that they would turn into something.

I started working in the studio at unusual hours, around 5 or 6 a.m. My sleeping habits had always been unconventional, and the previous years of touring had left me in a perpetual but useful state of jet lag. One morning, on the way back from driving Sonny to school, I was thinking about how the British prime minister David Cameron had been saying in the media that he was a fan of The Smiths. I thought it was odd that he had decided to namedrop The Smiths, as anyone who was a fan of the band would know we were against everything he and the Conservative party stood for. I wasn't having it that he was a fan, but if he wanted to say that he liked The Smiths, what could I do about it?

My friend who looks after my social media had been coaxing me to use Twitter for quite some time in order to engage more with people and let them know what I was doing. I considered Twitter to be a bit of fun at best, and whenever I used it I was usually as surreal and frivolous as possible. Without thinking too much about it, I picked up my phone and typed, *David Cameron, stop saying that you like The Smiths, no you don't. I forbid you to like it.* Satisfied that I'd made my protest, I went to take a nap.

A couple of hours later, the phone rang and I was woken

up by a call from Joe. He didn't realise that I'd been asleep, and he said in his usual understated manner, 'What do you want me to do about all the requests I'm getting? Do you want me to follow any of it up?' I didn't know what he was talking about, and asked him what he meant. 'The Cameron thing,' he said, 'the Twitter business, it's crazy.' While I'd been asleep the tweet I'd sent had completely blown up. It was being retweeted by thousands of people and had been picked up by the press all over the world. I got out of bed and saw my phone was full of messages. There were emails from my PR asking me to do interviews with everyone from BBC News to the *New York Times*. When I'd gone to sleep I had around 10,000 followers, and when I woke up I had 30,000.

It was totally bemusing, and also very funny. The idea of anyone 'forbidding' someone else to like anything was very amusing to me, but I did appreciate the opportunity to pull David Cameron up for making a claim on The Smiths. He had tried to co-opt the band and appear credible by association, and through social media I'd been able to respond to it in my own way. There were a lot of fans who didn't like the prime minister, and they were genuinely irked that he was aligning himself with the band, and the overall reaction to what I'd done was one of widespread hilarity and glee.

I rolled along with it for a while, and it was interesting to witness some of the more disappointing aspects of our society that come out on social media, and to see just how aggressive some people love to be. There was the inevitable reaction from some scathing types who were eager to vent and saying things like, *Where the hell does Johnny Marr get off forbidding anyone to like his music?* And better still: *I bet Johnny Marr wouldn't give back the £10 Mr Cameron spent on buying The Queen Is Dead*. I was amazed. Anyone who didn't see any humour in the situation, regardless of their politics, had to be a bit stupid, and anyone who seriously thought that David Cameron had actually bought *The Queen Is Dead* had to be very stupid indeed. The only thing to do was to have some fun. Sonny and I would spend the car journey to school every day coming up with things for me to say. We'd be sitting in traffic, composing tweets and falling around in hysterics. I would write something and then say, 'No . . . no . . . I can't say that, some people will kick off,' and she'd add something extra that would make it even funnier and then dare me to send it: *Dear Lord, please forgive me for making fun of the government. They are really nice and doth be very kind to poor people and students. Amen*. Minutes later I'd get a torrent of abuse from humourless morons accusing me of being a rock star socialist heathen, and we'd reply, *Oh, and also their fans doth have a brilliant sense of humour. Thank you . . . Amen*.

The David Cameron situation picked up more and more press interest over the following weeks, to the point where Mr Cameron himself was called on to comment during Prime Minister's Questions in the House of Commons. The Labour MP Kerry McCarthy stood up and said that Mr Cameron must be feeling upset about being banned from liking The Smiths, and then added, 'The Smiths are, of course, the archetypal student band. If he wins tomorrow night's vote, what songs does he think the students will be listening to? "Miserable Lie", "I Don't Owe You Anything" or "Heaven Knows I'm

Miserable Now"?' Mr Cameron took the opportunity to show his true indie cred: 'I expect that if I turned up I probably wouldn't get "This Charming Man".' Good one. It was all very jolly and I thought it was totally bizarre.

The vote Kerry McCarthy was referring to in her question to the prime minister was the proposed bill to increase the tuition fees for a university education from £3,290 to £9,000, even though there had been a promise not to do so in the run-up to the election. The coalition went back on that promise, and it brought students out all over the country in organised protests. British students had been betrayed by the deputy prime minister and leader of the Liberal Democrats, Nick Clegg, and their future was in jeopardy as they faced more cuts in education and crippling long-term debt. Fifty thousand demonstrators marched through London, and I was proud to see the students make a stand and call the politicians to account for their broken promises. It's a rare thing and I thought they were honourable. Things came to a head in Parliament Square on the day that the new laws were passed, when the police came down on the students using a tactic called 'kettling', where they corral people into a confined area and hold them against their will for hours in the cold. The students bravely held on to their convictions though.

The day after the Parliament Square protest, I was sent a photograph of a protestor called Ellen Wood who was confronting the police and wearing a Smiths T-shirt. I looked at the photograph and it took me a few seconds to grasp what I was seeing. A young woman in total defiance, facing down a force more powerful than herself but which appeared weaker because of her conviction and belief in what was right. It was incredible. I stared at the photograph again, her stance, the Houses of Parliament. I thought at first it must have been photoshopped, but it was absolutely real. The significance of her wearing the Smiths shirt made quite an impact on me. It occurred to me that, aside from the music we made, that picture could be the most powerful testament to The Smiths' legacy. I saw the Houses of Parliament behind the girl in the Smiths shirt and I reckon that pop music doesn't get much more powerful than that. That a group I had started by knocking on a door would end up being that symbolic was staggering. The only other person I knew who might comprehend it the same way was Morrissey, and so I sent him the picture by email. There'd been no contact between us for a long time, but it made sense to me and I thought it was a fitting opportunity to make a friendly gesture. I got a reply within minutes. He hadn't seen the picture and he was equally as surprised and impressed by it. Our communication continued for a day or so, some pithy remarks went back and forth, and although I felt I'd created a moment of friendship, on some level I felt an air of disaffection and distrust remained between us. It was a shame.

I continued working every day and the songs started to pour out. Very quickly I had what I felt was a good album, although I wasn't sure exactly how I would present it. I did know that I didn't want to join someone else's band, and I thought the music should be energetic, and sound good on the way to work or school. Now that I was based back in England I felt like I was reconnecting with my musical roots and the values of the bands I was into when I was starting out. I wanted two guitars with loud drums, and lyrics that reflected what I saw going on around me – something I came to think of as 'outside music'. It seemed that a lot of rock music had suddenly become extremely earnest, and too concerned with expressing some inner turmoil deep down inside, some personal malaise we all shared – as if all modern music had to be about conquering adversity as we all stand as one in a field. What was this communal distress that everyone was singing to the skies about? I thought it might be good to do something that was about other things – cities, environment, society, other people.

I had an idea about the way we fetishise technology, and I wrote a song about a man who wins the lottery and swaps his wife for a cardiac machine with which he has a loving relationship. Another song, called 'Say Demesne', was inspired by a street in Manchester where teenage prostitutes work; and from a TV show I saw in America about children who'd had surgery in order to help them become famous, I wrote a song called 'Sun and Moon'. A few weeks into the process my co-producer James Doviak said to me, 'This is a solo record, right?' I didn't know the answer to that. I'd assumed that I would go under the name of The Healers, and it was only when Doviak suggested it that I thought about going under my own name. I lived with the idea for a couple of weeks and it made sense. When the time came to find the other band members, I enlisted Doviak to play second guitar and keyboards, and I invited Iwan Gronow and Jack Mitchell, who I'd produced when they were in Haven, to play bass and drums. Jack and Iwan were not only friends, but the best rhythm section around as far as I was concerned, and it was good that my band wasn't just me and some hired hands.

The album was recorded in Manchester, New York and Berlin, and the picture on the cover was taken in Berlin by my friend Mat Bancroft when we were walking under a bridge as the sun came up. Mat took out his camera, and said, 'Do something that shows how you feel about your life.' I thought about the question and then started walking like I was on a tightrope, trying to keep my balance. Mat took the picture and said, 'That's the album cover.'

I called the album *The Messenger*, but two days before I was due to deliver it to the record company I decided that something was missing. I was happy that it was banging and 'outside music', but it felt like it needed something personal about my life. I came up with a tune on the guitar, and I got the band over and we finished the music in a day, which left me one day to write the words and sing it. I listened to the music, and the feeling of it made me think of the day when I decided to leave school and walked around town with Angie, dreaming of being in a band. A day when I imagined my future was there for me, if I was prepared to go for it and do what it took. I was working on that feeling, and then I realised I could sing the story of that day: *Left home a mystery, leave school for poetry*. I sang it and I asked Sonny to put a background vocal on it, as she'd done on some other songs on the album. It brought a good dimension to the song, and as we were mixing the track Nile came over and suggested a final guitar part for the instrumental section. I thought he should play it, and what he did was perfect. 'New Town Velocity' made it on to the album and it became a lot of people's favourite.

You can have a lot of considerations when you're making a record: is it as good as the previous one? Should it sound different from the others? Will people like it? And on it goes. It makes sense to have some ideas about what you want to achieve, and different people have different motivations. I went into my solo record very deliberately, with just a few considerations, and I ignored anything else. The first was that I wanted to write songs that I thought would be exciting to play live in concert. This meant that any ideas that might come up in the studio which we couldn't recreate as a four-piece would be dismissed. I'd got to make records with a lot of different bands over the years, and I'd started to like touring and travelling more and more as time went on. I really appreciated the live experience later on in my career, which was a good thing, and what I did live became more of a priority. I like the physical act of being onstage. It charges you as it drains you, and it's a powerful thing to be surrounded by the volume of the music. And when it's all over and I'm sitting on the bus, I shut right up and watch everyone else's post-gig excitement and feel fairly serene. Something else I wanted for my solo record was that fans would like it, which may seem very obvious, but you can go into a creative endeavour with the intention of challenging expectations and wanting to break away from what you're known for, and that's something that I've done a lot. I've always believed that it's the prerogative of any artist to not be typecast and to experiment all they want, but if you're carrying around an attitude about it when you're older to the point where you dismiss what you do best, then you're ignoring your good luck and you need to drop it. I decided that if my songs came out sounding naturally like me and felt right, then that was fine. I would leave it to the audience to decide.

When I finally became a solo artist I had an audience. It's extremely gratifying to find that a lot of people have stayed with me throughout all the different things I've done, and it's an amazing thing to know that there are people who have grown up with you. Some of my audience were in school when they first heard me in The Smiths, and the music I've made over the years has been a soundtrack to their lives. My audience love guitar music, they know what I'm about, and they're glad that I'm still doing it. There were a lot of young people at my shows too who had come to The Smiths years after we broke up, or who had been introduced to me through The Cribs and Modest Mouse. It all made for a good mix of people.

Once I started playing shows with my band, we got on a serious roll and wanted to be the best live band around. It seemed to me to be a good ambition. Fronting a four-piece new wave band with a guitar was natural and not terribly different from what I'd done in my teens. Singing with Modest Mouse and The Cribs had been good practice, and I knew how I wanted to sound. There's so much mythology around singing, the most common myth being that unless a song is delivered with the utmost emotion and sincerity then it's not authentic. I don't hear any histrionics in The Velvet

Underground, or any crooning in the Buzzcocks, and the singers that have inspired me – Ray Davies, Patti Smith, Debbie Harry, Eric Burdon – don't go in for any of that stuff, they're cool.

My gigs were a rousing affair from the off. The album was a hit, and me and my band played all the new stuff as well as my favourites from the past. All the solo songs worked live, which meant that when it came to playing songs by The Smiths or Electronic I felt I'd represented my current direction well enough, and playing the old songs became a celebration and gave the crowd something they knew and loved. I would be asked if playing Smiths songs was a hugely emotional thing for me, or cathartic, but those moments are as much about the audience as they are about me. When I do 'There Is a Light That Never Goes Out' or 'Please, Please, Please, Let Me Get What I Want' I'm giving everyone something they love. It's about the power of music and what it means in people's lives. Some people would inevitably compare the way I do Smiths songs to Morrissey, which is as redundant as it is absurd. I can't imagine what everyone's reaction would be if I stepped up to the microphone during one of my shows and delivered a Morrissey impression. It wouldn't even be funny; I have no idea what that would be.

Enjoying touring made me want to go around the world as much as I could, and for a while I didn't stop. We went to America a few times, and Australia and Japan, as well as around the UK, and then did it again and again. In 2013 I went back to play Glastonbury. I'd been back before with Modest Mouse and The Cribs, but for some reason that year felt like a real return. The weather was glorious and people knew the new songs, and when I played the old ones there was no stage invasion, just a lot of people sitting on their mates' shoulders, singing along with tears in their eyes. These days I've got my own tour bus, although I'd still be OK with showing up in the old white Merc.

Travelling and working so much inspired me, and before I finished touring with *The Messenger* I was making another album, called *Playland*. I would write songs on the road and then record them in between dates. In London I was recording in a studio by the river. I had put down an instrumental track that I liked, but didn't have the words. It was late at night and I went for a walk, and in the maze of concrete and glass I came across some drunk, obnoxious City types gorging on a cash machine, totally oblivious to a young couple sitting freezing on the floor with a blanket around them. After deflecting some of their moronic jibes, I walked away, imagining a scenario where one of them woke up to find they were homeless, having merely dreamt their status. I walked back to the studio with the song 'Speak Out, Reach Out' ready to go: *Sophisticated minds, you are your country, situated in a line in my city, reach out to get what you want 'cos all you've got is all there is.* Joe encouraged me to pursue my lyrical preoccupations: he liked how I was inspired by the Beats, and he thought I was really on to something with the new stuff. The title *Playland* came from a book called *Homo Ludens* by a Dutch writer named Johan Huizinga, about the role of play and creativity in society, which I married to my memories of the seedy arcade of the same name in

Piccadilly Gardens in the seventies. When it came out, *Playland* became my second Top 10 solo album, and the first single, 'Easy Money', turned out to be one of the most successful songs I've ever released.

Going solo also meant doing a lot of interviews, and it was interesting for me to see how much I'm considered to be a political artist. It's partly due to the stance taken by The Smiths, but it may also be due to the fact that there appear to be so few musicians these days who have an interest in voicing political opinions or social concerns. I come from a generation for whom the issues in society and the way the establishment operates is expected to be commented on by musicians. My coming of age in Britain during the Thatcher years, and observing subsequent events, only strengthened my belief that the powerful always act in favour of the privileged, and will forever treat the less fortunate in society as inferior in order to maintain inequality. It's not about me standing on a soapbox. When you're identified as having political ideals, there's an assumption in some places that you're always looking to criticise, but if you come from a working-class background and find yourself being asked about inequality then you're bound to have a view. I also consider it to be the prerogative of the artist to make fun of the establishment. Otherwise, what's the point?

It's difficult in interviews to avoid repeating yourself when you're asked the same questions all the time. In my case, the entirely predictable thing that everyone knows is coming is: 'Will The Smiths ever re-form?' I've had thirty years of head-scratching with that question, and on occasion even had some fun with it. It's bizarre that an interviewer might actually be thinking that the answer could be: 'Yes, we've just decided to re-form this morning. Now let me tell you about it.' The other thing about that question is that I have to assume that the person asking it has never once seen any of my interviews, because if they had they'd have seen me already answer it in every way possible. I've tried to avoid being all heavy and saying, 'No way, over my dead body,' because if I do I know the main headline will be: 'Marr Says He'd Rather Die Than Re-form Smiths'. And if I choose to say, 'Well, you never know, I'd like to see the fellas,' then I know I'll have a month of 'Marr Says Smiths Might Re-form' all over the place, which is worse. What most other artists would do is to have someone inform all journalists, 'No questions about The Smiths,' but then it appears that you've got some big problem and can't handle talking about your past. You can't really win. It used to frustrate me, but it doesn't any more. You just have to hope that the journalist is a bit clued-up on and cares enough not to ask such a predictable question, but if not, at least nowadays I can say 'Google it', which is quite helpful.

Awards are a funny thing. You wait for thirty years for one to show up, and then a load of them come at once, or something like that. I never got an award when I was in The Smiths, but when I put *The Messenger* and *Playland* out I was suddenly presented with quite a lot of them. I'd been to ceremonies in the past and was happy to present awards to other musicians, as it was always well deserved and meant a jolly-up with people I rarely got to see. I didn't ever crave awards myself or need them for self-worth or validation, because I only get that from what I do. The thing I find interesting about musicians getting awards, as opposed to actors or television people, is that musicians aren't really supposed to give a fuck about getting them, because rock culture is built on the idea of rebellion. In the television and film industry it's different, because winning an award is taken as an accolade and a sign of quality and success. When I'm asked in interviews about awards there's sometimes a trace of cynicism, but all I know is that when I'm standing in a room, applauding Pete Townshend or Ray Davies for getting an award, I'm thinking, 'I appreciate what you've done and I'm happy to be here to honour you,' so whenever I've received awards I take the gesture in the same spirit and I'm genuinely honoured to look out and see a roomful of people who I respect all happy for me and wanting me to know it.

The ultimate awards ceremony is the Oscars. *Inception* was nominated for four, and I was pleased for everyone who was involved in the movie. I'd been warned that the Oscars would be excruciatingly boring, but I found it very entertaining. The thing about the red carpet is that you're expected to look into every camera and talk into every microphone that's stuck in your face about films you've not seen, to people who are not listening, and who suddenly vanish as soon as someone more famous arrives, which is every minute. The other thing about the red carpet is it's very, very long, so I decided that I would pass the time by critiquing every outfit that I saw. It was good — fabulous, actually — those gowns really are impressive. Scarlett Johansson was the winner, in a maroon lace Dolce & Gabbana.

In 2007 I was made a professor of popular music by Salford University, which was something that I didn't see coming, and it meant I had to give an inaugural lecture. I called the lecture 'Always from the Outside: Mavericks, Innovators and Building Your Own Ark', and it was about infiltrating the music industry, and examined the idea that some people have that the music business is a kind of specific physical place furnished with thick carpets and sexy lighting where dreams automatically come true, and that you need a specially appointed insider to gain you admittance. I put forward the idea that almost all innovations in pop culture have been facilitated by outsiders with no previous experience but who possessed a vision and maverick spirit, people like Brian Epstein, Andrew Oldham, Malcom McLaren, Joe Moss and Rob Gretton, who were the entry point or portal to a successful career for so many important bands. Giving a lecture was another leap into the unknown, but people seemed to like it, and although it was a lot of work, it was worth it. A couple of years later I received a Doctorate of Arts by Salford University, which means that I'm both a doctor and a professor, although no one's ever called me either yet. I was also made an honorary patron of the University Philosophical Society by Trinity College Dublin, which I thought was great as I'm in such company as William Yeats, Samuel Beckett and Helen Mirren.

All of these things are amazing for someone who's known for playing the guitar, and the most amazing thing of all was to be invited to an audience with His Holiness the Dalai Lama as an official friend of Tibet, which came about after I had helped to arrange an event for the Dalai Lama a couple of years before. His associates had heard that I'd given my support to the Freedom for Tibet movement, and were aware that I would put their flags over my amps. I was shown into a room with Angie and a few other people, and the Dalai Lama thanked us for our support. It was fairly humbling and quite a surreal experience, and he didn't ask me if The Smiths were going to re-form, which I thought was very cool.

One of the privileges of having your own band is that you get to invite your favourite people to join you onstage. I've been invited myself to be a guest so many times by other musicians, so it's a nice thing for me to be able to return the compliment, and a nice thing for the audiences too. Ronnie Wood, who I always love to play with, my friend Kevin Drew from Broken Social Scene, Neil Finn, Robyn Hitchcock, Billy Duffy and Noel Gallagher have all got up to play encores with me. Bernard Sumner and I re-formed Electronic for a night when he joined me for 'Getting Away with It', and it became something of a tradition that whenever I played in New York Andy Rourke would come onstage and play a couple of Smiths songs. It's always a special thing for us. There's something that happens when we play together that works exactly the same as it did in when we were in The Smiths.

My son Nile has played with me onstage and on record. He and Sonny grew up around artists and guitars, and he taught himself to play when he was young. He started out doing his own solo shows, and spent his teenage years playing wherever he could and learning to be a songwriter. He put his first band together after we moved to Portland, and got involved in the

Pacific Northwest scene before starting to release records with his band, Man Made. He works constantly and lives between Manchester and Portland, but spends most of his time travelling with his band in their van. Sonny sang backing vocals on songs like 'European Me', 'Dynamo', 'Upstarts' and 'Easy Money'. She lives in London where she works in publishing and sometimes plays a Dakota red Fender Mustang guitar. My kids are often asked about what it was like growing up around The Smiths, but they were born a long time after the band had ended. They learned about The Smiths from the outside world. I didn't talk to them about it much or go in for the old war stories, and they weren't asking to hear them. We were all busy with whatever we were involved in at the time, and kids never live in the past. Nile and Sonny grew up around Modest Mouse and The Cribs, and they think of those bands as family. They know whatever they want to know about The Smiths; they're of a different generation, and they have their own tastes and opinions on it all.

Too Late to Stop Now

When I got to Manchester on the *Playland* tour, I played at the Apollo. It had been a dream of Joe's that I should play there, as he knew all about my history with the place as a boy and because we'd never done it with The Smiths. There was another personal reason why Joe wanted to get to the Apollo. He had been diagnosed with cancer, and he knew he didn't have a lot of time. We saw each other and talked a lot when we got the news. He was adamant that the tour went ahead, and he was immensely proud of the way things had turned out for me. He saw the Apollo show as my homecoming, and he told me that he would be there even if it meant I had to bring him in an urn.

The day of the show, Joe married his long-term partner Sarah, and we all got off the tour bus in the morning and went to the ceremony. It was a great day, and later, when it was time to play, I walked out at the Apollo for the triumphant homecoming show that Joe had wanted, as he stood on the side of the stage and beamed with pride. It was perfect, he got to see it and he loved it, and at the end of the night the whole of the Apollo sang 'There Is a Light That Never Goes Out' to him and Sarah. As I walked off the stage I went over to him and he hugged me and said, 'Well done, Johnny . . . not bad for a kid with a guitar.' I remembered something he used to say when we first started out, and I told him, 'Too late to stop now, Joe. Too late to stop now.'

Joe battled his illness right up to the last night of the *Playland* tour. He hung on until the very last show was over. He continued to be my manager and was looking after me right up until he died. Joe's death left a hole in my life that will never be filled. He was more than a manager, he was my mate, and he had such a specific way of doing everything that to know him meant to know a philosophy, and a philosophy doesn't die.

'Not bad for a kid with a guitar': I thought about that phrase a lot. When I met Joe and introduced myself as a 'frustrated musician', it was because I was. When you're young and starting out, the thing you crave most is to be heard, and to get the chance to do what you love. Fame and money and status are dreams, but being heard is what you need. You need it because you've worked at trying to get good enough and you have to know if you're right. If you get to be heard and find out that you're right, you can communicate your ideas and visions about everything to people who you hope will like it, people like you, and that is being an artist. I grew up looking for a way to make the world more exciting and more comprehensible, and I was fortunate enough to find a way to do it with something I loved. It didn't mean that life became instantly easy or any less incomprehensible, sometimes it made things harder, but it gave me a direction and a passion and that's all you need.

There was a time in my career when I was referred to as 'a journeyman' or 'gun for hire', as if joining bands, playing the guitar on people's records and collaborating with my favourite artists was anything other than totally great. My choices have always made sense to me. I followed a mission that I was lucky enough to be given as a kid, and my nature always stayed the same. I was first known for being in a very big band, and it was everything I'd dreamed and more. I worked hard to put it together and then make it a success with the others, and as great as we were, The Smiths could only ever have lasted as long as we did because of the differences in my and Morrissey's personalities. I understand the appeal and security of staying with the same group for forty years, but I couldn't ever imagine doing it myself. It was never in my stars to be doing the same thing for ever. I'm good at running groups and I've done it since being a kid, but I was always my own entity and I always needed to feel free. I wanted to keep getting better and learn about all the different ways of creating guitar music, and the only way I knew how to do it was to take things as far as I could in whatever situation I was in, and then move on. I've had the best job in the world. I've joined my favourite bands with my favourite people, and my heroes became my friends. I love my work and I've always appreciated the good luck that's come with it.

I've never found out why I was so attracted to the guitar as a kid and why it had to accompany me through life. Being a guitar player has been my identity, to the outside world and to myself. It's been that way since I saw my first one in a shop window as a five-year-old boy, and I've never known life any other way since that moment.

Building my own signature guitar was a total obsession. Once I had a prototype I used it in every situation I could think of to make it as versatile as possible. I gigged it and gigged it while constantly making improvements, and after playing hundreds of shows with it I brought it into the studio, and then took it to another level with orchestras on film soundtracks. By the time I'd finished it, my signature Jaguar had evolved into what I consider to be perfection, and it was only then that I gave it to Fender to remake it faithfully so that every one with my name on is identical to mine.

When it finally became available, the Fender Johnny Marr Jaguar received the award for Best International Instrument, and that felt like a real achievement.

I can't say what it is that's happened in my life that I'm most proud of: the bands I've been in, finding the love of my life, my kids, the songs, or having a flower named after me. For a Mancunian-Irish kid with a guitar, it's all's been pretty good. I may be most proud of the fact that I'm still doing what I've always done, and I hope I always will. It's something to be proud of, that – and having my own guitar named after me, and painted white, the same as the one I got at Emily's.

Acknowledgements

Writing this book has been an interesting and enjoyable experience and I'm glad to have done it. I'd like to thank everyone at Century for making it happen and Susan Sandon for her time and expertise in helping to guide the poetic spirit. Thanks are also due to Carrie Thornton and Graham Sim.

Many thanks to Dave Cronen for management and to Derek Fraser, Andy Booth and Pat Savage for all the help day in, day out, and to Mat Bancroft, Jane Arthy and Andy Prevezer and all at Tibor Jones for the great work and support.

Special thanks to my family and to Bill and Mary Brown for all the love and understanding, and especially to Nile and Sonny for being such great people who make me proud; and to the friends who've been with me for so long and who've played an important part in my story: Jon Savage, Fiona Skinner, John and Kathy Featherstone, Neil and Sharon, Andy

Rourke, Zak, Liz Bonney and Lee Spencer, Christine Biller, Leslee Larson, David Palmer, James Hood, Guy Pratt and Mark Mahoney. You know I love you. And thanks to my bandmates – James, Jack and Iwan – for being the best.

I'd like to take this opportunity to acknowledge all the guitar techs and road crews who've worked with me over the years, especially Bill Puplett for taking such great care of my guitars and for doing such a wonderful job in helping me build my signature Jag.

Finally, I'd like to say thank you to all the people who have bought the records and come to the shows, and who have been with me through all the twists and turns. I hope you've enjoyed it as much as I have.

Picture Credits

The author and publishers have made all reasonable efforts to contact copyright holders for permission, and apologise for any omissions or errors in the form of credit given. Corrections may be made in future reprints.

Section 1

Page 1, top – Courtesy of Manchester Libraries, Information and Archives, Manchester City Council
Page 8, all – © Pete Hope

Section 2

Page 1, top left – © Paul Slattery
Page 1, below – © Paul Slattery
Page 2 – © Eugene and Willa Watson/National Portrait Gallery, London
Page 3, top right – © *Guitarist* magazine, 1983
Page 4 – © Angie Marr

Page 5 – © John Fairweather
Page 6, all – © Andrew Catlin
Page 7, all – © Angie Marr
Page 8 – © Paul Slattery

Section 3

Page 1, top – © Angie Marr
Page 2, top – © Angie Marr
Page 3, below – © Charles Dickins
Page 4, all – © Angie Marr
Page 5, all – © Angie Marr
Page 6, top – © Jeff Katz
Page 6, below – Every possible effort has been made to track down
        the original photographer
Page 7, top – © Angie Marr
Page 8, below – © Jon Shard

Section 4

Page 1, top – © Angie Marr
Page 1, below – © Loren Jansch
Page 2, top – © Jon Shard
Page 2, bottom – © Mick Rock 2003, 2016
Page 3, top – © Pat Graham
Page 3, middle – © Pat Graham
Page 3, below – © Wendy Lynch Redfern for *Under the Radar*
        magazine
Page 4, top – © Pat Graham
Page 4, below – © Oli Scarff/Getty Images
Page 5, top – © Dan Massie
Page 5, below left – © Capital Images
Page 5, below right – © Pat Graham
Page 6, top – © Angie Marr
Page 6, below – © Richard Henry
Page 7, top – © Lawrence Watson
Page 7, below – © Marc McGarraghy
Page 8 – © Niall Lea

All other photographs are from Johnny Marr's private collection.

Index

431

447